QUEER JEWS, QUEER MUSLIMS

QUEER JEWS, QUEER MUSLIMS

RACE, RELIGION, AND REPRESENTATION

EDITED BY ADI SALEEM

Wayne State University Press
Detroit

© 2024 by Adi Saleem. All rights reserved. No part of this book may be reproduced without formal permission.

ISBN 9780814350874 (paperback)
ISBN 9780814350881 (hardcover)
ISBN 9780814350898 (e-book)

Library of Congress Control Number: 2023940088

Cover design by Shoshana Schultz.

Published with the assistance of a fund established by Thelma Gray James of Wayne State University for the publication of folklore and English studies.

Wayne State University Press rests on Waawiyaataanong, also referred to as Detroit, the ancestral and contemporary homeland of the Three Fires Confederacy. These sovereign lands were granted by the Ojibwe, Odawa, Potawatomi, and Wyandot Nations, in 1807, through the Treaty of Detroit. Wayne State University Press affirms Indigenous sovereignty and honors all tribes with a connection to Detroit. With our Native neighbors, the press works to advance educational equity and promote a better future for the earth and all people.

Wayne State University Press
Leonard N. Simons Building
4809 Woodward Avenue
Detroit, Michigan 48201-1309

Visit us online at wsupress.wayne.edu.

For Elliott

Contents

Introduction: Why Jewish, Muslim, *and* Queer?   1
Adi Saleem

I. Boundary Crossings and Intersectionality

1. Queer-Jewish-Muslim: Constructing Hyphenated
   Religious Identities through Tactics of Intersubjectivity   25
   Katrina Daly Thompson

2. Queer Disguises: Jewish Women's Performance of Race
   and Gender in the Colonial Maghreb   51
   Edwige Crucifix

3. "A Living Tableau of Queerness": The Orient at the
   Crossroads of Genre and Gender in Proust's *Recherche*   75
   Amr Kamal

II. Public Discourse and Identity

4. Queering the Abrahamic Scriptures   105
   Shanon Shah

5. A Corpus-Assisted Analysis of the Discursive Construction
   of LGBT Muslims and Jews in UK Media   127
   Robert Phillips

viii   Contents

III. Building Community, Forging Solidarity

6. Religious Life Is Life Together: Ritual, Liminality, and
Communitas among Queer Jews in Postsecular Britain   147
Matthew Richardson

7. Eid Parties, Iftar Dinners, and Pride Parades:
Navigating Queer Muslim Identity through Community   179
Elizabeth Johnstone

Afterword: Lessons in Historical Nominalism   205
David M. Halperin

Contributors   219
Index   221

Introduction

Why Jewish, Muslim, *and* Queer?

Adi Saleem

To study the long history of Jews and Muslims in Europe is to study the history of racialization, racism, imperialism, colonization, exploitation, expulsion, genocide, and extermination. From the *limpieza de sangre* (blood purity) statutes, first established in 1449 in Toledo, Spain, to the more recent French concept of *Français de souche* (French by roots/lineage), by way of eugenics and Nazi Germany's Nuremberg Laws, Jews and Muslims, among other racialized populations, have frequently found themselves at the center of white European obsessions with racial purity, often to deadly effect. At various junctures of European history, Jews and Muslims, even after conversion to Christianity (as in the case of *conversos/marranos* and *moriscos*), remained racialized and marginalized as Jews and Muslims. Then, as now, religion could not be conceptually separated from race. On the two 1492s—the Reconquista and the so-called discovery of the so-called New World—Ella Shohat suggests that "anti-Semitism or Judeophobia, along with anti-infidelism or Islamophobia, provided a conceptual framework projected outward against the indigenous peoples of Africa and the Americas."[1] At the same time, however, European discourses and practices of anti-Blackness in and between Africa and the Americas would also provide a conceptual and practical framework for the further elaboration of antisemitism and Islamophobia (two branches of what we might call Orientalism). Between the *cristiano viejo* and the *Français de souche* lies a long European history of constructing the civilized European subject as white and Christian in opposition to a range of inferiorized others. Much like gender must be continuously and repetitively performed in order to give it a sense of stability, the equation of humanness with Europeanness (and, thus, whiteness) would be repeatedly performed by force to the point where the human could be overdetermined by the European, with devastating consequences.[2] The racialization and, as Santiago Slabodsky puts it, the "barbarization" of Jews, Muslims, Natives, and Africans share a fundamental commonality: "throughout modernity imperial powers created networks of colonized described as barbarians and these networks, especially in our spatial framework, often included Jews."[3] This is not a narrative you will encounter within official histories of European nations that prefer a linear progression from obscurity to enlightenment, erecting an artificial boundary between European history and "world" history, between the history of the European continent (at what point did Europe become Europe and, thus, separate from Asia, and at what point did Europeans begin to see themselves as European?) and the history of the colonies, as if what happened "there" could be separated from what happened "here," as if "there" was not always "here." Indeed, to paraphrase Stuart Hall, this is the outside history that is inside the history of Europe.[4]

Engendering/Racing

The construction of Jews and Muslims as separate races that were/are inferior, inimical to white, Christian Europe, and therefore needing to be controlled or exterminated, reflects the interplay between the nascent European concepts of race and religion in early modern Europe. The dehumanization or infrahumanization of Jews and Muslims and Native Americans and Africans that went along with these concepts is a shared story, one that cannot be fully understood in isolation. Indeed, with *Orientalism*, Edward Said remarked that he was writing the story of the "strange secret sharer of Western anti-Semitism."[5] Examining the figure of the Jewish "Muselmänner" in Auschwitz, Gil Anidjar contends that "Muslim" could only become a signifier for "Jew" in this deadly context because there was some level of interchangeability in the European imaginary between "Semites," as a racial category constructed in opposition to "Aryans."[6] Numerous other scholars have devoted much attention to the interrelations between antisemitism and Islamophobia, Jews and Muslims, in Europe. A recent edited volume on the topic is subtitled with a tentative "A Shared Story?"—a question that the contributors' essays, looking at cases from a variety of locations in Europe, from Iberia to the Balkans, seem to answer in the affirmative.[7] The interrelation between antisemitism and Islamophobia in Europe is not merely historic but remains a key element in contemporary European racism. Sometimes, the interrelation is more subtle, as in the "theory" of *grand remplacement* (great replacement), popularized by French white nationalist Renaud Camus, which draws on classic antisemitic themes to claim that "elites" are conspiring to replace the white population with non-white immigrants, primarily Muslims. Other times, it is far more obvious, as when effigies of Orthodox Jews were burned at a 2015 anti-Muslim rally in Wrocław/Breslau, a city whose Jewish community was once the third largest in Germany before being almost entirely exterminated during the Holocaust. Writing from the United States, I cannot forget the alternating chants of "Jews will not replace us" and "You will not replace us" by white supremacists in Charlottesville, Virginia, in 2017. As a tiny minority in the United States, Jews cannot replace anyone by themselves. What those neo-Nazis meant was that Jews will not replace "us" with people of color. Without the history of the Semites (and the Aryans) and the history of barbarization (and colonization/civilization), without the *Protocols of the Elders of Zion* and the great replacement theory, we cannot fully understand and combat contemporary white supremacy. No wonder Fanon emphasized the intersection between antisemitism and Negrophobia: "Quand vous entendez dire du mal des Juifs, dressez l'oreille, on parle de vous."[8]

It should not be controversial to state that the figures of the Muslim and Jewish "other," as racialized, inferiorized, and persecuted subjects, have been co-constitutive in modern European thought over several centuries. Many Jews and Muslims from a variety of geographic and temporal locations understand this and resist in their own ways the white supremacy and coloniality that lie at the heart of their intersecting oppressions. Yet, despite an abundance of scholarship, particularly in the last few decades, and the compendium of European antisemitism and Islamophobia from the Middle Ages to the present, pointing to the shared history and present of Jews and Muslims in Europe, contemporary discourse, aided by the invention of the "Judeo-Christian," tends to position Jews and Muslims as inherently separate, irreconcilable, and antagonistic groups.[9] This ahistorical view of Jewish-Muslim relations, influenced by a reading of the Israeli colonization of Palestine that transforms colonization into ethnoreligious "conflict," continues to drive a wedge between Jews and Muslims in the twenty-first century and contributes to obscuring the intersecting forms of oppression that continue to affect all our lives. The chapters in this book challenge and go beyond this narrative of Jewish-Muslim polarization and conflict.

In addition, processes of racialization and barbarization have long functioned through hierarchical notions of gender and sexuality. The idea of two, distinct genders and biological dimorphism, as well as distinct, hierarchical gender roles, was constructed as a marker of civilization and the absence of which as a sign of barbarism. The late María Lugones, a pioneer in the field of decolonial feminism, introduced the concept of the "coloniality of gender," building on Aníbal Quijano's concept of "coloniality of power," precisely to examine our dominant system of gender today in terms of its imposition through European colonization. For Quijano, the concept of the coloniality of power helped explain how the concept of race—and subsequently the scientific elaboration of distinct, hierarchical races—was a fundamental part of the inauguration of a nascent colonial/capitalist/modern world system that involved the extraction and expropriation of natural resources and the exploitation of "inferior" races. Lugones's contribution to this line of inquiry was to highlight the importance of gender to this picture. She writes, "Understanding these features of the organization of gender in the modern/colonial gender system—the biological dimorphism, the patriarchal and heterosexual organization of relations—is crucial to an understanding of the differential gender arrangements along 'racial' lines."[10] This is the historical and contemporary reality of "gender ideology" and not the moral panic around pronouns and gender theory / *la théorie du genre* whipped up by the far right and the so-called gender-critical movement in North America and Europe. On a recent flight from Detroit to Amsterdam, I found myself discussing the complexities of postcolonial life in Africa, Asia, and the diaspora with a fellow passenger from Kenya. Kikuyu, he told me, does not have gender-defining pronouns. The same is true of Malay, and of most Austronesian languages, I added. How do people coming from these linguistic and cultural contexts even begin to make sense of the sheer horror that even the word "pronouns" seems to illicit in Ron DeSantis and his ilk? The sexual politics of this contemporary surge of fascism, we concluded, has its roots in an older colonial history.

If colonization and racism—which is to say, inequal colonial and racial power relations—are necessary conditions for the modern capitalist world system, gender—which is to say, inequal gender relations—and sexuality—which is to say, the imposition of heterosexual norms—too play a predominant role. Just as European colonizers classified entire groups of people into distinct races, with implications for the level of dignity and autonomy they "deserved," so too did they erase a global diversity of indigenous understandings of what came to be called gender and sexuality. From the diverse corporeal expressions of various Native American peoples (sometimes subsumed under the umbrella term *two-spirit*) to the Buginese *bissu*, today's frameworks of gender and sexuality, rooted in heteropatriarchy and coloniality, were neither "natural" nor universal. Moreover, even the category and the concept of gender itself, as Oyèrónkẹ́ Oyěwùmí demonstrates in her groundbreaking book *The Invention of Women: Making an African Sense of Western Gender Discourses* (1997), are not universal. Instead of a direct relation between body and identity (as in our contemporary dominant framework of gender), precolonial Yoruba society saw a variety of identities that were not related to anatomy. It was, Oyěwùmí explains, the imposition of colonial heteropatriarchy that led to "the emergence of women as an identifiable category, defined by their anatomy and subordinated to men in all situations."[11] Scholars like Oyěwùmí have helped us understand that, just as race is about racing social relations (rather than describing a "natural" or inherent quality), gender is better understood as an ongoing cultural and historical set of processes.

Alternative Epistemologies

Yet, in place of an epistemological and ontological diversity of corporeality, social roles, and desire, the world, in the era of European domination, was divided into two on the basis of European gender and sexual norms, which various colonial administrations would naturalize, normalize, and legislate. The "civilized" understood gender as a binary in which heterosexuality and heteropatriarchy were the organizing principles. Consequently, deviations, whether real or imagined, from this norm could be deployed as proof of a lack of civilization and evolution, thus justifying the need for control and/or extermination. Placed within such a context, we can clearly apprehend the sexual and racial politics that underpin the horrific photographs that emerged from the Abu Ghraib prison during the early stages of the US-led invasion of Iraq. The torture carried out by US soldiers at Abu Ghraib on Iraqi men relied on the construction of "the Muslim body . . . as pathologically sexually deviant and as potentially homosexual, and thus . . . as a particularized object for torture."[12] The linking of sexual deviancy to "savagery," in other words, "sexual colonization," was an essential feature of European imperialism in the Americas, Africa, and Asia from 1492 onward.[13] The exact parameters of sexual colonization differed from time to time and place to place, but the link between racial inferiority and gender/sexual practices remained central. The history of the term *berdache* provides an illuminating example of how this configuration of savagery and deviance also links European Islamophobia/Orientalism and European imperialism and genocide in the Americas:

> Of French origin, "berdache" translates as "kept boy" or "boy slave": that is, as a subordinate male (young, or read as youthful) who is imagined to have been turned into a sexual slave by adult men, and as a result to have been psychically if not also physically feminized. In this early modern French and Spanish usage, the term purportedly translated a word from Farsi, which in its own right appeared to be reporting to Europeans that Middle Eastern or Muslim societies were a source of this form of violent adult male coercion of young men into effeminizing sexual relations. . . . Immediately after achieving the Reconquista of the Iberian Muslim caliphates, Spanish conquistadores met Indigenous Americans through this racialized, imperialist, and Orientalist narrative. . . . In turn, because "berdache" invoked not just one person but an imagined male sexual economy, its colonial usage in the Americas actually projected sexual immorality onto Indigenous men collectively. In this way, colonizers deployed "berdache" or similar stories about gender or sexual transgression among Indigenous men to justify violating and assimilating Indigenous *peoples* under colonial patriarchal rule: attacks on Indigenous manhood that targeted gender diversity proved crucial to establishing colonial rule. . . . The gendered story of "berdache" functioned by altering identity for

all Indigenous people and for European invaders, while facilitating broad establishment of a colonial and patriarchal social order.[14]

With *berdache*, we get a glimpse of how casting an entire group of people as deviant, in terms of gender or sexuality, can serve an important role in justifying and establishing colonial rule. Is this surprising? Hardly. As mentioned earlier, if 1492 marks the so-called discovery of the so-called New World, it also marks the Reconquista and the Alhambra Decree. By dubiously situating the historiographical origin of *berdache* in Southwest Asia and North Africa (SWANA), while applying a generalized framework of immoral and deviant sexual desire to Indigenous peoples, European colonizers effectively produced their own sexual identity as moral and civilized through an erasure of precolonial understandings of gender and desire. The importance of the concept of *berdache* for European colonizers must be understood relationally: "knowing European manhood's boundaries to be porous and needing reinforcement, and meeting Indigenous possibilities that threw such boundaries into question, early conquerors invoked berdache as if assigning a failure to differentiate sex to Indigenous people, but they did so to define sexual normativity for them all."[15] In effect, the *berdache* frame served two purposes: first, it provided a veneer of stability to a fragile European masculinity, and, second, it allowed Europeans to portray non-Europeans, whether in the Americas or SWANA, as morally depraved and therefore incapable of ruling themselves (or even being entitled to human dignity and stewardship of their own lands). Colonization (and exploitation, expropriation, and extermination), in such a worldview, could be reframed as a moral obligation.

In contrast to these European norms, the Arab-Islamic world prior to the nineteenth century did not share the concept of "homosexuality" (and, thus, of the binary between homosexuality and heterosexuality) as a distinct sexual identity. Same-sex desire was instead understood as one aspect of human sexuality, among others. Premodern Arab-Islamic societies had a more fluid and flexible attitude toward expressions of corporeality and sexual desire than in Western Christendom. Indeed, while some Islamic jurists condemned same-sex relations, many others did not. This is not to validate the Orientalist fantasy of a decadent and sexually permissive Orient, however. Additionally, rather than taking the perspective that there was simply a discrepancy between the practice and the theory of same-sex desire, the intellectual historian Khaled El-Rouayheb suggests that there was a "multiplicity of ideals that coexisted in the Arab-Islamic world in the early Ottoman period" that would eventually be superseded by the European concept of homosexuality, which implies a particular epistemology and ontology, imposed through colonization.[16] Focusing on the lived experiences of queer Muslims, Scott Kugle argues that the very existence, presence, and persistence of contemporary queer Muslims who challenge any incommensurability between Islam and their sexuality serves as a reminder of a long, varied past of a "love [that] over flows the boundaries of eros and sexuality," one that is woven into the rich tapestry of what we might call the Islamic tradition.[17] Moreover, as the gay Imam and anthropologist of religion Ludovic-Mohamed Zahed writes, "It turns out that, not only does Islam play a central role in the identities of many queer Muslims, but that the identities of individual queer Muslims have undeniably occupied a central place in Islam, from the beginning."[18] From the figure of the *mukhannath* and the *ghulamiyya* to the practice of *nazar ila'l-murd* and the Urdu term *amrad parasti*, Islamic history is replete with examples that challenge the reductive view that one often encounters in contemporary discourse that Islam—as if there were a singular, definitive *Islam*—forbids homosexuality.

Similarly, the Jewish tradition offers a range of other ways of understanding and categorizing what we call gender and sexuality today. While the Western male-female gender binary is present in the Torah and the Talmud (as *zakhar* and *nekevah*), the Talmud also recognizes four other categories, namely, *androgynos*, *tumtum*, *aylonit*, and *saris*. However, the feminist theologian Rachel Adler warns that this categorization—and her caution applies as well to the Islamic case—is fraught with potential pitfalls. First, these categories may express a desire to diagnose and taxonomize nonconformity to a norm. Second, there remains a debate on whether these categories "actually present us with a spectrum of genders or merely a hierarchy in which the heterosexual male is predictably at the top and others are ranked according to their possession or possible possession of male characteristics."[19] Still, the very fact that there is a clear tradition, both in Islam and Judaism, of complicating, if not always going beyond, a gender binary suggests an understanding and recognition of the constructedness of these very categories. This implicit recognition of constructedness lies in stark contrast to the normalizing, hegemonic category of gender in modern

Europe. In other words, the concept of social constructionism, rather than being only rooted in Kantian or Marxian theories, may be characteristic of a particular impulse within Jewish and Muslim interpretive traditions. As Max Strassfeld suggests in *Trans Talmud* (2022), "Perhaps the rabbis invoke these categories to grapple with the regulation of the body and the limits of the halakhic enterprise itself."[20] Besides, to combine the insights of Zahed ("the identities of individual queer Muslims have undeniably occupied a central place in Islam") with Strassfeld's analysis of gender in rabbinic literature, it *is* significant, in terms of both historiography and contemporary politics/poetics, that "the rabbis chose to situate nonbinary people at the heart of rabbinic discussions of sex and gender."[21] The importance of this discussion, at least to me, is not so much to suggest that there can be a return to some precolonial form of Islam and Judaism that possesses a more capacious understanding of gender and sexuality but rather to suggest that the normalizing and naturalizing impulses of the modern gender (male-female) and sexual (heterosexual-homosexual) binary betray a particular, rather than a universal, epistemology. In the afterword to this book, the classicist and queer theorist David M. Halperin argues that studying classical antiquity "in all its unsystematic specificity" necessarily leads to the undoing of "all the ideologies that have been constructed on its ostensible foundation and in its name—the Eurocentrism, the white supremacism, the various ethnonationalisms, the racisms, the chauvinisms, the parochialisms, and the many reactionary varieties of identity politics (white, male, European, elitist identity politics, even chauvinist gay and lesbian identity politics)." Similarly, to look back and draw on a variety of figures and figurations in the diversity of Islamic and Jewish traditions is thus fundamentally about looking forward and imagining new possibilities with our queer Jewish and Muslim ancestors, among others, who certainly exceeded the categories constructed to make sense of them. To those concerned with the charge of anachronism, I am compelled to echo Strassfeld: "Some of us may be forced to live more fully within the bounds of these murderous ontologies. I therefore claim, for both myself and my kin, the use of any and all anachronisms, close readings, and fanciful-if-tenuous connections available to disrupt and imagine otherwise."[22] Simply put, there are other ways to understand, to make sense, to live, to share, to enjoy, and to be human that far exceed the limits of modern-colonial epistemology—and we will get there however we can.

Queering Jewish-Muslim Relations

The comparative study of the experiences (and representations) of Jews and Muslims within Euro-American modernity can help unravel the intimate relationship between race, religion, gender, and sexuality and modernity, capitalism, and coloniality. In contemporary public discourse, race, religion, gender, and sexuality are often taken for granted as distinct, coherent, and even natural categories organizing social life and relations. The context for the emergence of these categories, which I have sketched above in relation to modernity/coloniality, is often occluded. What impact does this occlusion continue to have today? For starters, the insistence on a clean, clear-cut separation between race and religion allows racism against Muslims to be cast as not actually racism. In contrast to just a hundred years ago, racism is today understood by most whites as "bad." However, by restricting the definition of racism to interpersonal prejudice based on skin color, the structural and systemic nature of racism (and its centrality to both European nation-states and our international order), which is to say, the most significant aspects of racism, remains obscured. In effect, a purely interpersonal-prejudice definition of racism allows a variety of practices, such as the surveillance of Muslim communities, the indiscriminate banning of citizens of majority Muslim countries, or the over-policing of "certain" neighborhoods, to be glossed over, while including absurdities like anti-white racism. In such a perspective, systematic violence against Muslims is not racism but merely a precautionary measure against a suspicious group of people motivated by a particularly dangerous, politico-religious ideology. In such a perspective, Islamophobia is not racism because Islam is not a race but a political religion ("radical Islam," "political Islam," "Islamism," and so on). Accordingly, Islamophobia becomes a moral obligation, which, perhaps not coincidentally, was how Europeans justified (and, to some extent, continue to justify) colonialism. As the French feminist Elisabeth Badinter argues, "We shouldn't be afraid of being called Islamophobic."[23] Against this reality, white nationalist commentators in Europe and the United States have been promoting the absurd idea that, due to Muslim immigration, there are areas in Europe and the United States that are dangerous, "no-go zones" for whites. This meaningless definition of racism stems from the evacuation of systems and structures from the concept of racism and the delinking of race from religion. This cynical usage of racism to the detriment of minoritized racialized people is also an important aspect of contemporary racism.

Despite the geographical, ethnic, and linguistic diversity of the global Muslim population, Muslims tend to be racialized in different but similar ways in Europe and the United States. Whether it is as *maghrébins* in France, "Asians" in the United Kingdom, or "Arabs" in the United States, with all the nuances related to the different colonial and imperial histories of these countries, there is a history of Muslim racialization—which rendered Muslims "Asiatic," "Turks," "Mohammedans," "Arabs," and so on, with a range of implications—that has shaped and continues to shape the perception of Muslim barbarism, licentiousness, and backwardness. Between British general Charles Napier (1782–1853), who described the Talpur in Sindh as a "barbarian power [that] continually menaces British India," and former US deputy national security adviser K. T. McFarland (1951–), who declared, after the US assassination of the Iranian general Qasem Soleimani, that, in contrast to the American "default position" of peace, the "normal state of condition [for 'Middle Easterners'] is war," the figure of the Muslim in Euro-America has long been racialized as inferior, violent, and needing to be controlled.[24] A hundred years separates Napier's death and McFarland's birth, but they are joined in a colonial continuity. To make sense of this continuity, to make sense of the consistency with which racial animus toward Muslims is often justified in religious terms, we must contend with the fact that neither in the past nor in the present has the concept of race ever been separate from the concept of religion, or as Gil Anidjar eloquently puts it, "The very distinction between race and religion is an effect of the historical movements we are still trying to grasp."[25] Indeed, the concept of *limpieza de sangre*, as an early form of systematic racialization and discrimination, constructs religious difference (Muslim and Jewish) as an immutable difference located in the blood. This is not to say that the modern concepts of race and religion are indistinguishable but that they are both "co-constitutive in their distinctiveness" and "co-concealing categories."[26]

Another description of the Talpurs proffered by Charles Napier provides us an entry point into another aspect of racialization, namely, its relation to ideas about gender and sexuality: "Their zenanas were filled with young girls torn from their friends, and treated with revolting barbarity. In fine, the life of an Ameer was one of gross sensuality, for which the labour and blood of men were remorselessly exacted, the honour and happiness of women savagely sacrificed!"[27] Scholars such as Leila Ahmed, Marnia Lazreg, and Lila Abu-Lughod have charted how various imperial and colonial powers have sought to justify their actions through a selective concern for women's rights.[28] Deploying what Leila Ahmed calls colonial feminism—or what Sara Farris has more recently termed femonationalism—at various junctures in history, US, UK, and French governments have justified invasions and colonization by casting Afghans, Egyptians, and Algerians as oppressive to women.[29] Such a framework is succinctly summarized by Gayathri Spivak: "white men saving brown women from brown men."[30] This framework does not only apply to justify imperialism outside Euro-America's borders, however; it also applies within European nation-states and the settler colonies of North America wherein certain racialized spaces are constructed as no-go zones for white men, (white) women, and (white) LGBT+ individuals. This spatial intersection between racing, gendering, and sexing is aptly captured, in the French context, by the title of Mehammed Mack's book on sexual nationalism: *Sexagon* (2017). The term "sexagon," referencing hexagon, a colloquial synonym for metropolitan France, succinctly describes how assumptions about gender and sexuality can be deployed to construct certain racialized groups as threatening, "unassimilable," and diametrically opposed to the values of the nation. In this way, a cynical and selective concern about gender and sexual equality is wielded to exclude and marginalize non-white people, particularly those racialized as Muslim.

None of this is unique to Muslims in the past and present. Just as Islamophobia often functions through assumptions about dangerous or deviant sexualities and genders, so too has antisemitism long been associated with ideas about the sexual and gender deviancy and degeneracy of Jews. In *Slandering the Jew: Sexuality and Difference in Early Christian Texts* (2013), Susanna Drake examines early Christian literature to convincingly argue that the depiction of Jews as sexually deviant, licentious, and diseased becomes a central theme in early Christian texts by the fourth century. Crucially, Drake demonstrates how these depictions were found not only in religious texts but also in legal texts and legislation. In both cases, Jewish sexual deviancy was constructed as a disease that threatened the healthy body of Christianity. The supposed physical degeneracy/deficiency of Jews was used to make claims about the intellectual and moral degeneracy/deficiency of Jews. As such, "Jews were portrayed both as perpetrators of [sexual/moral] violence and as subject to a justified—even necessary—Christian violence."[31] With obvious differences, this construction of Jewish sexual deviance animates Judeophobia and antisemitism in Europe through various time periods, from early Christianity and the Middle Ages to the nineteenth and twentieth centuries. It is not so much that there are similarities between the Jewish and Muslim case but that the experiences of Jews and Muslims in Europe are part of a larger racial, colonial system of control in which gender and sexual norms play a central role. These ideas about our supposed degeneracy tell us nothing about what it means to be Jewish or Muslim in any time period or in any place, but it tells us a great deal about "the ongoing legacy and political impact of Western, Christian, and European ideologies: Orientalist, colonialist, anti-Semitic, and Islamophobic."[32]

Even so, contemporary discussions about Jews and Muslims in Europe and North America tend to proceed from a rigid, binary assumption of Muslim aggression and Jewish victimhood (an exemplar in this genre is Pierre-André Taguieff's *La nouvelle judéophobie* [2002]). What is often absent is a reckoning with the intertwined histories and presents of Islamophobia, antisemitism, racism, coloniality, misogyny, and homophobia. Occasionally, this does enter public discourse, as when Adam Shatz penned a letter responding to Kamel Daoud's 2016 op-ed castigating "the sexual misery in the Arab-Muslim world."[33] Shatz reminded Daoud of his uneasiness at such a characterization that reminded him of classic antisemitic tropes of sexual deviancy and degeneracy: "Jews, as you well know, were themselves considered a strain of illness; and European anti-Semites in the 19th century, at the very moment of emancipation, were extremely preoccupied with the sexual customs of Jews and with the dominance of Jewish men over women."[34] The kind of Jewish-Muslim intersectional memory that Shatz demonstrates in his letter is all too rare in public discourse. Accordingly, this present book represents an exercise in queer Jewish-Muslim intersectionality and an attempt to bring a set of more nuanced interventions into the contemporary study and discussion of Jews and Muslims both within and without academia. Perhaps it represents an attempt to respond to the challenge that David Halperin issued to queer theory in 2003: "If queer theory is going to have the sort of future worth cherishing, we will have to find ways of renewing its radical potential—and by that I mean not devising some new and more avant-garde theoretical formulation of it but, quite concretely, reinventing its capacity to startle, to surprise, to help us think what has not yet been thought."[35] That is why we are talking about Jewish, Muslim, *and* queer.

This Book

Queer Jews, Queer Muslims is a collection of chapters from a variety of disciplinary and interdisciplinary perspectives examining the interrelated experiences and representations of Jewish and Muslim minorities in Europe, while triangulating the Jewish-Muslim dyad with a third variable: queerness. The focus on Islam and Judaism is important for several reasons, including the similarly racialized (and gendered and sexualized) positions of Jews and Muslims in European pasts and presents, the cultural and theological similarities, and the often polarized, oppositional representations of Jewishness and Muslimness (often as a function of conflicting transnational allegiances). In North America and Europe, Islamophobia increasingly functions by constructing Muslims and Islam as inherently hostile to LGBT+ people, women, Jews, and, more generally, liberals/ liberalism. By bringing together academics from different disciplines, this collection takes a comparative approach to study the convergences and divergences in the representations and lived experiences of Jewish and Muslim gender and sexual minorities in Europe and North America. In doing so, we critically examine and challenge the construction of Muslims and Islam as inherently hostile to LGBT+ issues and to Jews.

The chapters in this collection are divided into three sections: "Boundary Crossings and Intersectionality," "Public Discourse and Identity," and "Building Community, Forging Solidarity." In addition to these chapters, an afterword by David M. Halperin frames this book within a broader discussion of queerness and historical nominalism. The three sections of *Queer Jews, Queer Muslims* are interconnected, with each building upon the themes and insights presented in the preceding sections. The first section lays the foundation for the rest of the book by exploring the complexities of navigating multiple racialized, gendered, and sexual identity categories. The chapters in this section, from different disciplinary perspectives, examine the intersecting forces of race, religion, gender, and sexuality through a perspective rooted in intersectionality and the straddling of/crossing between multiple identities and boundaries imposed by dominant norms and expectations. The second section builds on this by examining how representations of queer Jews and Muslims are constructed and deployed in the public sphere. The chapters in this section interrogate the ways in which scriptural texts and media discourse shape perceptions of Jewish and Muslim gender and sexual minorities and how these representations have the potential to significantly impact the lived experiences of queer Jews and Muslims by either limiting or expanding the space available for the expression of nonnormative Jewish and Muslim sexualities and corporealities. Importantly, this section highlights how Jewishness and Muslimness are often constructed in opposition to each other and how these configurations have an impact on lived experiences. The final section brings the themes of the book to a conclusion by examining the (separate) efforts of queer Jews and Muslims, in the contemporary period, to organize themselves and form communities as a way of forging solidarity in the face of multiple forms of oppression and marginalization. The chapters in this section explore a variety of strategies and tactics deployed by queer Jews and Muslims to build networks of solidarity and communion. Importantly, with these chapters, we gain a sense of how queer Jews and Muslims may be forging new forms of cultural citizenship that provide us with alternatives to hegemonic demands of assimilation and integration.

The first section, "Boundary Crossings and Intersectionality," begins with a chapter by linguistic anthropologist Katrina Daly Thompson on two queer individuals who both identify, in different ways, as queer, Jewish, *and* Muslim. Drawing on an analysis of interviews and talk-in-interaction at a queer-inclusive mosque and in online progressive Muslim spaces, Thompson examines the ways in which these two queer-Jewish-Muslim individuals construct intersectional identities in interaction. The second chapter is by literary scholar Edwige Crucifix, who examines how same-sex desire was reclaimed in novels by Maghrebi women writers during the French colonial period. Crucifix examines authors Elissa Rhaïs and Blanche Bendahan to demonstrate how these novels sought to challenge the racial and sexual strictures of colonialism, while negotiating their own complicated colonial positions. The final chapter of the first section is written by Amr Kamal, a professor of French and Arabic, who reexamines Proust's magnum opus. Seizing on a brief remark by Edward Said that describes Orientalism as "a living tableau of queerness," Kamal deftly analyzes a wide range of references to Jewishness and Muslimness and queerness in *La Recherche*. Kamal asks and answers why and how the Orient (in its Jewish, Muslim, and queer articulations) functions as both an impending threat and a source of desire in *La Recherche*. The Orient, Kamal argues, represents a way for Proust to disrupt the normative narrative of French national history. "Proust," Kamal writes, "uses Orientalist imaginary as a form of queering to deconstruct French national identity and culture." These three opening chapters differ in methodology, theoretical framework, and primary sources, but they are each concerned with interactions, interrelations, and intersections between Jewish, Muslim, and queer identifications.

The second section, "Public Discourse and Identity," contains two chapters that focus on (scriptural and media) discourse and identity. The first chapter, written by sociologist Shanon Shah, revisits the interconnections between Jewish and Muslim scriptures in order to explore the tension between, on the one hand, the lived experience and spirituality of queer Muslims and, on the other, normative claims of Islamic authority. In doing so, Shah also adopts a creative approach to the issue by asking and reflecting on a series of deeply personal questions, such as the extent to which queer Jews and Muslims are curious about each other and read each other's texts together or the extent to which his own approach is a product of his particular insider-outsider position as a gay Muslim and a scholar of religion whose approach to spirituality is unabashedly hybrid. By reflecting on these questions, Shah takes us on a veritable journey through the heart of identity construction, knowledge production, and religious and spiritual experience. The second chapter in this section is written by cultural and linguistic anthropologist Robert Phillips, who explores how UK media discursively constructs LGBTQ Jewish and Muslim identities. Drawing on corpus linguistics and discourse analysis, Phillips systematically examines mainstream media coverage of LGBTQ Jews and Muslims from 2000 to 2018. In doing so, Phillips makes a unique contribution to the study of Islamophobia and antisemitism in mainstream media coverage by examining the particular ways in which doubly minoritized individuals (in this case, queer Jews and Muslims) are represented in British media.

The final section, "Building Community, Forging Solidarity," is devoted to, on the one hand, the efforts of queer Jews and Muslims to build community and forge solidarity and, on the other, the significant challenges such endeavors face. The first chapter by social anthropologist Matthew Richardson introduces readers to a unique queer Jewish space in London (and a number of puns): Buttmitzvah. The event, Richardson explains, is dubbed "the ultimate cumming of age party," which puts the "Oy Gay! into the ancient teenage Jewish ritual, [Bat] Mitzvah." Buttmitzvah, however, is not merely another raunchy London club night. Drawing on ethnographic research, Richardson proposes that the event represents a liminal space for attendees to construct and maintain queer Jewish social solidarity in the face of antisemitism, heterosexism, and postsecularism. Richardson argues that it is precisely the "anti-structural quality" of the event that allows the queer Jewish participants to resist and subvert broader hegemonic power structures, while consciously engaging in "identity affirmation" and "celebration." The final chapter of the book, written by independent scholar Elizabeth Johnstone, focuses on queer Muslim community building and identity construction. Drawing on original research conducted in the United Kingdom, Johnstone carefully examines the impact of targeted support groups and networks created by and for queer Muslims. By placing these initiatives in the context of Islamophobia and queerphobia in the United Kingdom, this chapter captures the high stakes involved. Through her analysis, Johnstone suggests that such groups and networks participate in creating new forms of queer Muslim citizenship and thus provide alternatives to hegemonic demands of acceptance and integration.

Together, these chapters examine, first, historical and contemporary representations of queer Jews and Muslims in a variety of texts, images, and media and, second, queer Jews and Muslims from an anthropological perspective, focusing on subjectivities and collectivities. In doing so, the book sheds light on the interconnected nature of cultural/political representation and individual/collective lived experience. By placing the question of gender and sexuality at the heart—and not merely as a subsection—of (ethno-)religious identity and spiritualties, the volume queers binary and oppositional understandings of Jewishness/Judaism and Muslimness/Islam in order to, *inshallah*, *be'ezrat hashem*, broaden the horizon of Jewish and Muslim coexistence and, more important, co-resistance. After all, the colonialism, racism, sexism, queerphobia, and transphobia that are all part and parcel of the power structures of our contemporary world are killing all of us—some quicker and more directly than others—Jewish and Muslim alike.

Notes

1 Shohat, "The Sephardi-Moorish Atlantic," 52.
2 See Wynter, "Unsettling the Coloniality of Being/Power/Truth/Freedom," and Wynter, "No Humans Involved," for a longer discussion of how humanness came to be overdetermined by Europeanness/whiteness and the resulting consequences of such an overdetermination.
3 Slabodsky, *Decolonial Judaism*, 59.
4 Hall, "Old and New Identities, Old and New Ethnicities," 70.
5 Said, *Orientalism*, 27–28.
6 Anidjar, *The Jew, the Arab*, 138–49.
7 Renton and Gidley, *Antisemitism and Islamophobia in Europe: A Shared Story?*
8 Fanon, *Peau noire, masques blancs*, 98.
9 See Nathan and Topolski, *Is There a Judeo-Christian Tradition?*
10 Lugones, "Heterosexualism and the Colonial/Modern Gender System," 190.
11 Oyěwùmí, *The Invention of Women*, 124.
12 Puar, *Terrorist Assemblages*, 87.
13 Morgensen, *Spaces between Us*, 36.
14 Morgensen, "Cutting to the Roots of Colonial Masculinity," 43–44.
15 Morgensen, *Spaces between Us*, 37.
16 El-Rouayheb, *Before Homosexuality in the Arab-Islamic World*, 155.
17 Kugle, *Living Out Islam: Voices of Gay, Lesbian, and Transgender Muslims*, 229.
18 Zahed, *Homosexuality, Transidentity, and Islam*, 116.
19 Adler, "Queer Jews Talking Their Way In," 10.
20 Strassfeld, *Trans Talmud*, 188.
21 Strassfeld, *Trans Talmud*, 194.
22 Strassfeld, *Trans Talmud*, 88.
23 France Inter, "Elisabeth Badinter : Il ne faut pas avoir peur de se faire traiter d'islamophobe," *L'invité de 8h20 : le grand entretien*, January 6, 2016. www.radiofrance.fr/franceinter/podcasts/l-invite-de-8h20/elisabeth-badinter-il-ne-faut-pas-avoir-peur-de-se-faire-traiter-d-islamophobe-8630081.

24 Napier, *The History of General Sir Charles Napier's Conquest of Scinde*, 15; McFarland, "On Fox, Former Trump Official Claims the Middle East's 'Normal State of Condition Is War.'"

25 Anidjar, *Blood*, 62.

26 Anidjar, *Blood*, 62; Anidjar, *Semites*, 28.

27 Napier, *The History of General Sir Charles Napier's Conquest of Scinde*, 24.

28 See Ahmed, *Women and Gender in Islam*; Lazreg, *The Eloquence of Silence*; Abu-Lughod, *Do Muslim Women Need Saving?*

29 See Farris, *In the Name of Women's Rights*.

30 Spivak, "Can the Subaltern Speak?" 48.

31 Drake, *Slandering the Jew*, 100.

32 Hochberg, "'Remembering Semitism' *or* 'On the Prospect of Re-Membering the Semites,'" 193.

33 Daoud, "The Sexual Misery of the Arab World."

34 Shatz, "The Correspondence of Kamel Daoud."

35 Halperin, "The Normalization of Queer Theory," 343.

Works Cited

Abu-Lughod, Lila. *Do Muslim Women Need Saving?* Cambridge, MA: Harvard University Press, 2013.

Adler, Rachel. "Queer Jews Talking Their Way In." *European Judaism* 49, no. 2 (2016): 6–13.

Ahmed, Leila. *Women and Gender in Islam: Historical Roots of a Modern Debate*. New Haven: Yale University Press, 1992.

Anidjar, Gil. *Blood: A Critique of Christianity*. New York: Columbia University Press, 2014.

———. *The Jew, the Arab: A History of the Enemy*. Stanford: Stanford University Press, 2003.

———. *Semites: Race, Religion, Literature*. Stanford: Stanford University Press, 2008.

Daoud, Kamel. "The Sexual Misery of the Arab World." *New York Times*, February 12, 2016. www.nytimes.com/2016/02/14/opinion/sunday/the-sexual-misery-of-the-arab-world.html.

Drake, Susanna. *Slandering the Jew: Sexuality and Difference in Early Christian Texts*. Philadelphia: University of Pennsylvania Press, 2013.

El-Rouayheb, Khaled. *Before Homosexuality in the Arab-Islamic World, 1500–1800*. Chicago: University of Chicago Press, 2005.

Fanon, Frantz. *Peau noire, masques blancs*. Paris: Editions du Seuil, 1952.

Farris, Sara R. *In the Name of Women's Rights: The Rise of Femonationalism*. Durham, NC: Duke University Press, 2017.

France Inter. "Elisabeth Badinter : Il ne faut pas avoir peur de se faire traiter d'islamophobe." *L'invité de 8h20 : le grand entretien*, January 6, 2016. www.radiofrance.fr/franceinter/podcasts/l-invite-de-8h20/elisabeth-badinter-il-ne-faut-pas-avoir-peur-de-se-faire-traiter-d-islamophobe-8630081.

Hall, Stuart. "Old and New Identities, Old and New Ethnicities." In *Essential Essays, Volume 2: Identity and Diaspora*. Durham, NC: Duke University Press, [1991] 2018.

Halperin, David. "The Normalization of Queer Theory." *Journal of Homosexuality* 45, no. 2–4 (2003): 339–43.

Hochberg, Gil. "'Remembering Semitism' or 'On the Prospect of Re-Membering the Semites.'" *ReOrient* 1, no. 2 (2016): 192–223.

Kugle, Scott Siraj al-Haqq. *Living Out Islam: Voices of Gay, Lesbian, and Transgender Muslims*. New York: New York University Press, 2014.

Lazreg, Marnia. *The Eloquence of Silence: Algerian Women in Question*. New York: Routledge, 1994.

Lugones, Maria. "Heterosexualism and the Colonial/Modern Gender System." *Hypatia* 22, no. 1 (2007): 186–209.

Mack, Mehammed Amadeus. *Sexagon: Muslims, France, and the Sexualization of National Culture*. New York: Fordham University Press, 2017.

McFarland, KT. "On Fox, Former Trump Official Claims the Middle East's 'Normal State of Condition Is War.'" Media Matters, January 8, 2020. www.mediamatters.org/outnumbered/fox-former-trump-official-claims-middle-easts-normal-state-condition-war.

Morgensen, Scott L. "Cutting to the Roots of Colonial Masculinity." In *Indigenous Men and Masculinities: Legacies, Identities, Regeneration*, edited by Robert Alexander Innes and Kim Anderson. Winnipeg: University of Manitoba Press, 2015.

———. *Spaces between Us: Queer Settler Colonialism and Indigenous Decolonization*. Minneapolis: University of Minnesota Press, 2011.

Napier, William Francis Patrick. *The History of General Sir Charles Napier's Conquest of Scinde*. London: Charles Westerton, 1857.

Nathan, Emmanuel, and Anya Topolski, eds. *Is There a Judeo-Christian Tradition? A European Perspective.* Berlin: De Gruyter, 2016.

Oyěwùmí, Oyèrónkẹ́. *The Invention of Women: Making an African Sense of Western Gender Discourses.* Minneapolis: University of Minnesota Press, 1997.

Puar, Jasbir. *Terrorist Assemblages: Homonationalism in Queer Times.* Durham, NC: Duke University Press, 2007.

Renton, James, and Ben Gidley, eds. *Antisemitism and Islamophobia in Europe: A Shared Story?* New York: Palgrave Macmillan, 2017.

Said, Edward W. *Orientalism.* New York: Pantheon Books, 1978.

Shatz, Adam. "The Correspondence of Kamel Daoud." World Policy, February 26, 2016. worldpolicy.org/2016/02/26/the-correspondence-of-kamel-daoud/ (now unavailable).

Shohat, Ella. "The Sephardi-Moorish Atlantic: Between Orientalism and Occidentalism." Between the Middle East and the Americas: The Cultural Politics of Diaspora, edited by Ella Shohat and Evelyn Alsultany, University of Michigan Press, 2013, pp. 42–62.

Slabodsky, Santiago. *Decolonial Judaism.* New York: Palgrave Macmillan, 2014.

Spivak, Gayatri Chakravorty. "Can the Subaltern Speak?" In *Can the Subaltern Speak? Reflections on the History of an Idea,* edited by Rosalind Morris. New York: Columbia University Press, [1988] 2010.

Strassfeld, Max K. *Trans Talmud: Androgynes and Eunuchs in Rabbinic Literature.* Berkeley: University of California Press, 2022.

Taguieff, Pierre-André. *La nouvelle judéophobie.* Paris: Mille et une nuits, 2002.

Wynter, Sylvia. "No Humans Involved: An Open Letter to My Colleagues." *Forum N.H.I.: Knowledge for the 21st Century* 1, no. 1 (1994): 42–73.

———. "Unsettling the Coloniality of Being/Power/Truth/Freedom: Towards the Human, After Man, Its Overrepresentation—An Argument." *CR: The New Centennial Review* 3, no. 3 (2003): 257–337.

Zahed, Ludovic-Mohamed. *Homosexuality, Transidentity, and Islam: A Study of Scripture Confronting the Politics of Gender and Sexuality.* Translated by Adi Saleem Bharat. Amsterdam: Amsterdam University Press, 2019.

PART I

BOUNDARY CROSSINGS AND INTERSECTIONALITY

1

Queer-Jewish-Muslim

Constructing Hyphenated Religious Identities through Tactics of Intersubjectivity

Katrina Daly Thompson

Judeo-Islam is all about the work that the hyphen does. It is the positing of imbroglio as opposed to tidiness.

—AARON HUGHES, "INTERVIEW"[1]

With the hyphen . . . between "Jewish and Muslim," we are, baruch hashem, alhamdulillah, reunited.

—BRIAN KLUG, "JEWISH-MUSLIM: WHAT'S IN A HYPHEN?"[2]

Introduction

Like normative conceptions of binary sex and gender, scholars and lay-people alike often treat religious identities as bounded categories: one must either be male or female, a man or a woman, and, if religious, one must select one label: Christian, Jewish, Muslim, or whatever. To identify with more than one religion, like identifying as intersex, non-binary, or gender fluid, is a rather queer thing to do. Many researchers have dismissed the idea that one could be both Jewish *and* Muslim, often viewing Jews and Muslims through biological metaphors as different "species"—a view that Aaron Hughes has recently critiqued.[3] This chapter takes a queer anthropological approach to entangled queer-Jewish-Muslim identities and relationships, first in reviewing the existing literature and then by examining how two contemporary individuals involved in queer-inclusive Muslim groups navigate their hyphenated religious identities, practices, and heritages.

In line with this chapter's epigraphs, I reinstate the hyphen that once "made possible such terms as 'Judeo-Muslim' and 'Arab-Jew,'" but was dropped from common use in the West in favor of "Judeo-Christian," and add *queer* to it, arguing for a queer-Muslim-Jewish understanding of entangled identifications.[4] Following anthropologist Margot Weiss, I use *queer* here to "signify transgression of, resistance to, or exclusion from normativity, especially but not exclusively heteronormativity."[5] Ara Wilson draws our attention to Weiss's phrase "not exclusively," which "stresses the intersectional nature of queer perspectives, meaning that prevailing sex/gender norms are not isolated axes of social systems" but intertwine with others—including, in the two cases I examine here, religion, race, and ethnicity.[6]

While not using *queer* exclusively to refer to identity, both I and the two people whose discourse I examine in this chapter *do* consider ourselves queer. David, a gay intersex male-presenting person in Toronto, is Jewish but attends a queer-inclusive mosque nearly every Friday, sometimes even giving the sermon. Keegan, a gay Arab non-binary person who grew up in Iraq and Syria and now lives in Southern California, identifies as both Jewish and Muslim and is an active participant in a queer-inclusive Muslim online group. After reviewing some of the scholarly work that has rendered hyphenated religiosity queer and thus illegible, I turn to David's and Keegan's framing of their queer-Jewish-Muslim experiences. I use analysis of interviews with both of them, a sermon David gave during Friday prayers, and Keegan's posts in an online progressive Muslim group to explore the various ways in which the two use "tactics of intersubjectivity" to construct hyphenated religious and other identities in interaction.[7] In addition to understanding *queer* as part of David's and Keegan's self-identifications, I argue that their Jewish-Muslim-ness is itself queer and allows for new, queer ways of understanding complex religious identities that exceed normative binaries.

On the Permeability of Boundaries

Jewish and Muslim cultural syncretism has been well documented but usually treated as distinct from religion. Ella Shohat, in her work on the "Judeo-Muslim" and "Arab-Jew," describes "a kind of transregional geo-cultural Jewish space, from the Mediterranean to the Indian Ocean . . . under the aegis of the larger Islamic world," within which Jews traveled and exchanged goods and ideas while retaining their Jewishness and were "shaped by Arab Muslim culture, while also helping shape that culture in a dialogical process."[8] Mark Mazower describes Jewish men in Salonica who adapted aspects of Islamic law to their own needs and adopted Muslim sartorial and tonsorial customs.[9] In the provocatively titled chapter "On the (Im)Possibility of Muslim Jews," Yair Wallach asks, "If we think of Jewish as nationality and Muslim as belonging to a faith community, are these two categories necessarily mutually exclusive, or could they overlap? Could a Muslim join the Jewish nation without converting? Could a Jew convert to Islam and remain a Jew in nationality?"[10] Such questions rest on the normative assumption that if we think of Jewish as belonging to a faith community then Jewish and Muslim *are* mutually exclusive.

While scholars often depict cultural boundaries between Muslims and Jews as nonexistent, they nevertheless tend to treat "religious borders" as "clear-cut."[11] Hughes's *Shared Identities* beautifully demonstrates that in the early period of Islam "no characteristics could be described as singularly Jewish or Muslim, primarily because neither group existed or at least not on the Arabian Peninsula."[12] Yet, the assumption of clear-cut boundaries is so taken for granted that, even in the face of contradictory evidence, scholars continue to depict Muslims and Jews as binary opposites. Thus, in the face of evidence that Jews converted to Islam but retained some of their Jewish beliefs and practices, scholars have referred to their conversion as "nominal" rather than considering the possibility that they believed in elements of both traditions.[13]

While Hughes focuses on the period of Islam's emergence in the Arabian Peninsula, showing that boundaries between Islam and Judaism were blurry, scholarship on later periods and other places has continued to depict Islam and Judaism as separated by firm boundaries. For example, the Dönme in Turkey arose from followers of the Jewish convert to Islam Sabbatai/Shabbetai Zevi (1626–76), forming a whole community of "Muslim Jews."[14] Yet, many researchers question the Dönme's religious identity. Scholars have described Zevi mainly in negative terms—"a spiritual schizophrenic," "torn between two religions," in "a state of inner turmoil," leading a "double life."[15] His followers, too, like early Jewish converts, are depicted as "nominal Muslims," only "ostensibly Muslim," "by no means genuine converts," or "caught in the crack," in an "internal tug-of-war" between two religious identities.[16] Gil Anidjar refers to the title of his own article "Muslim Jews" as "somehow implausible," an "unnecessary" phrase of null value—"the name of a fiction" used to refer to those who convert to Islam but remain "Jews at heart."[17] Even Hughes argues that "the line between Jew and Muslim is perhaps more fixed and impermeable than it has ever been."[18]

Examining queer-Muslim-Jews reveals that the line is more like a hyphen, more permeable than it may seem. Some individuals refuse to be contained by orthodox binaries, and this refusal allows them to queer their religious beliefs, practices, and identities. As "Nikos" Hannan-Stavroulakis, a Turkish descendant of the Dönme, told Alpert: "Sunni Orthodox Muslims find [the Dönme] not really Muslims. Jews find them not Jews."[19] Nikos didn't tell Alpert much about how the Dönme view themselves, but his comment hints at the possibility of a syncretic approach to religion—the possibility of practicing both Judaism and Islam in ways illegible to those concerned with orthodoxy. We also find syncretism in Henk Driessen's study of shrines in precolonial and colonial Morocco, where both Muslims and Jews visited the same shrines and venerated the same saints.[20] These examples suggest that having some distance from "orthodox" religion makes blurring the boundaries between religions more imaginable.

Works "devoted to micro topics in Jewish-Muslim relations," Hughes argues, have increased "our knowledge of localized interactions between Jews and Muslims in specific geographical locales" but without contributing much to broader, theoretical understandings of the purported boundaries between religious or other identities.[21] In contrast, I argue that individual cases, when read queerly, can point to the non-binary nature of Jewish-Muslim-ness well beyond the formative period of Islam that Hughes examines. In his ethnographic study of Moroccan Jews, André Levy describes a presumptive gay man, George, whose "indifference to gossip" about his sexuality "attested to an overall outlook that ignored community pressures, including those around relationships with Muslims," who were welcomed into George's home but not into the homes of other Jews Levy knew.[22] Pointing toward links between queer gender performance and queer religiosity, in his interview with Alpert, Nikos also draws parallels between the Dönme and "transvestites."[23] (Unfortunately, Alpert focuses on the "stigma" of cross-dressing rather than its subversive potential.)

And there are other hints of queer boundary crossers in what we might call the hyphenated Jewish-Muslim archive. In his recent biographical work on Hugo Marcus (1880–1966), a gay German Jew who converted to Islam but remained active in the Jewish community, Marc David Baer writes that Marcus's religious identity "should give us cause to rethink where the boundary between 'Muslim' and 'Jew' lies" and "helps us to queer Jewish and Islamic Studies simultaneously."[24] Yet, through commas, the title of the book—*German, Jew, Muslim, Gay*—renders each aspect of Marcus's identity separable from the others. In contrast, hyphens would have made more explicit the extent to which these categories intersected with one another.

"Seen on occasion studying the Koran while wearing the *tefillin* (phylacteries) of the pious Jew," Zevi was not unlike the two contemporary queer-Muslim-Jewish individuals I introduce below.[25] Queer boundary disruption is useful here as a framework because it helps us pay attention to gender-sexuality-race-religion intersections, sites where boundaries can still be made porous. Through this framework, in the remainder of this chapter, I turn to two contemporary examples. Keegan's and David's experiences, while "micro examples," exemplify the ways in which queer transgression of gender, race, and religious normativities allows interfaith relationships and religious idiosyncrasy to flourish.

Ethnographic Context, Participants, and Methods

I met Keegan and David while conducting multisited ethnographic research in several interconnected Muslim groups and mosques loosely affiliated with what others have called "the progressive Muslim movement."[26] When I began the project in January 2016, I conceived of it as a study of progressive Muslims, but I have since come to consider them "nonconformist Muslims." I use this label similarly to the way I defined *queer* above, reflecting these communities' radical inclusion of anyone who considers themselves a Muslim, even those who transgress some (or many) normative Islamic interpretations. Although not everyone involved in these groups is queer in terms of sexuality or gender, *queer* is central to their practices and discourse because of participants' nonconformity with dominant Muslim norms, including their religious pluralism.[27] Across all of the groups in which I conducted participant observation, members are predominantly Muslim but welcome non-Muslims like David. Many identify as lesbian, gay, bisexual, trans, non-binary, queer, or some combination of these categories.

As a queer convert and self-identified "progressive Muslim," I am a longtime member of the Facebook group of Muslims for Progressive Values (MPV), founded in 2007, where I first met Keegan.[28] Via Skype, I had occasionally prayed with the El-Tawhid Juma Circle Toronto Unity Mosques (El-Tawhid for short) during Friday prayers before beginning my research, visiting in person, and meeting David. Many MPV members are involved in groups that meet in person for prayer or other spiritual practices, religious discussions, or socializing, including El-Tawhid. Since 2009, El-Tawhid has functioned as a "pop-up mosque" every Friday in Toronto.[29] Their congregational prayers are also open to the global nonconformist community, initially via Skype, later by live video through Facebook, and now—since COVID-19—by Zoom.

I met David in September 2016 during my first in-person visit to El-Tawhid; during my second visit in June 2019, I recorded David giving the sermon. About a week later, we met up for an interview at Toronto's Allen Gardens, and since then we have stayed in touch by email. "If I'm introducing you to readers in something that I'm writing, how would you like me to describe you, or how would you introduce yourself?" I asked.

"Well, the first word that came to my mind is princess," David said with mock seriousness, making me laugh. "But I really don't know." David thought for a moment before offering this description: "Arab-Jewish guy negotiating a place within progressive Islam within Toronto." Although David used the word *guy*, has a typically male name, and self-describes as "male-presenting," David is intersex, prefers to be referred to as a person rather than a man, and asked me to use the real name David rather than any third-person pronouns.[30] Although, in Canada, people see David as "dead-fish-belly white," David does not identify as such "because my Arab Jewish community includes people who wouldn't be able to pass as white."

David also lived in Europe for six years, "where I found out that Europeans don't think of North Africans as white, and to people in Europe, particularly places that have large North African populations, . . . I was identifiable as not-white." David's understanding of North African racialization resonates with Alastair Bonnett's work on how Middle Eastern and North African self-understandings have evolved from earlier conceptions of themselves as "white," in contrast to sub-Saharan or darker-skinned Africans, toward Arabness as a form of resistance to European domination.[31]

While I've spent time with David in person, I know Keegan, who uses *they/them* pronouns, mostly through online spaces. I first encountered Keegan in January 2018, when they joined MPV, a large (19,000+ members) online group and nonprofit organization for progressive Muslims of which I've been a member since 2009, just two years after the group began. Keegan is a pseudonym similar to their real name—which they legally changed, having rejected a "very masculine" Arabic birth name in favor of one Keegan describes as a "more non-binary name."

> It's also a nonreligious name, you know? I don't think it's fair that, that I am identifying with a specific name that is only exclusively for one religion, one race, one gender, 'cause this is not who I am.

A few months after Keegan joined MPV, we met in person at the June 2018 West Hollywood Pride parade, where we both marched with the Los Angeles chapter of MPV, which included members of the MPV Facebook group and others. Subsequently, Keegan and I became friends on social media, and in March 2020 I interviewed them over Zoom. Keegan came to the United States as a refugee from Iraq in 2011 and is now a US citizen. In their first post to MPV in January 2018, Keegan introduced themself as "an LGBTQ community member and out to the community as a Gender Fluid Muslim activist." Just a few months later, in June, Keegan added another layer to their identity, coming out to the group as "Muslim-Jewish Queer" and punctuating their exclamation with a rainbow-flag emoji, a symbol of LGBTQ pride.

In the remaining sections, I examine my interviews with both Keegan and David, Keegan's posts in MPV, and one of David's sermons at El-Tawhid. I do so using Bucholtz and Hall's "tactics of intersubjectivity" framework to understand how they position themselves in relation to

Islam, Judaism, and queerness, or as I put it here, *queer-Jewish-Muslim-ness*. David's and Keegan's use of such tactics, I argue, enables them to articulate understandings of Islam and Judaism that depend not on abstract, orthodox interpretations of either religion but rather on their own "local, contingent, and contextually specific acts," which are crucially linked to their queerness.[32]

The tactics of intersubjectivity articulated by Bucholtz and Hall include three dimensions along which to examine how identification emerges in interaction: "sameness versus difference, genuineness versus artifice, and institutional recognition versus structural marginalization."[33] With regard to the three "positive" tactics (the first pole in each binary), David and Keegan use *adequation*—the construction of "social sameness"—to present similarities between Jewish and Muslim traditions and practices. Both use *authentication* to link themselves to their Jewish ancestors and those ancestors' interfaith relationships. David also uses *authorization* to legitimate involvement, as a Jew, in Muslim religious practices. But both only use one "negative" tactic: *distinction*, marking their difference from various normative identities and practices. Evaluating these differences positively, David and Keegan valorize anti-normativity, thereby marking themselves and their practices as *queer*.[34] Ultimately, I argue, it is this queerness—which is entangled with but not limited to their gender and sexual nonconformity—that allows them to claim relationships to both Judaism and Islam.

Adequation

Both Keegan and David use adequation, an interactive tactic through which people emphasize individual or group similarities, albeit in slightly different ways. Keegan, on the one hand, emphasizes the similarity between "Muslim" and "Jewish" as identities an *individual* might hold and construct through discourse and depicts practices from both religions as offering them ways to be a faithful religious person. David, on the other hand, emphasizes similarities between Jewish and Muslim *communities* and communal traditions.

In both MPV and our conversation, Keegan used a tactic of adequation, presenting the social categories *Muslim*, *Jewish*, and *queer* as "sufficiently similar" to coexist within a single individual, erasing the social boundaries between them.[35] While I already knew from Keegan's online posts that they are a "Muslim-Jewish Queer," they explained their complex, layered identity further during our March 2020 interview.

> I identify both as Muslim and Jew since I was born in [a] bi-faith, or multi-faith family, interfaith. . . . I am a queer person, an immigrant, a refugee, a war survivor. Somebody who still believes in God, oddly enough, even after all I've been through.

In Keegan's online post, the hyphen in "Muslim-Jewish" contributed to this adequation as well, resonating with this chapter's epigraphs. When Keegan said "oddly enough," "even," and "actually" to introduce their belief in God and, more broadly, religion, they acknowledged that some people would see a distinction between their religiosity and their experiences of discrimination as a gay and gender fluid person. Still, they obscured the differences between these experiences.

Keegan incorporates religious practices from both Islam and Judaism into their life, suggesting that the practices are similar enough in purpose to achieve Keegan's spiritual goals. Not only does Keegan pray the traditional Muslim *salat* five times a day and pay *zakat*, a form of Islamic charity, but they also observe the Jewish Sabbath:

> I still do Shabbat, Sabbath, on Fridays. Very interesting[ly], I still celebrate both Muslim and Jewish holidays. . . . I still have both, from both religions, I still have things that I consider religious. . . . Both of them are really important for me in my life, to believe in them, and to identify with them, and to do them also. . . . I do believe those are religious ideas, not just traditional ideas. Like, I don't have to do it anymore, I don't have to pray five times a day anymore if I am not religious. I don't have to do Shabbat anymore if I'm not religious. But those things actually help me, help me move on with my life, and keep my spirits up, keep my faith up, keep my trust up.

Keegan's four-time repetition of the word *both* contributes to the adequation of the two religions. Moreover, by distinguishing between *religious* and *traditional* ideas, Keegan equates Jewish and Muslim practices *as religious*; Keegan is not merely a Muslim with some Jewish heritage but rather a Muslim-Jew, someone who practices both religions.

Whereas Keegan presented Judaism and Islam as existing equally within themself, in our interview, David focused on historical relationships between Jews and Muslims. Drawing on a personal "messy" Tunisian-Jewish background, David depicted Judaism and Islam as similar enough that there was "flow" between them. In Jewish communities of the Maghreb, David said, "labels for which religion you belong to had . . . to do with where your family was, but there was an interaction or flow between the religions." David presented a romanticized, dehistoricized, and somewhat essentialized view of the Maghreb's Jewish communities, but one that meshed with David's nostalgia. "I feel connections to the Muslim community, as Jewish, and sort of think that I, we, enrich each other."

Personal involvement in both Jewish and Muslim communities actualizes David's approach to them as similar despite their differences. David is active in Toronto's Jewish community, especially in "mystical Judaism," and has also taken part in the city's queer Muslim community for almost twenty-five years. David's involvement in the latter began in 1997 through Salaam, a social/support group for queer and trans Muslims launched in the early 1990s.[36] In 2003, David started to volunteer for the international conference for LGBTIQ Muslims that Salaam cohosted in Toronto and then for the annual interfaith "Peace Iftar" (an evening meal to break the fast) that Salaam still cohosts.[37] David cited the annual interfaith iftar as an example of the "way things interconnect" between Jews and Muslims: the organizers envisioned it as "an iftar that would invite the broader community, Muslims, non-Muslims, observant, [and] non-observant." David also compared it to the "Peace Seders" led by "members of the progressive Jewish community, where they would invite members of the Muslim community in a space to gather, pray, eat, and to be able to form relationships that are the necessary basis before you can even start talking about solving the problems" of Israel and Palestine. David uses adequation to present the Peace Iftars and the Peace Seders as similar events involving food, focusing on interfaith networking, and sharing the same broader political aim.

David also represented certain Muslim and Jewish practices as so similar as to be mistaken for one another, even for David to be mistaken for Muslim.

What I'm wearing now is a type of skullcap. Sometimes I wear a *kufi*, which is very North African but also mainly associated, in North America, with people who are Muslim. But it's a sort of thing that I'll have people, strangers on the street, come up to me and say "As-salamu alaykum." And the proper thing to do is not to say, "Oh no, I'm not Muslim!" That's really kind of insulting to them. I say, "Wa alaykumu s-salam."

David presented North African Muslim and Jewish sartorial practices as sufficiently comparable to confuse North Americans, even Muslims. David doesn't mind being mistaken for a Muslim, and David's use of an Arabic greeting associated with Muslims further adequates David with Muslims. While David mentioned (not) "passing" in reference to his Jewish Maghrebi ancestors above, David should not be understood as "passing" for Muslim: David does not conceal a "true" Jewish identity or claim a Muslim one.[38] Nevertheless, just as David benefits from white privilege despite not attempting to pass, in more subtle and less substantive ways, David benefits from being read as Muslim.

Another way that David adequated Jews and Muslims was through the use of spoken Arabic and Hebrew equivalencies. The second time I visited El-Tawhid, in June 2019, David was the *khatib* (sermon giver). Following the mosque's prescribed format, David read aloud the opening words in both English and transliterated Arabic. In honor of Toronto Pride, which began that day, David recycled a sermon given in previous years as well, on the topic of "modesty and its relationship to Pride." The original sermon format document that the mosque provides to volunteer *khatibs* reads, "I begin with a prayer given to us by the Prophet Musa (Moses)." Most *khatibs* interpret the text as giving them a choice between saying *Musa*, as he is referred to in Arabic, or *Moses*, in English, rather than saying both forms. But on this day, David read, "I begin with a prayer given to us by the prophet Musa, Moshe," using both the Arabic and the Hebrew forms of Moses's name. Throughout the sermon, David used both the English *God* and the Arabic *Allah*, just as most Muslim *khatibs* do, emphasizing that the two words have the same referent, regardless of one's religion, similar to the way Keegan offered an interlinear translation, "Shabbat, Sabbath," in describing their religious practices.

Authentication

In Bucholtz and Hall's framework, authentication refers to "the processes by which speakers make claims to realness," credibility, or truth—in other words, how they discursively verify their identity claims, often through "claimed historical tie[s] to a venerated past."[39] Through authentication tactics, Keegan and David demonstrate their ties to their present-day identities, Keegan as Muslim-Jew with dual ancestries and David as a North African Jew whose ancestors had close relationships and shared traditions with Muslims.

Despite having been raised Muslim, Keegan insisted on the right to call themself Jewish and enacted authentication by claiming Jewishness as (part of) their true identity.

> It is who I am. I think it's really important not to oppress your own identity, and to be proud of it no matter what, and to bring a new form [. . .] like to break the stereotype about both the Muslim and Jewish community. Like, for example, I do believe in the right of Israel to exist. But I also believe in the right of Palestinians to have their independent own states, with dignity. And this is really important, you know . . . when I speak about it [from the] perspective of a Jewish person, versus the perspective of an outsider. So I do believe that . . . my identity gave me a privilege to actually speak up about this issue. And people will listen to you when you are either Palestinian or Jewish, you know, when you talk about this issue, versus as somebody who's completely an outsider. [. . .] You know, this is just an example about why I think it's important to keep my identity.

In emphasizing the copula *is*, Keegan presented their Jewishness as indisputable. Similarly, using the (strictly speaking, unnecessary) adjective *own*—saying *your own identity* rather than merely *your identity*—emphasizes Keegan's claim to a unique subjectivity. Though Keegan does not explicitly address their queerness here, it is not hard to imagine that their argument about it being "really important not to oppress your own identity" also relates to their experience as a queer person. Claiming these various aspects of one's identity as authentic, Keegan suggests, also enables one to speak as a representative member of different groups. As an Arab, Keegan might be assumed to align with Palestinians, but claiming Jewishness as an authentic part of their identity allows them, in certain settings, to strategically align with Israelis and to talk about the Israeli-Palestine conflict from an authenticated, even authoritative, position. Religious identities, like all identities, are constructed through discourse as much as they are by participation in communities of practice.

Whereas Keegan used authentication tactics to verify their Jewishness, David used them to authenticate the "flow" between Jewish and Muslim communities discussed above. As part of the sermon mentioned above, David told a Mullah Nasruddin joke, having grown up with these humorous and pedagogical stories told throughout the Muslim world and, therefore, David implies, in Tunisian Jewish communities as well.[40] A more extensive example David used in our interview was the holiday Mimouna, a North African Jewish tradition in which Muslims played an essential part in the precolonial Maghreb.[41] Research suggests that Tunisians did not celebrate Mimouna, at least with that name, so David's knowledge seems unlikely to have come directly from Tunisian ancestors. David's description of Mimouna as a holiday that "actually require[d] two religious communities to be involved" seems heavily influenced by Harvey Goldberg's 1978 article, "The Mimuna and the Minority Status of Moroccan Jews," in particular. "I was raised with the nostalgia," David said, although whether that nostalgia was for Mimouna, in particular, or Jewish-Muslim interaction, in general, was unclear.

> And I'm trying to revive it. . . . My grandparents were both dead by the time I was five. But I hear the stories about the community and the friendships that used to exist. And again, when I do the reading or talk to Muslim people from the areas, they also talked about the nostalgia about the community that used to exist. . . . If you're holding the memories, you do have a point to rebuild.

Having clearly "do[ne] the reading," David, not surprisingly, presents a depiction of Mimouna that is based in nostalgia; Goldberg, too, uses his discussion of the holiday to emphasize "links between the Jewish celebration and Moslem [sic] cultural practices," though more recently André Levy has shown that most Moroccan Jews no longer involve Muslims in Mimouna.[42]

Through authentication via ancestry, both Keegan and David verify their identifications—Keegan as Jewish and David as a member of a Jewish community with close ties to Muslims. In both cases, we see not that authenticity is "an inherent essence" but instead that authentication is "a social process played out in discourse."[43] In other words, it matters not whether Keegan's or David's claims are verifiably accurate but rather how they use them in interaction.

Authorization

While both David and Keegan used adequation and authentication tactics, David also used *authorization*, the discursive representation or affirmation of oneself or others as legitimate and authoritative.

Interestingly, even though some Muslims treat Sufi practices as illegitimate in relation to mainstream (Sunni) Islam, David referred to Jewish Sufism in ways that authorized mystical practices in both traditions.[44] Having been involved with mystical Judaism, practices associated with Sufism or "mystical Islam" appealed to David. Around the same time that the interfaith iftars started, David began participating in Sufi circles for zikr, the rhythmic repetition of God's names or attributes in Arabic, a few times a month at the private home of our mutual friend El-Farouk, a gay Muslim immigrant who cofounded El-Tawhid.[45] In 2009, the zikr circle evolved into El-Tawhid. I asked David, "Can you say a little bit more about what you get out of attending El-Tawhid since you don't identify as Muslim? . . . Is it mostly community, or is there a religious or spiritual aspect for you?" David answered:

> There is a spiritual aspect for me. I'm not sure about the division between community and spirituality. . . . I enjoy praying with other people, so at some parts of the prayers, I put in Jewish prayers. Yeah, I don't think I'd separate out creating a community from being in the presence of God. They're together. It is a view, also based on my readings, that there is a history within Islam that—I wouldn't say so much that I'm reclaiming as that I'm aware that it's there and it's always been there—that there is a tradition of Jewish Sufis.

It is worth noting that David's answer offers another example of adequation, this time between Muslim and Jewish prayers, such that one can simply be "put in" in place of the other. David went on to give two examples of Jewish Sufis: Zalman Schachter-Shalomi, whom David described as the founder of a Jewish Sufi order, the Jewish Renewal Movement, and Maimonedes.[46] Describing the latter, David told me:

> He was a prominent Jewish philosopher and writer in Andalusia, who wrote in Judeo-Arabic. And he's pretty much a central liturgical authority within Orthodox Judaism. He wrote something called *The Guide to the Perplexed* [1955], but he was also prominent within Muslim circles. And at one point of his life, they weren't sure whether or not he had actually converted to Islam or not. But his sons were members of the Jewish Sufi order, and there was a tradition, following him, of the lineage of Jewish Sufis. So . . . the idea of Sufism was one of the areas where kabbalistic Jews and mystic-inclined Muslims would be able to get together and share, . . . existing in relationship to each other, without losing the self.

In referencing these Jewish Sufis, David uses adequation to establish similarity between the Sufi practices of Muslims and Jews. At the same time, such references serve the purposes of authentication, positioning David as a rightful heir to a tradition of interaction between Jews and Muslims or Sufis that has "always been there." That both Schachter-Shalomi and Maimonedes were not only Jewish Sufis but also in positions of authority—as a founder of Sufi order and as a "prominent" and "central" philosopher, respectively—also means that mentioning them serves the purpose of authorization, the affirmation of David's identity through structures of institutionalized knowledge.

Another way that David practiced authorization was in discussing the religious permissibility of a Jew giving the sermon at the mosque's Friday prayers. Before doing so, David had wanted to be sure it was permissible within both traditions.

> I checked out with Jewish authorities first. Yes, it is permissible under Judaism, and it is permissible under, again, the form of Islam that

exists in the Maghreb, . . . for non-Muslims, for Jews, to be able to give speeches to Muslim congregations on religious topics, and for Muslims to listen to non-Muslim people on religious topics.

While it's not clear what sources David used to check what is permissible in Maghrebian Islam, certainly it is permissible within the queer framework of El-Tawhid, which similarly seeks authorization for its queer practices in various Muslim traditions and offers authorization to others seeking it.[47] Having such authorization was important to David because of "the idea of being a good guest." But David continued:

> El-Tawhid is a space for Muslims. . . . I have to be aware . . . that it is a place for queer Muslims. I'm gay enough to participate; I'm welcome in the community, but I'm not there to crowd out other people. . . . I think it's important for me to be able to say that . . . there's actually an Islamic tradition that would allow me to give a khutbah [sermon]. However, I will not ask to give the call to prayer. That is something that is specific [to Muslims]. . . . There are things that [are] okay, and there are things that are not okay. Leading prayer, doing the call to prayer, those are things that you couldn't do traditionally. There's no tradition of them being by non-Muslims.

Acknowledging the limits to what a Jew could do at the mosque further authorized David as someone who respects the ideological structure of religious laws in both traditions. Both David and Keegan accept some forms of orthodoxy and reject others. As is the case in El-Tawhid, in MPV, and in the wider nonconformist Muslim movement that is the subject of my larger ethnography, retaining some reverence for some elements of "tradition" is a way to authorize the rejection or queering of other elements.[48]

Queer Distinctions

So far, we have seen how Keegan and David used "positive" tactics to construct sameness between Jews and Muslims, the genuineness of their ties to these communities, and, in David's case, institutional recognition for Jewish involvement in Muslim practices. Here I turn to how both of them used one "negative" tactic, *distinction*, which "involves distancing oneself from an identity that contrasts or conflicts with that being constructed."[49]

In Keegan's case, they repeatedly distinguish between themself as liberal and others as illiberal. In an MPV post, Keegan described their experience growing up in a "judgmental Muslim community" where they were not "accepted as openly queer." Feeling rejected by Muslims, Keegan briefly converted to Christianity but still found he "was too gay for them." Eventually, Keegan wrote, "I decided to claim back my Muslim identity." Although Keegan now lives as "openly queer" in the United States, they wrote, "I am still not fully accepted or acknowledged by my community," meaning the Muslim community of the Southern California city where they currently live. After describing ongoing activism against Muslim homophobia there, Keegan concluded, "Starting today, I'm no longer apologetic of my identity." Throughout this post, Keegan made distinctions not only between themself and homophobic Christians and Muslims but also between their past self—on a "journey to be accepted as an openly queer" by exploring different religions—and their current self, now "proud to be an Openly Muslim-Jewish Queer!"

In our interview, Keegan also used the distinction tactic to depict other Iraqi Jews as different from Keegan's family. Explaining why Judaism was initially more about cultural identity than religiosity for Keegan, they offered several factors that had prevented them from learning more about practicing Judaism. Keegan didn't grow up in a religious household, they said, differentiating themself from their irreligious parents. Moreover, outside of the home, there were no opportunities to learn more about Judaism, which the Iraqi government suppressed. "It was not allowed to be openly Jew[ish] or to practice in general. The Jewish community was really small—like you can count them on your fingertips," Keegan said, wiggling the fingers on both hands. The small size of the Iraqi Jewish community evidenced both its oppression by the government and Keegan's lack of access to Jewish people from whom they might have learned. Keegan also told me that Iraqi Jews are "ultraorthodox," so Keegan believed they would not welcome an outsider wanting to learn more about Judaism, perhaps especially a queer person. Here the unspoken distinction was between ultraorthodox Jews and those like themself. "And, of course, in [Iraqi] schools, we only learn about Islam," Keegan said, making a distinction between an oppressive Iraq and an imagined, more liberal, religiously pluralist community where Keegan presumably would have preferred to live.

We saw earlier that Keegan adequated their practice of *salat* and their observance of Shabbat. But Keegan also distinguished themself from more orthodox Muslims and Jews, laughing while saying, "Maybe I don't do it the perfect way or the orthodox way." One could read this as a tactic of illegitimation, but I understood Keegan *not* to see themself or their practices as illegitimate in any way but rather to distinguish themself from those who are concerned with orthodoxy.

While Keegan used distinction to mark themself as different from orthodox and homophobic Jews and Muslims, David did so to distinguish between Islam itself and El-Tawhid in particular and between certain aspects of Islam and Judaism. Despite being a "deeply-embedded guest" at El-Tawhid, David has no desire to convert to Islam.

> I'm talking about my membership in a Muslim community, but I'm also a very active member in my own Jewish community, where I participate strongly and enthusiastically. . . . I would say that I feel El-Tawhid is my community more than Islam is my community.

Another reason for not converting, David told me, is that there are "some basic things where I agree with kabbalistic Jewish understandings of the world and strongly disagree with mainstream Islamic understandings." As an example, David explained that in Islam,

> the concept of Prophet, in particularly Sufi terms, is a person who is able to hear God because they are more pure and more noble and closer to God. Which means there's fewer veils between them and God. So this is a person God can speak to.

In contrast, in the Jewish tradition, David said, there are many examples of prophets who were "not very nice people"; the message is more important than the messenger. "I can identify more with a prophet who's somebody who's not necessarily pure and good and noble, but still does God's will," David told me. "And that's one of the things that I feel . . . [is] an essential difference between how I understand Judaism and how I understand Islam."

In fact, David finds being different from others at the mosque spiritually valuable:

> I know for a lot of people, religion is a comfort. I prefer religion to be a challenge. And so it's a thing like, I go into the space, and I have to be mindful. I have to be mindful of who I am; I have to be mindful of where I'm coming from, I have to be mindful of where other people are coming from, I have to be paying attention, I have to be trying to be the best person I can be. And that for me is something very deeply, deeply spiritual that, that awareness and the effort to be a better person is for me what it means to be in a spiritual place.

David also discussed the value of being different in the Pride sermon I recorded in June 2019. Speaking of obedience to social structures, David said,

> It's an obedience that consists of changing oneself to fit in what's already being determined by other people what our place is. This isn't duty; this is *shirk*. This is *shirk* disguised as duty.

By using the Arabic Islamic concept *shirk* (worshipping anything other than God), David showed authority as someone knowledgeable about Islam. Simultaneously, David made a distinction between *shirk* and duty, arguing that trying to fit into oppressive norms is being obedient to others rather than to God. Rather than trying to fit in, David said, we should appreciate the beauty of those trying to be their authentic selves, like those at Pride. "This joy and self-acceptance is what God wants," David concluded, encouraging congregants to value our and others' queer differences.

Conclusion

Both David and Keegan emphasize what Jews and Muslims, Jewishness and Muslimness, and Judaism and Islam have in common despite their differences. David's description of Jewish-Muslim interaction is in keeping with scholarly depictions of the Maghreb and other parts of the Muslim world discussed above. However, being mistaken for Muslim adds a further, more personal layer to the adequation David uses. We saw that, despite having "white" skin, David does not identify as white because David's Tunisian ancestors could not "pass" and because David was perceived as not-white when in Europe. The fact that people usually read David as white and sometimes as Muslim further adds to the slipperiness of the identity categories we discussed. David slips not just between being identified as a member of one religious community or the other but also between racialized identifications: white in Toronto, not-white in Europe. Whereas David slips back and forth between categories, Keegan goes further; their adequation of Jewish-Muslim identity and spiritual practices *within a single individual* marks a radical departure from typical representations of Jews and Muslims as being separate categories to begin with.

Past research has tended to treat Judaism and Islam as clearly defined and distinct religious identities throughout history and in diverse locations. In contrast, in this chapter, we see evidence of individuals and sometimes whole communities that blur these binaries. Valuable recent work by Aaron Hughes provides strong evidence that those boundaries were not clear to begin with yet leaves intact understandings of their contemporary impermeability.[50] David's and Keegan's experiences illustrate that Jewish-Muslim identities are still less bounded than most people think and that queerness opens up a space to rethink taken-for-granted binaries. In their cases as well as those in other times and places, being able to blur those binaries, whether in self-identification, religious practice, interfaith relationships, or some combination thereof, is made easier by some distance from orthodoxy: praying at interfaith shrines, taking part in mystical Judaism or Sufism, having atheist parents, or leaving an oppressive country. Whether transgressing, resistant to, or excluded from religious normativity, queer boundary crossers transform our understanding of religious identities and reveal their intersections with the other complex identities we embody.

Queer discourse plays a vital role in the construction of nonnormative religious identities and practices. David's and Keegan's identifications are concerned not with their differences to a religious Other, as much previous work on Jews and Muslims would lead us to expect, but instead with their opposition to orthodox, normative forms of both Judaism and Islam that would disallow their hybrid identifications. By making such queer distinctions, those who identify as Muslim *and* Jewish, like Keegan, or as Jews who belong to Muslim communities, like David, avoid any sense of "tug of war." Instead, they construct similarity rather than difference within themselves and their communities, and difference only from those who oppress them. Just as the Dönme were "transvestites," Hugo Marcus gay, David intersex, and Keegan gender fluid, constructing hyphenated queer-Muslim-Jewish identities both links these categories and plays on the spaces between them. In the space of the hyphen, we can tactically and intersubjectively create similarities across and within difference—or, as David put it, "existing in relationship to each other, without losing the self."

Notes

1 Hughes, "Interview with Aaron W. Hughes, Author of Shared Identities."
2 Klug, "Jewish-Muslim."
3 Hughes, *Shared Identities*.
4 Shohat, *Taboo Memories*, 341.
5 Weiss, "Always After," 628.
6 Wilson, *Queer Anthropology*, 7.
7 Bucholtz and Hall, "Theorizing Identity in Language and Sexuality Research"; Bucholtz and Hall, "Identity and Interaction."
8 Shohat, *Taboo Memories*, 335.
9 Mazower, *Salonica, City of Ghosts*.
10 Wallach, "On the (Im)Possibility of Muslim Jews," 331.
11 Baer, "Muslim Encounters with Nazism and the Holocaust," 145–46.
12 Hughes, *Shared Identities*, 4.
13 Wasserstrom, *Between Muslim and Jew*.
14 Anidjar, "Muslim Jews."
15 Alpert, *Caught in the Crack*, 15; Scholem, "The Crypto-Jewish Sect of the Dönmeh (Sabatians) in Turkey," 63.
16 Meri, "Historical Themes," 28; Scholem, "The Crypto-Jewish Sect of the Dönmeh (Sabatians) in Turkey," 63, 150; Alpert, *Caught in the Crack*, 25.
17 Anidjar, "Muslim Jews," 2, 6; Scholem, "The Crypto-Jewish Sect of the Dönmeh (Sabatians) in Turkey," 142.
18 Hughes, *Shared Identities*, 16.
19 Alpert, *Caught in the Crack*, 87.
20 Driessen, "A Jewish-Muslim Shrine in North Morocco."
21 Hughes, *Shared Identities*, 2.

22 Levy, "Striving to Be Separate," 1598.

23 Alpert, *Caught in the Crack*, 295.

24 Baer, "Muslim Encounters with Nazism and the Holocaust," 147; Baer, *German, Jew, Muslim, Gay*, 21.

25 Alpert, *Caught in the Crack*, 15.

26 Safi, "Introduction: Islamic Modernism and the Challenge of Reform"; Duderija, "Construction of the Religious Self and the Other"; Kugle, *Homosexuality in Islam*.

27 Thompson, "Making Space for Embodied Voices, Diverse Bodies, and Multiple Genders in Nonconformist Friday Prayers"; Thompson, "Queering Language Socialization"; Thompson, "Becoming Muslims with a 'Queer Voice.'"

28 Following Valentine, *Imagining Transgender*, I use a mix of pseudonyms and real names for both the individuals and groups with which I conducted research, depending on participants' preferences.

29 Petersen, "Pop-up Mosques, Social Media Adhan, and the Making of Female and LGBTQ-Inclusive Imams."

30 In an earlier publication (Thompson, "Making Space for Embodied Voices"), I regret that I used an incorrect pronoun for David.

31 Bonnett, "Who Was White?"

32 Bucholtz and Hall, "Theorizing Identity in Language and Sexuality Research," 494.

33 Bucholtz and Hall, "Theorizing Identity in Language and Sexuality Research," 494.

34 Weiss, "Discipline and Desire."

35 Bucholtz and Hall, "Theorizing Identity in Language and Sexuality Research," 495.

36 Khaki, "Expanding the Gender Jihad."

37 Salaam Canada, www.salaamcanada.info/, accessed August 5, 2020.

38 Beydoun and Wilson, "Reverse Passing."

39 Bucholtz and Hall, "Identity and Interaction," 601–2.

40 Suresha, *Extraordinary Adventures of Mullah Nasruddin*.

41 Goldberg, "The Mimuna and the Minority Status of Moroccan Jews"; Levy, "Happy Mimouna"; Levy, "Striving to Be Separate."

42 Goldberg, "The Mimuna and the Minority Status of Moroccan Jews," 85; Levy, "Striving to Be Separate."

43 Bucholtz and Hall, "Identity and Interaction," 605.

44 Schmidt, *Islam in Urban America*; Safi, "Introduction: Islamic Modernism and the Challenge of Reform"; Rasiah, "Towards Muslim Pluralism"; Rozehnal, *Cyber Sufis*.

45 Khaki, "My Story"; Khaki, "Expanding the Gender Jihad"; Chung, *Accidental Activist*.

46 Blann, *When Oceans Merge*.

47 Thompson, "Queering Language Socialization."

48 Thompson, *Muslims on the Margins*.

49 Jones, "'If a Muslim Says "Homo," Nothing Gets Done,'" 114.

50 Hughes, *Shared Identities*.

Works Cited

Alpert, Reuven. *Caught in the Crack: Encounters with the Jewish Muslims of Turkey*. Spring Valley, NY: Wandering Soul Press, 2002.

Anidjar, Gil. "Muslim Jews." *Qui Parle* 18, no. 1 (2009): 1–23.

Baer, Marc D. *German, Jew, Muslim, Gay: The Life and Times of Hugo Marcus*. New York: Columbia University Press, 2020.

———. "Muslim Encounters with Nazism and the Holocaust: The Ahmadi of Berlin and Jewish Convert to Islam Hugo Marcus." *American Historical Review* 120, no. 1 (2015): 140–71.

Beydoun, Khaled A., and Erika K. Wilson. "Reverse Passing." *UCLA Law Review* 64, no. 2 (2017): 282–355.

Blann, Gregory. *When Oceans Merge: The Contemporary Sufi and Hasidic Teachings of Pir Vilayat Khan and Rabbi Zalman Schachter-Shalomi*. Rhinebeck, NY: Adam Kadmon Books, 2019.

Bonnett, Alastair. "Who Was White? The Disappearance of Non-European White Identities and the Formation of European Racial Whiteness." *Ethnic and Racial Studies* 21, no. 6 (1998): 1029–55.

Bucholtz, Mary, and Kira Hall. "Identity and Interaction: A Sociocultural Linguistic Approach." *Discourse Studies* 7, no. 4–5 (2005): 585–614.

———. "Theorizing Identity in Language and Sexuality Research." *Language in Society* 33, no. 4 (2004): 469–515.

Chung, Jinung. *Accidental Activist: El-Farouk Khaki*. YouTube, 2020. youtu.be/drjBVKhiOfs.

Driessen, Henk. "A Jewish-Muslim Shrine in North Morocco: Echoes of an Ambiguous Past." In *Sharing Sacred Spaces in the Mediterranean Christians, Muslims, and Jews at Shrines and Sanctuaries*, edited by Dionigi Albera and Maria Couroucli. Bloomington: Indiana University Press, 2012.

Duderija, Adis. "Construction of the Religious Self and the Other: The Progressive Muslims' Manhaj." *Studies in Contemporary Islam* 10, no. 1–2 (2008): 89–120.

Goldberg, Harvey E. "The Mimuna and the Minority Status of Moroccan Jews." *Ethnology* 17, no. 1 (1978): 75–87.

Hughes, Aaron W. "Interview with Aaron W. Hughes, Author of Shared Identities." Reading Religion, November 19, 2017. readingreligion.org/content/interview-aaron-w-hughes-author-shared-identities (now unavailable).

——. *Shared Identities: Medieval and Modern Imaginings of Judeo-Islam.* New York: Oxford University Press, 2017.

Jones, Lucy. "'If a Muslim Says "Homo," Nothing Gets Done': Racist Discourse and In-Group Identity Construction in an LGBT Youth Group." *Language in Society* 45, no. 1 (2016): 113–33.

Khaki, El-Farouk. "Expanding the Gender Jihad: Connecting the Dots." In *A Jihad for Justice: Honoring the Work and Life of Amina Wadud*, edited by Kecia Ali, Juliane Hammer, and Laury Silvers, 167–72. Self-published, 48HrBooks, 2012.

——. "My Story: An Interview with El-Farouk Khaki." In *Progressive Muslim Identities*, edited by Vanessa Karam, Olivia Samad, and Ani Zonneveld, 149–66. West Hollywood: Oracle Releasing, 2011.

Klug, Brian. "Jewish-Muslim: What's in a Hyphen?" *JMRN Review.* July 14, 2020. https://sites.lsa.umich.edu/jmrn/hyphen/.

Kugle, Scott. *Homosexuality in Islam: Critical Reflection on Gay, Lesbian, and Transgender Muslims.* Oxford: Oneworld, 2010.

Levy, André. "Happy Mimouna: On a Mechanism for Marginalizing Moroccan Israelis." *Israel Studies* 23, no. 2 (2018): 1–24.

——. "Striving to Be Separate: The Jewish Struggle for Predictability in Casablanca." *Anthropological Quarterly* 93, no. 1 (2020): 1579–606.

Maimonides, Moses. *The Guide to the Perplexed.* Translated by Michael Friedlander. New York: National Academy for Adult Jewish Studies of the United Synagogue of America, 1955.

Mazower, Mark. *Salonica, City of Ghosts: Christians, Muslims, and Jews, 1430–1950.* 1st Vintage Books ed. New York: Vintage, 2006.

Meri, Josef (Yousef). "Historical Themes: Muslim–Jewish Relations in the Medieval Middle East and North Africa." In *The Routledge Handbook of Muslim-Jewish Relations*, edited by Josef Meri, 15–34. New York: Routledge, 2016.

Petersen, Jesper. "Pop-up Mosques, Social Media Adhan, and the Making of Female and LGBTQ-Inclusive Imams." *Journal of Muslims in Europe* 8, no. 2 (2019): 178–96.

Rasiah, Harun. "Towards Muslim Pluralism: Dialogue and Discord in Contemporary Sri Lanka." In *Emergent Religious Pluralisms*, edited by Jan-Jonathan Bock, John Fahy, and Samuel Everett, 123–44. Palgrave Studies in Lived Religion and Societal Challenges. Cham: Springer International Publishing, 2019.

Rozehnal, Robert. *Cyber Sufis: Virtual Expression of the American Muslim Experience*. London: Oneworld Academic, 2019.

Safi, Omid. "Introduction: Islamic Modernism and the Challenge of Reform." In *Voices of Islam, Volume 5: Voices of Change*, edited by Omid Safi, xvii–xxxiv. Westport, CT: Praeger, 2007.

Schmidt, Garbi. *Islam in Urban America: Sunni Muslims in Chicago*. Philadelphia: Temple University Press, 2004.

Scholem, Gershom. "The Crypto-Jewish Sect of the Dönmeh (Sabatians) in Turkey." In *The Messianic Idea in Judaism and Other Essays on Jewish Spirituality*, 142–66. New York: Schocken Books, 1971.

Shohat, Ella. *Taboo Memories, Diasporic Voices*. Durham, NC: Duke University Press, 2006.

Suresha, Ron Jackson. *Extraordinary Adventures of Mullah Nasruddin: Naughty, Unexpurgated Stories of the Beloved Wise Fool from the Middle and Far East*. Maple Shade, NJ: Lethe Press, 2014.

Thompson, Katrina Daly. *Muslims on the Margins: Creating Queer Religious Community in North America*. New York: NYU Press, 2023.

——. "Becoming Muslims with a 'Queer Voice': Indexical Disjuncture in the Talk of LGBT Members of the Progressive Muslim Community." *Journal of Linguistic Anthropology* 30, no. 1 (2020): 123–44.

——. "Making Space for Embodied Voices, Diverse Bodies, and Multiple Genders in Nonconformist Friday Prayers: A Queer Feminist Ethnography of Progressive Muslims' Performative Inter-Corporeality in North American Congregations." *American Anthropologist* 122, no. 4 (2020): 876–90.

——. "Queering Language Socialization: Fostering Inclusive Muslim Interpretations through Talk-in-Interaction." *Language & Communication* 74 (2020): 29–40.

Valentine, David. *Imagining Transgender: An Ethnography of a Category*. Durham, NC: Duke University Press, 2007.

Wallach, Yair. "On the (Im)Possibility of Muslim Jews." In *The Routledge Handbook of Muslim-Jewish Relations*, edited by Josef Meri, 331–50. New York: Routledge, 2016.

Wasserstrom, Steven M. *Between Muslim and Jew: The Problem of Symbiosis under Early Islam*. Princeton, NJ: Princeton University Press, 1995.

Weiss, Margot. "Always After: Desiring Queerness, Desiring Anthropology." *Cultural Anthropology* 31, no. 4 (2016): 627–38.

———. "Discipline and Desire: Feminist Politics, Queer Studies, and New Queer Anthropology." In *Mapping Feminist Anthropology in the Twenty-First Century*, edited by Ellen Lewin and Leni M. Silverstein, 168–87. New Brunswick, NJ: Rutgers University Press, 2016.

Wilson, Ara. "Queer Anthropology." In *Cambridge Encyclopedia of Anthropology*, 2019. http://doi.org/10.29164/19queer.

2

Queer Disguises

Jewish Women's Performance of Race and Gender in the Colonial Maghreb

Edwige Crucifix

Introduction

As famously argued by Edward Said, the imposition and sedimentation of imperialism over the "Orient"—through brute force, administrative policies, and cultural production—relied on an inherently sexualized and gendered construct. Orientalism, Said tells us, was "an exclusively male province" whose feminized object of concupiscence was born from and reproduced through a "male power-fantasy."[1] In the colonized Maghreb, the feminization of the Orient as a land of military and sexual conquest had deep symbolic and material consequences ranging from hyperbolically erotic depictions of harems, baths, and bodies in the art and literature that circulated both in France and in the colonies, to the most abject acts of colonial rape and sexual violence.[2] Through the sedimentation of colonial policies and of the imperial imaginary, the Maghreb took shape as a sexual "rational utopia" (a term Liat Kozma uses in reference to the red-light district of Bousbir), a symbolic and geographic locus where the fantasy of sexual encounter with (and domination of) the colonized Other could be enacted safely.[3]

While the sexualization of the Orient relied on a profoundly patriarchal and heterosexual dynamic, the hypersexualization of the Maghreb further licensed voyeuristic practices and sexual acts that would not have been tolerated in the metropole, as if the colony's sexual surplus warranted a certain degree of "deviancy." Same-sex liaisons in particular (then believed to take place frequently between the French and locals) were consequently "excused" by the climate, military life, the seclusion and unavailability of heterosexual partners, the fear of venereal diseases, or even the physical constitution and mores of the *indigènes*.[4] Combined with the imperial impulse to segregate local populations into domitable ethnic groups, the sexualizing of North Africa produced its own set of erotico-racial stereotypes, propagated through visual arts, literature, scientific publications, and medical treaties.[5] Relying on artificially impermeable ethnic, religious, linguistic, or racial delineations, these stereotypes included, for instance, the "Belle Juive," the "Alouette Naïve," or the "pédéraste Arabe," often depicted as alluring prostitutes, eager to enter into sexual contact with Europeans, and, importantly, to engage (sometimes exclusively) in same-sex relations.[6] Such stereotypes—which appear at the same time as products of hyper-heteronormative dynamics and as queer figures—anchored the image of the Maghreb as a land of erotic exploration and, further, as a haven for homosexual encounters.[7]

Facing the vast cultural production of such stereotypes (be it as a distorted echo or a response), the understudied works of Maghrebi women writers often reveal a complication of gender and sexuality as it was constructed in the colonies. Subverting gender performance and reclaiming same-sex desire became an attempt for the first generation of Francophone Maghrebi female writers to resist colonial stereotypes and to engage with their own complicated positions—most notably in the case of Jewish women. Contrary to what has been assumed by some scholars, Maghrebi female writers in the colonies did not only depict sexual desire and Oriental femininity to appeal to their metropolitan audience—though it was certainly part of their marketing strategy. Rather, gender and sexuality are treated as unstable categories, whose (often improper) performance becomes the ground for self-determination and even for the articulation of anti-patriarchal and anti-imperial sentiment. In these texts, gender and sexuality are often presented as "disguises" whose fluidity reveals the instability (and even absurdity) of other identity categories. Contending with Marjorie Garber that the blurring of gender often "indicates a *category crisis elsewhere*," as she states in her seminal study on the meaning and practices of cross-dressing, I propose to read queer disguises in these texts as a symptom and critique of the "pénible et constante ambiguïté" of North African Jewish identity, as it was most specifically felt by Maghrebi Jewish women.[8]

Due to imperial assimilation policies and to the widespread influence of the Alliance Israélite Universelle—one of the first and largest educational institutions for girls in the Maghreb—Jewish women were, overall, educated in schools and in French about one or two generations earlier than women in other autochthonous groups in the Maghreb.[9] As a result, they constitute the (often disregarded) first wave of Francophone Maghrebi female writers, authoring a sparse but important oeuvre, comprising novels, poetry, and theater, of both religious and secular inspiration. Jews had long been considered by the French as the most likely candidates for assimilation, a process that took its strongest form in Algeria with the 1870 Décret Crémieux, granting Algerian Jews French citizenship. The *décret* was welcomed almost universally by French and Algerian Jews alike, causing them to embrace Frenchness absolutely and rapidly and to abandon their language, clothes, and traditions in favor of French equivalents, resulting in what Benjamin Stora has famously identified as an "exile" from their own Maghrebi Jewish identity.[10]

Jewish women's access to authorship and publication marks a radical shift in their condition, crystallizing a moment of both unprecedented alienation and unprecedented agency. Caught in a bind, Jewish women engaged with gender performance and same-sex attraction to reshape their relationship to the "Other" and to express their sense of hybridity (both a racialized and gendered category), questioning social norms and their bond to metropolitan France. This is striking in Elissa Rhaïs's *Le mariage de Hanifa* (1926), where two women's desire for the same man morphs into a reciprocal attraction and questions racial delineations, and in Blanche Bendahan's radical *Messieurs, vous êtes impuissants* (1961), a dystopian novel where justice will be brought through sexual reassignment and miscegenation. In this corpus, queer characters and relations (often a pretense, a display, or a disguise) automatically question the bounds of other identity categories but, moreover, the very notion of "category itself."[11] Queer disguises become both a literary technique and a symbol to threaten the delineation of gender and race in the North African colonies.

Queer Maghreb: (Homo)Sexual Policies and Imaginaries in Colonized North Africa

By the nineteenth century, Robert Aldrich notes, "French observers were well aware of homosexual practices in their colonies" and of "networks of contacts and places of sociability" where they could engage in them.[12] In North Africa, they "widely believed that all Arabs enjoyed homosexual contacts, both with each other and with foreigners."[13] Consequently, the Maghreb—presented simultaneously as the epitome of patriarchal oppression and as a territory for sexual experimentation—had become a sexual utopia whereupon to project and act out their wildest fantasies. Lucienne Favre, a French *colon* in Algeria, attests to this fact in a candid description of Algiers's casbah in 1933. Without condemning homosexual love itself, she understands the relationship between *indigènes* and European men as being shaped primarily by an imperial dynamic. In her mind, older Europeans are responsible for the "corruption" of younger Algerian boys whose "sincere" love they debase with their metropolitan "snobisme":

> La pédérastie en Afrique du Nord, n'aurait rien de particulièrement ignoble s'il ne s'y était adjoint récemment un élément de peu de foi fourni par la métropole. Ainsi apparaissent aux alentours de la Casbah de la prostitution masculine, certains européens particulièrement indésirables. . . . Le grand inconvénient, c'est qu'ils amènent dans ce désir à rebours, dans cet amour réputé anormal mais susceptible de fougue, de fringale, de sincérité tout comme l'autre, leur faux besoin, leur envie d'avoir envie, en un mot, leur snobisme.[14]

To Favre, the homosexual desire of the European visitors lacks authenticity and seems rather prompted by circumstances. The relationship she depicts is corrupted by its contractual nature, limited to what she perceives as the inherently exploitative power structure of colonial prostitution.

This depiction of homosexual love in Algiers is inscribed in a larger outlook on same-sex relations and desires in the French colonies, what Boone calls the "homoerotic subtexts embedded in Orientalism."[15] Far from being an irreconcilable contradiction, the coexistence of heteronormativity and homoeroticism, of anti-Arab and pro-*indigènes* sentiment, at the heart of France's imperial project was in fact constitutive of Orientalist discourse extending beyond the boundaries of North Africa and even beyond the colonial period.[16] Colonial expansion—which relied on a central sexual metaphor—in turn, widened the sexual scope of the metropole when "European explorers and adventurers came into contact with cultures in which sexual relations between men and between women . . . were not subject to the same kind of legal, medical, and religious condemnation as in the West."[17] Starting in the nineteenth century, medical treatises, cultural accounts, travel guides, and studies attempted to map out and systematize sexual practices in the colonies. Same-sex relations were of particular interest to the French. In the wake of Ambroise Tardieu's massive and influential study on French "pederasty and prostitution," numerous authors attempted to apply his teachings to colonized subjects. Among them was Adolphe Kocher, who conducted invasive examinations on the anus and genitals of Algerian men and boys, in an attempt to identify the physiological and ethnological characteristics of the Arab "pederast."[18] For Kocher and his colleagues, homosexuality was before all a racial matter, allowing them to conclude that "the Arab" (a qualifier employed abusively to encompass all inhabitants of North Africa) was indeed an "inveterate pederast," whose inclination, therefore, stood contrary to the circumstantial or "situational" homosexuality of the European, understood as a kind of overseas aberration ("la pédérastie est avant tout une question de race . . . l'Arabe est un pédéraste invétéré").[19]

The elaboration of such categories, far from undoing the sexualized dynamics of imperial domination, only served to further assert them. In medico-legal studies about same-sex practices in the Maghreb, authors generally reused Tardieu's distinction between "active" and "passive" pederasty, concluding that the Arab man was by nature a "passive sodomist" ("un sodomiste passif"), feminized by his attire, clothes, and behaviors.[20] The Arab pederast was almost universally depicted as an androgynous, lithe boy, ready to succumb to European appetites and be conquered by a more "male" desire. In this respect, the stereotyped "Arab pederast" was still an apt object for Said's Orientalist "male power-fantasy," being not only feminine but feminized, stripped of his masculinity. In a region where, in the mind of many authors, Islam had made women inaccessible to Europeans, feminized men could be mentally constructed as the next best thing to act out their masculine domination.

Same-sex desire among women was traditionally evoked to serve a similar purpose. Sapphic undertones were omnipresent in Orientalist

56 Edwige Crucifix

depictions of the harem, as famously exemplified by Ingres's *Bain Turc*, an eroticized rendition of Lady Montagu's much tamer account of female sociability in Ottoman bathhouses.[21] Much like the colonial construction of the "pederast," the sapphic harem of the Orientalists simultaneously relied on the oversexualization of the feminine and the emasculation of its male actors, depicted here as muscular but sexually impotent eunuchs.[22] While most studies and accounts of same-sex desire focused on men, doctors, scientists, and ethnographers similarly alluded to instances of female homosexuality (or *tribadisme*) between local and European women, though the subject clearly did not elicit much medico-legal concern. Kocher mentions the case of a woman named Ouali-bent-Zaout, tattooed with both the name of a French male lover and the portrait of a female one, noting in passing that "au sein *gauche* se remarque un portrait de femme française qui était son *amie* à Laghouat. Cette prostituée se livrait au saphisme."[23] Same-sex relations between women were understood as the result of European influences, in a way that both maintained the hyper-femininity of Oriental women and crystallized their position as objects of Western desire. Arène Sextius even asserts that same-sex relations were virtually inexistant among Arab women, given their supposed lack of erotic fantasy.[24] To prove his point, he adds, with utmost seriousness, that the Arabic expression for cunnilingus (which he reserves to intercourse between women) is "yakoul el guenfouz" (an approximation of القنفذ يأكل), translated as "manger le hérisson."[25] This expression, he notes, is clear proof that the act itself is never practiced, since Arab women are notoriously "carefully shaved." If this practice ever takes place, he adds, "on peut dire que l'éducation européenne est passée par là ; d'ailleurs, les liaisons lesbiennes sont presque toujours mixtes."[26]

However, if the colonial discourse on same-sex desire was constitutive of France's inherently patriarchal imperial project, it also provided the ground for the artistic and material exploration of alternative forms of gender performativity and sexual experiences. Recalling Kozma's characterization of Bousbir, the oversexualization of the Maghreb through Orientalist aesthetics and colonial typologies created a form of homoerotic utopia (or even "pornotopia" in the words of Jaap Kooijman) whose material existence depended on an imaginary projection and that was ironically sanctioned and safeguarded by the existence of imperialist structures. This utopia, displayed both in the metropole and in the colonies, attracted numerous French artists and intellectuals throughout the nineteenth and twentieth century, including the likes of André Gide, Jean Genet, Yves Saint-Laurent, Roland Barthes, Colette, and Lucie Delarue-Mardrus.

For women, the "queerness" of the Maghreb was attractive not only for its homoeroticism but also for affording new possibilities in the performance of gender. In France, the spectacular and sexualized nature of the Orient could offer queer women a venue to express their unconventional sexuality through an exuberant masquerade. For Emily Apter, the "outing" of one's sexuality could thus be permitted (and even condoned) through a complex performative imbrication whereby the Oriental disguise would become the expression of one's queerness, as in the case of Colette or Ida Rubinstein.[27] In North Africa, the subversion of gender norms was further afforded (or even demanded) by colonial life and local customs. Indeed, in the colonies, French women found themselves at the encounter of imperial and patriarchal hierarchies, remaining "inferior" to their fellow male *colons* but enjoying a "superior" status to the *indigènes*. While North African colonies afforded them unprecedented professional and social opportunities, they were also confronted with the limitations traditionally placed upon women in the Maghreb.[28] In order to gain greater mobility in the Orient, some European women partook in an act of double "drag" by cross-dressing as Arab men.[29] Among the many artists, journalists, and travelers who practiced cross-dressing, Isabelle Eberhardt is certainly the most famous and most striking example, adopting a completely parallel persona as Mahmoud el-Mouskoubi (Mahmoud the Moscovite).[30] Isabelle's disguise had a phenomenal impact on later European female travelers, leading to an almost cultlike veneration, which Apter dubbed the "Eberhardt complex."[31]

As can be seen in these examples of "deviant" sexuality and gender performance, the combined influence of the colony's imaginary representations and material reality contributed to construct an alternative vision and experience of the colonized Maghreb as a queer space, in both Orientalist and colonial discourse. The construction of the Maghreb's excessive and deviant sexuality, however, took shape within the patriarchal structure of French imperialism, and in fact often in echo with it, reinforcing the heteronormative paradigms of imperialism and Orientalism. At the same time, it also provided Europeans with an opportunity and a space to act out same-sex desire and nonconforming gender presentations,

58   Edwige Crucifix

especially in the case of French women, both in the metropole and in the colonies.

Doubly Queered: Discovering One's Own Hybridity

In parallel to and in echo of such depictions, the first generation of Maghrebi Francophone women writers fed on the construction of the Maghreb as a queer and oversexualized signifier, often subverting gender and sexual norms in the colonies in order to question their own identity. A striking example of this subversion was Rosine Boumendil, an Algerian woman who wrote under the pseudonym of Elissa Rhaïs and whose work enjoyed remarkable popular success in the 1920s, before the dwindling appeal of exotic narratives caused it to fall "into oblivion."[32] Rhaïs's own trajectory is a *rocambolesque* story in itself, relying on an enticing authorial travesty since her introduction to the French public was done under the guise of a Muslim woman having escaped from a harem.[33] Rhaïs's novels, like her life, question the bounds of what it meant to be Jewish in colonial Algeria (before and after the Décret Crémieux) and in imperial France: two settings where she could not find her place without resorting to a masquerading act.

As an echo of Rhaïs's own situation, the characters of her story are often caught in the crossfire of multiple communities, torn by desires that prove irreconcilable with the groups to which they "belong." Most evidently, her novels often stage tensions between North African Muslim and Jewish populations, as in *La Fille des Pachas*, a tragedy à la *Romeo and Juliet* where the star-crossed lovers are a Muslim woman and a Jewish man, whose forbidden desire for each other can only end in a bloodbath. But beyond addressing "the extraordinary taboo that separates Jews and Muslims in colonial Algeria," Rhaïs also wrote about social tensions resulting from France's colonial presence.[34] In the same novel, she addresses colonial antisemitic sentiment, explicitly referring to the Algerian "crise antijuive" of the 1890s, a series of events prompted both by the general discontent of many *colons* opposed to the Décret Crémieux and by the *affaire Dreyfus* raging in the metropole, which provoked the sudden rise to power of Max Régis's infamous "ligue antijuive" in Algiers.[35] In *Les Juifs*, her most celebrated novel, Rhaïs further depicts the chasm that divides Parisian Jews and their North African coreligionists, observing that the latter's culture and way of life bring them much closer to their Muslim neighbors.

While never adopting an explicitly anticolonial position (and sometimes even celebrating France's imperial influence), Rhaïs's novels offer a constant depiction of colonial tensions and problematic identities. In this complicated constellation, gender too is often portrayed as an unstable category, both reinforcing existing tensions and creating its own. Such instability is striking in *Le mariage de Hanifa*, where it is rendered through a complex web of feminine desire, shaped and frustrated by social and racial divides. The knot of the intrigue and the root of the tragedy concerns the absence of Hanifa's handsome cousin Said, gone to wage war in France, which ignites the jealousy of three enamored women around this hollow object of desire: Westernized Hanifa, Oriental Lalla Nefissa, and "negress" Fakhite, a Bedouin servant. This feminine triangulation of desire is emptied out when its masculine target is taken away by an androgynous *mère-patrie*. The intrigue, then, is carried almost solely by the rivalry and closeness that develop among the three women. At the apex of the triangle, Hanifa attracts the ire and jealousy of the other two.

Hanifa, who has been educated in a French school, is repeatedly presented as some sort of cultural hybrid, at the same time "une vraie petite Française" and a "jeune fille Arabe parfaite."[36] Her highly problematized cultural hybridization—a progressive process in the novel that elicits numerous remarks from her French peers, her family, and her rivals—is accompanied and dramatized by a complication of her gender presentation. Her cousin Said is in fact seduced by her ambiguous identity, which is not only racial and cultural but also sexual, as the encounter of French and Arab accents on Hanifa troubles her appearance:

> Hanifa était assise à son bureau. Deux tresses aux épaules, un tablier noir qui l'enveloppait entièrement, les pieds dans des pantoufles de faille bleue, elle ressemblait en effet à une vraie petite française. Elle parut délicieuse à Sidi Said sous ce vêtement quasi masculin, qui donnait à sa physionomie douce quelque chose d'un peu ferme.[37]

In this depiction, Hanifa's identity is mediated and transformed by the French costume she wears, a disguise that does not hide her femininity but rather disturbs it. In her "almost" masculine performance of Frenchness,

60   Edwige Crucifix

Hanifa effectively sports a double disguise that causes her to be doubly queered in her cousin Said's eyes. This recurring gesture in Rhaïs's work can also be found in her novel *La Riffaine*, where the character of Aïcha, the pasha's favorite spouse and a Senegalese *métisse*, is similarly queered by the male gazer. Here, too, the pasha is seduced by the reimagined layer of Frenchness that he imposes upon her, prompting another sexually ambiguous observation:

> Chaque fois qu'il contemple ces yeux, ces yeux verts d'une eau magnifique, il imagine le beau et élégant colonial français qui fut le père d'Aïcha. De lui, elle a toute la finesse, la noblesse et l'esprit. Active, délicate, artiste et sage, avec son corps exquis, Aïcha est très française par certains côtés. Elle est très orientale aussi, ayant la soumission résignée de la concubine.[38]

In both passages, the characters' hybridity, their cultural and social ambiguity, is rendered through a parallel instability of race and gender. In a fashion that recalls the "vamp" Orientalism of the metropole's Belle Époque, it is paradoxically the disguise that reveals the most intimate "truth" about those wearing it—which "outs" them, so to speak—by pointing to their unfitness within preestablished categories. While relying on the dynamics of Orientalism, the fluctuation of desire thus subverts its expected course. What is attractive is precisely undefined and ambiguous figures rather than the "feminized" Orient symbolized by Hanifa's rivals. In *Le mariage de Hanifa*, it is the double queering of the eponymous character that produces her sexual appeal, which attracts Said's reciprocal desire and the reader's sympathy, standing in stark contrast with desexualized Fakhite, as was expected, but also with hyper-feminine, hyper-Oriental Lalla Nefissa. The latter even berates her for appearing unveiled in front of Said, in a gesture that she interprets as a betrayal of her identity and her community. Hanifa's French costume thus causes her to be literally "découverte," uncovered and discovered both, outed and revealed to the eyes of Said and of the reader in her complex identity.

The double-queering process at the center of the intrigue is further dramatized by the effect it has on Fakhite and Nefissa. As the object of Said's lust, Hanifa causes her rivals' attention to turn back upon her, as a weird slippage in the novel's economy of desire. For Fakhite in particular, loving Said appears to be nothing but a pretense. Fakhite is a Bedouin orphan girl from Hanifa's hometown, the same age, but from a very poor family. What she truly seeks seems to be Hanifa's love and recognition, which, tragically, never come. Indeed, for all her angelic generosity, Hanifa does not love Fakhite, whom she finds rather incommoding. Although she does pity her for her poverty, she never goes so far as considering Fakhite her equal. Eventually, in what is to her a final act of mercy and to her beneficiary an ultimate humiliation, she allows Fakhite to work as her servant. Fakhite's position of absolute dependence translates into her consequent racial and sexual *déclassement*, causing her to discover herself as inferior to Hanifa and to realize with righteous anger that she has been excluded from the novel's romantic economy. In a highly symbolic scene, she glances at herself in her rival's mirror only to discover her downfall through the superimposed reflection of blond, blue-eyed Hanifa, in contrast to whom she perceives herself as a "négro," a racially inadequate and masculinizing descriptor:

> Les regards de Fakhite se portaient alors sur ses jambes maigres et brûlées, sur ses bras olivâtres. . . . Quand elle se trouvait chez Hanifa, vite, elle allait se regarder dans la glace de l'alcôve. Elle voyait avec horreur sa tignasse terne et crépue comme celle d'un négro, sa bouche large et sa figure de misère.[39]

This mirroring scene further subverts the dynamics of desire in the novel, as Fakhite's love for Said and desire for Hanifa's affection morph into the fantasy of a literal union with Hanifa, one in which they would become one and the same. The episode allows Fakhite to not only compare herself to Hanifa but to see her own racial and sexual value through Hanifa's eyes. The slippage of desire allows her to cross through the looking glass and discover herself as thoroughly undesirable.

This slippage of desire, an "inversion" in the sense that it is turned back upon one's gender and eventually upon oneself, further offers an interesting counterpoint to the dominant discourse of French women writing in colonial North Africa and fantasizing about their "encounter" with Oriental women, as displayed by the work of Marie Bugéja, the wife of a French *colon* who authored numerous books about the condition of North African women. Bugéja's entire feminist endeavor relies on the ambivalent similarity she establishes between European and North African women, as it simultaneously rejects the possibility of identification and relies on a projection of reciprocal desire. In order to match her own fascination for the other, the *séduction orientale* (the unapologetic title of one of her novels), there needs be a *séduction occidentale*. Recounting an episode in which she was invited to dinner by Algerian women in *Nos soeurs musulmanes* (1921), she exits "avec la certitude que les femmes musulmanes, ces cloîtrées qui vivent en dehors de la société moderne sentirent s'ébaucher dans leurs âmes un rêve encore obscur mais séduisant ; elles se plaisent à nous imiter et sont prêtes à nous aimer."[40] Assimilation, here, clearly relies on the sharing of gender in a complex imbrication of mimesis, desire, and love. Maintaining the divide she set out to undo, Bugéja's project is doomed to fail. Her feminist commitment to her "Muslim sisters" remains dependent on racial considerations as she proves unwilling to relinquish the hierarchical superiority granted to her in the colonial setting.

In many ways, *Le mariage de Hanifa* echoes the failure of reciprocity in female desire but reaches a very different conclusion. Indeed, Fakhite's obscure desire for Hanifa (to be close to her, to be recognized by her as an equal, and, eventually, to *be* her) drives her to a crime of passion. On the eve of Hanifa's wedding day, Fakhite slips into her room and kills her. In the novel's romantic economy, the murder scene appears as a morbid simulacrum of the long-awaited wedding night promised by the title, as it is Fakhite who visits Hanifa in her marital bed and honors their bond. In killing her, Fakhite avenges a social unbalance. She has been freed from her servitude, although it is to embrace a beggar's life of misery and adventure.[41] With Hanifa gone, Fakhite is no longer her "dark reflection" with the ending reinterpreting the mirroring scene in light of the reflective colonial relationship studied by Homi Bhabha, whereby the colonizer is "tethered to . . . the shadow of colonized man, that splits his presence, distorts his outline, breaches his boundaries, repeats his action at a distance, disturbs and divides the very time of his being."[42] The relationship between Westernized Hanifa and racialized Fakhite becomes a representation of colonial relations, and the house in which they live, a stage for imperial alienation. Through the lens of gender, Fakhite is able to exorcize her racial and sexual frustration to undo this aberrant dichotomy. The double queerness of the characters and the accompanying slippage of desire have thus the double effect of revealing the instability of imperial identity categories (to others and to oneself) and of giving female characters the agency to self-identify against them—with the cynical caveat that this freedom might lead to their disappearance.

"Inverted" Utopias: Queer Disguises to Straighten the World

Published over thirty years after *Le mariage de Hanifa*, Blanche Bendahan's bizarre *Messieurs, vous êtes impuissants* is a futuristic novel written during the Algerian war of independence, a particularly unstable context for Jewish communities, whose massive departure from the region would soon follow. Recounted in Bendahan's characteristic tongue-in-cheek style, the story is set in the year 2005 in an "inverted" society where people's names are in *verlan* and where both love and biology have been mechanized to the extreme. Reminiscent of the multifaceted surveillance of sexual behaviors practiced by Kocher and the colonial administration, public policies are exerted through a network of *Instituts médico-légaux*, which provide their customers/citizens with various serums and treatments to give them the appearance of eternal youth. The story's main protagonist, humorously named Nicole Nycravatt, is a filmmaker and aficionada of the 1950s, a period known to her contemporaries as "la sale époque." She stands both as a figure of resistance to the times in which she lives (as displayed by her refusal to "invert" her name and her taste for the past) and as its purest product. The novel opens with her wedding night, as she expects the delivery of Gregorio Talmor, a mail-ordered husband who is set to take her virginity—a precious though incongruous rarity for a woman her age, observes the narrator. Thwarted by the machinations of rivals, Nicole and Gregorio cannot be "properly" married, and the entire novel—somewhat recalling the plot of *Le mariage de Hanifa* —is, in fact, a deferral of this awaited wedding night, as Nicole and others find themselves caught in a series of erotic and romantic imbroglios, scientific experiments, and interstellar plans to destroy Earth.

Bendahan's own voice rings clear in the narration, making it apparent that her playful elucubrations are above all a way to criticize contemporary mores. Among the numerous societal ills she deplores are women's "pseudo" emancipation, often depicted as yet another form of servitude, and the prevalence of homosexuality; she files "pédérastie" among other "choses détéstables."[43] While her point of view is rather conservative, it is precisely through the depiction and exploration of such "dystopian" sexualities that the novel carves out a space for its sexual, societal, and political revolutionaries, set to tackle the world's greatest ills. Among these luminaries are Sixfrancs Clardou, an "inverti," and Riema Dolicho, a "hermaphrodite" born female but "modifi(ée) sexuellement, dans le sens de la masculinité" to comply with her misogynistic father's wishes.[44] Both characters join forces in an attempt to end racism once and for all through a project of global proportions.

Subverting the dystopian biopower of the *Instituts médico-légaux*, Sixfrancs conspires to inject the world's population with the blood of Jewish and Black children he adopted, hoping to prove that "les races pures n'étaient qu'un mythe."[45] With Riema's complicity, he is able to test out his plan on her father, a man who spends his days hidden in a cave, where he writes racist pamphlets. In their Tangiers laboratories, "inverti" Sixfrancs and "hermaphrodite" Riema become the symbolic parents of a new humanity, one where races have been abolished through miscegenation, concluding in triumph:

> Ainsi la redevenue internationale Tanger avait rempli au mieux sa mission d'internationalité. Ainsi encore l'éternelle question du rapprochement des races était résolue une fois pour toutes ; le monde allait cesser enfin de se débattre dans ce conflit shakespearien : être ou ne pas être . . . un Juif, un Nègre, ou autre.[46]

Their plan can be interpreted as a radical take on "intermarriages" (*mariages mixtes*), a central concern for lawmakers and French feminists throughout the colonial period.[47]

From an extradiegetic point of view, the characters' ambiguous sexual and gender identity is a clear echo to their project of racial hybridization.[48] Its role is even stronger within the story, as it is precisely Sixfrancs's and Riema's queerness that allows them to carry out their plan, giving Riema the "male" capabilities she needs and deviating attention from Sixfrancs's activities. It is at least in these terms that Riema herself asks for Sixfrancs's collaboration, noting that "vous êtes aussi peu mâle que je suis peu femelle ; donc nous sommes faits pour nous entendre, et nous entr'aider."[49]

The necessity of queerness to the miscegenation process is further suggested by the fact that both characters shift gender and sexual identity at the end of the novel: Sixfrancs revealing that he is in fact not a homosexual and Riema becoming "une femme cent pour cent."[50] This final inversion accompanies a more general turn back to "normalcy" as the world, almost destroyed by extraterrestrial forces, gets back on its feet, symbolized by a final ceremony where every character's name gets un-inverted. Similarly "set straight," Sixfrancs and Riema even discover that they are irrepressibly attracted to one another. The novel ends in a romantic flurry where all the protagonists are finally assembled and paired in a series of amorous matches. The shift, of course, signifies that normalcy leaves no place for same-sex desire and for non-binarity. But it also indicates that Sixfrancs and Riema's plan, while it was being carried out, necessitated that their sexual and gender identity be generally "ambiguous," that they sport a queer disguise, as this fluidity eventually permitted the abolition of old racial categories and, in fact, of races altogether.

Sixfrancs and Riema's endeavors are echoed by those of Bainur and Soifranc, Nicole's pacifist twin brothers, long gone missing before the protagonist finds them again in the secret Himalayan laboratory from which they have devised a solution to achieve world peace. Concluding that violence and domination are male attributes, they engineer a scientific method to incapacitate the men of the world, causing their bodies to bend over at a right angle and making them incapable of any sexual arousal. Nicole's explicitly asexual twin brothers (often referred to as "eunuchs" and the only characters in the novel who do not get paired with the opposite sex at the end) make an even more bizarre couple than Sixfrancs and Riema. Instead of engineering a new mixed-race humanity, in their desire for peace, they abolish sexual desire and reproduction, in a radical solution to the unending conflicts between East and West, which proves remarkably efficient:

> Ces messieurs d'Occident et d'Orient ont cessé, tout d'un coup, d'entrecroiser leurs défis ! On ne parle plus de guerres, petites ou grandes, froides ou chaudes, intérieures et extérieures, . . . (ils) se révèlent à l'usage, apathiques autant que des eunuques. . . . Pacifistes ? Le sont toujours les hommes qui ne sont plus vraiment des hommes. Conclusion : à quoi tiennent les révolutions, les conflits mondiaux ? Aux fonctions excrétrices d'une glande génitale masculine.[51]

Their pacifist project, referred to by the double entendre name of "mal sans nom"—which spreads as fast as its televised announcement "messieurs, vous êtes impuissants"—produces spectacular results and is only thwarted by a deus ex machina: a sudden meteor attack from Mars that destroys their laboratory and straightens at the same time men's physiognomy, the characters' sexuality, and the world's order.

Through both utopian projects, the inverted world can thus only be brought back to order by its most "inverted" dwellers, as Sixfrancs, Riema, Bainur, and Soifranc divert the course of the dystopian novel to bring about an ideal world of peace and tolerance. Like it was the case for Rhaïs, gender fluidity and same-sex desire serve here to advocate for a dismantlement of arbitrary racial categories. Gender and race are both treated as disguises whose subversion allows for a revelation. Bendahan herself addresses this same tension in a short avant-propos, where she confesses her own temptation to hide her Maghrebi Jewish name under "celui très catholico-aryen" of her mother. Her readers, she adds "s'ils veulent bien lire ce roman jusqu'au bout, . . . comprendront pourquoi" she was tempted to pick such a "nom de guerre" and finally rejected the idea.

While obeying somewhat conservative views, Bendahan uses the fluidity of race and gender in the text as a means to question both the racism and the patriarchal logics of colonial society that she faced herself.[52] The dystopian society depicted in the novel is the logical result of a hyperliberalization of heterosexuality, where the matrimonial enterprise has been reduced to its barest expression: a utilitarian transaction. Stuck in this supposedly emancipating logic, sex and love are no more than commodities (which can even be performed by "robots à tout-faire-l'amour-y-compris") and women themselves are reduced to their "valeur marchande."[53] The commodification of love and sex grants Nicole, one of the rare remaining virgins, an inordinate value, which unleashes the passion, jealousy, and violence of those around her. The novel's quest for a feminine pseudo-ideal (oscillating between virgin Nicole, Tildeclo, the only remaining woman with an unmarked rear end, and the robotically beautiful president of the "Etats-Unis" d'Europe) drives crowds to madness and bespeaks the absurdity of this hyper-heteronormative and exploitative model.

It is in cosmopolitan Tangiers, reimagined as a global metropole, that the literal recipe (a symbolic mix of blood) of a new order is born, bringing about an age of world peace and sexual harmony. Both the gender war (lead by Riema, who violently tortures and murders robots made to look like real men) and the race war are ended, through subversive gender performances: be they Sixfrancs's and Riema's queer disguise or the twins' asexual refusal to behave like "manly"—and thus murderous—men. It is this subversion that reveals the fantasy of race purity, allowing the inhabitants of Earth to face their commonality and finally love their neighbor "like themselves."[54] The queer disguise is necessary to "straighten" things up, in the literal redressing of men's bent bodies and in the adoption of a new world order.

Conclusion

Despite their widely different styles, both *Le mariage de Hanifa* and *Messieurs, vous êtes impuissants* narrate the story of a frustrated wedding night. In both novels, the deferral of this basest and most primordial of heteronormative rituals opens up the narrative space for the further subversion of gender and sexual performance (or, even, non-performance), be it in Fakhite's refusal to be erotically erased by her race or in Bainur and Soifrancs's asexual pacifism. Gender and sexuality appear as unstable disguises, which can be sported to seduce or, quite paradoxically, to reveal. Rather than a means to hide, the queer disguise is both the tool and the vector of a revelation, an unveiling, which shows what was previously invisible and disrupts the status quo. The instability of gender and sexuality, though they should be taken at face value, also serves to destabilize other identity categories. The queer disguise, as it reveals itself, also designates a racial disguise that does not correspond to any fixed reality.

The emancipating exercise of the masquerade tends, therefore, to its abolition: Fakhite cannot accept to be seen under her "negress" disguise just like Riema refuses that her father disguises others as Jews. Such identifiers are ultimately revealed as empty signifiers: freed from a logic of oppression and control, they become nothing more than an imposed mask. The final act or revelation, the inversion that concludes both novels, is thus a condemnation of the profound lie that has distorted society. Sporting the queer disguise to better drop it as the curtain falls appears as a show of resistance against colonial identity categories (the "epistemology of the imperial closet," so to speak). Through the complex interlocking

68   Edwige Crucifix

of same-sex desire and mimesis, sexual and gender performances allow for the creation of a "third term," what postcolonial theorists would call a third space: a locus for ambiguity or hybridity that resists imperial and patriarchal limitations.[55]

Notes

1   Said, *Orientalism*, 207.
2   Rape and sexual abuse were, for instance, widely practiced by the French army during the Algerian war of independence. Historian Raphaëlle Branche notes that Algerian women were frequently asked to show their genitals during police controls as the French government grew aware of their participation in the war and that Algerian women were generally considered like "women who could be raped" ("Des viols pendant la guerre d'Algérie," 127). One of the better-known victims of such acts was Djamila Boupacha, whose case was famously exposed and defended by Gisèle Halimi and Simone de Beauvoir.
3   Kozma, "Colonial and Post-Colonial Casablanca," 264. One of the most striking examples of the centrality of this sexual dynamic to colonial domination in the Maghreb was the transformation of Casablanca's red-light district into a prime tourist destination. Under French control from 1922 to 1953, Bousbir (as it was known) was a massive colonial project, designed not only for the enactment of French biopower but also for European enjoyment and titillation.
4   In a 2017 UN report on trafficking in women, Daniel Lee cites a 1935 police document that suggests that "homosexual prostitution was a thriving trade that functioned both in hotels and in family homes" ("Prostitution in Tunis," 230) and that a house for male prostitution named Étage Ouaki existed in Tunis's Medina. Lee adds that due to the inexistence of regulations for same-sex relations under French laws, the state found itself unable (or unwilling) to press charges.
5   On the different civil statuses in colonial North Africa, see Lorcin, *Imperial Identities*; and Weil, "Le statut des musulmans en Algérie coloniale."
6   Focusing on same-sex relations between men, Joseph Boone underlines the powerful attraction that homoerotic tropes—in spite of their historical instability—have continually exerted on European visitors to North Africa and to the Middle East since the early modern period. While

Boone proposes considering such homoerotic tropes as the product of "the cross-cultural interplay of homoerotic desires and taboo throughout history" (*The Homoerotics of Orientalism*, 52), Joseph Massad, in his review of the book, insists that they should be envisioned as results of orientalist discourse ("Edward W. Said and Joseph Boone's *The Homoerotics of Orientalism*").

7 In his study on queerness in the Maghreb, Jarod Hayes addresses the problematic use of the term "queer" to historically address sexuality and gender in North Africa, pointing to its embeddedness in Anglo-American culture. While recognizing this important point, this chapter abides by Hayes's use of the word "less as an adjective to describe sexual acts than as a verb to signify a critical practice in which nonnormative sexualities infiltrate dominant discourses to loosen their political stronghold" (*Queer Nations*, 7).

8 Garber, *Vested Interests*, 17; Memmi, *Portrait du colonisé, précédé de portrait du colonisateur*, 40.

9 About the changes succeeding in Jewish women's life during this period and the influence of the Alliance Israélite Universelle, see Laskier, "The Alliance Israélite Universelle and the Jewish Communities of Morocco, 1862–1962"; Reguer, "The World of Women"; Malino, "'Institutrices' in the Metropole and the Maghreb: A Comparative Perspective"; and Benichou Gottreich and Schroeter, *Jewish Culture and Society in North Africa*.

10 Stora, *Les trois exils : Juifs d'Algérie*.

11 Garber, *Vested Interests*, 17.

12 Aldrich, *Colonialism and Homosexuality*, 17.

13 Aldrich, *Colonialism and Homosexuality*, 329.

14 Favre, *Tout l'inconnu de la Casbah d'Alger*, 2015–16.

15 Boone, *The Homoerotics of Orientalism*, 6.

16 Todd Shepard has notably studied the long-lasting impact that colonial constructs of Arab men's sexuality bore on France in the 1960s—in the wake of Algeria's independence and in the midst of the so-called sexual revolution—whose orientalist echoes can be felt both in the discourse of the anti-Arab far right and that of the most liberal actors of the sexual revolution.

17 Aldrich, "Homosexuality in the French Colonies," 201.

18 In these texts, the word "pederasty" is employed to refer to same-sex acts and relations between men.

19 Jacobus X, *L'Amour aux colonies*, 167–68.

20 Kocher, *De la criminalité chez les Arabes au point de vue de la pratique médico-judiciaire en Algérie*, 170; Sextius, *De la criminalité des Arabes au point de vue de la pratique médico-judiciaire en Tunisie*, 152; Mouliéras, *Le Maroc inconnu: étude géographique et sociologique*, 50.

21 On this topic, see Yeazell, "Public Baths and Private Harems."

22 The colonial construction of the Maghrebi "pederast" bears interesting parallels to that of the Ottoman eunuch, another queer figure populating the orientalist imagination. For studies on the history of eunuchs in Ottoman harems and their perception by the West, refer to the works of Booth, *Harem Histories*; Toledano, *Kul/Harem Slavery*; and Hathaway, *The Chief Eunuch of the Ottoman Harem*.

23 Kocher, *De la criminalité chez les Arabes au point de vue de la pratique médico-judiciaire en Algérie*, 69–70.

24 Sextius, *De la criminalité des Arabes au point de vue de la pratique médico-judiciaire en Tunisie*, 156.

25 Abdelkebir Khatibi notes that the word "al-qanfûd" is part of the lexicon of Cheikh Nafzawi in the sixteenth century and used to designate "la vulve de la vieille femme décrépite" (*La Blessure Du Nom Propre*, 149), while Christelle Taraud reports that the word (in its Moroccan pronunciation) was part of the vocabulary of Bousbir prostitutes in the 1950s ("Jouer avec la marginalité").

26 Sextius, *De la criminalité des Arabes au point de vue de la pratique médico-judiciaire en Tunisie*, 156–57.

27 Apter, "Acting Out Orientalism," 105.

28 Lorcin, "Mediating Gender, Mediating Race," 45–46.

29 This practice was as much a way for women travelers to gain greater freedom of movement and avert unwanted attention as it was a playful experiment—since it seems unlikely that the disguise would always be convincing. European female travelers engaged in a wide spectrum of cross-dressing practices, from wearing a female Eastern outfit or a male European costume to sporting an Arab man's dress. Among the better-known European travelers who engaged in this practice of double cross-dressing were Suzanne Voilquin, Jane Dieulafoy, Rosita Forbes, Freya Stark, and Lady Esther Stanhope, who further insisted that her maids do the same.

30 Hedi Abdel-Jaouad, "Isabelle Eberhardt," offers an excellent overview of Isabelle Eberhardt's many social and literary disguises, noting how her performance of nomadism questioned existing power structures and paved the way for subsequent Maghrebi female writers.

31 Apter, "Acting Out Orientalism," 111.

32 Déjeux, "Elissa Rhais, Conteuse Algérienne (1876–1940)," 49.

33 The first complete account of Rhaïs's life and career is given by Jean Déjeux, "Elissa Rhais, Conteuse Algérienne (1876–1940)." For studies focusing on Rhaïs's "masquerade," see Apter, "Ethnographic Travesties, Alibis of Gender and Nation in the Case of Elissa Rhaïs"; Rosello, "Elissa Rhaïs"; Lorcin, "Manipulating Elissa"; and Crucifix, "An Orientalist Masquerade."

34 Brahimi, *Femmes arabes et soeurs musulmanes*, 40.

35 For a historical overview of this context, see Wilson, "The Antisemitic Riots of 1898 in France"; Iancu, "Les Juifs d'Algérie et de France pendant la crise antijuive algérienne (1897–1898)"; and Assan, "Dans la tourmente anti-juive."

36 Rhaïs, *Le mariage de Hanifa*, 47, 193.

37 Rhaïs, *Le mariage de Hanifa*, 47.

38 Rhaïs, *Le mariage de Hanifa*, 48.

39 Rhaïs, *Le mariage de Hanifa*, 200.

40 Bugéja, *Nos soeurs musulmanes*, 88.

41 Rhaïs, *Le mariage de Hanifa*, 242.

42 Bhabha, *The Location of Culture*, 62–63.

43 Bendahan, *Messieurs, vous êtes impuissants*, 193.

44 Bendahan, *Messieurs, vous êtes impuissants*, 22, 46.

45 Bendahan, *Messieurs, vous êtes impuissants*, 84.

46 Bendahan, *Messieurs, vous êtes impuissants*, 253.

47 Regarding "intermarriages" during the colonial period, see Déjeux, *Image de l'étrangère*; and Liauzu, "Guerre des Sabines et tabou du métissage." For an overview of "intermarriages" in the Maghrebi Jewish community in particular, see Katz, "Conversion, Intermarriage and the Legal Status of Jews in French Protectorate Morocco."

48 Bendahan, in a manner characteristic for the time, often conflates the two categories, declaring, for instance, several times that Sixfrancs, because of his sexual orientation, is not really a man.

49 Bendahan, *Messieurs, vous êtes impuissants*, 49.

50 Bendahan, *Messieurs, vous êtes impuissants*, 82.

51 Bendahan, *Messieurs, vous êtes impuissants*, 216.

52 Bendahan's first novel, *Mazaltob*, written much earlier in 1930, was already a scathing (and humorless) critique of the situation of Maghrebi Jewish women, depicting the bleak prospects and the constant sexism faced by the eponymous heroine, and clearly bore some autobiographical accents.

53 Bendahan, *Messieurs, vous êtes impuissants*, 12.

54 Bendahan, *Messieurs, vous êtes impuissants*, 221.

55 Garber, *Vested Interests*, 11.

Works Cited

Abdel-Jaouad, Hedi. "Isabelle Eberhardt: Portrait of the Artist as a Young Nomad." *Yale French Studies*, no. 83 (1993): 93–117.

Aldrich, Robert. *Colonialism and Homosexuality*. London: Routledge, 2003.

———. "Homosexuality in the French Colonies." *Journal of Homosexuality* 41, no. 3–4 (2002): 201–18.

Apter, Emily. "Acting Out Orientalism: Sapphic Theatricality in Turn-of-the-Century Paris." *L'Esprit créateur* 34, no. 2 (1994): 102–16.

———. "Ethnographic Travesties, Alibis of Gender and Nation in the Case of Elissa Rhaïs." In *Continental Drift: From National Characters to Virtual Subjects*. Chicago: University of Chicago Press, 1999.

Assan, Valérie. "Dans la tourmente anti-juive." In *Les consistoires israélites d'Algérie au XIXᵉ siècle*, 365–406. Paris: Armand Colin, 2012.

Bendahan, Blanche. *Messieurs, vous êtes impuissants*. Paris: Nouvelles Editions Debresse, 1961.

Benichou Gottreich, Emily, and Daniel J. Schroeter. *Jewish Culture and Society in North Africa*. Bloomington: Indiana University Press, 2011.

Bhabha, Homi K. *The Location of Culture*. London: Routledge, 2004.

Boone, Joseph A. *The Homoerotics of Orientalism*. New York: Columbia University Press, 2015.

Booth, Marilyn. *Harem Histories: Envisioning Places and Living Spaces*. Durham, NC: Duke University Press, 2010.

Brahimi, Denise. *Femmes arabes et soeurs musulmanes*. Paris: Tierce, 1984.

Branche, Raphaëlle. "Des viols pendant la guerre d'Algérie." *Vingtième Siècle. Revue d'histoire* 75, no. 3 (2002): 123–32.

Bugéja, Marie. *Nos soeurs musulmanes*. Paris: La revue des études littéraires, 1921.

Claude Liauzu. "Guerre des Sabines et tabou du métissage : les mariages mixtes de l'Algérie coloniale à l'immigration en France." *Les cahiers du CEDREF* 8–9 (2000): 259–80.

Crucifix, Edwige. "An Orientalist Masquerade: The Self-Exoticizing Gaze in the Works of Elissa Rhaïs." *MHRA Working Papers in the Humanities* 14 (2019): 29–37.

Déjeux, Jean. "Elissa Rhais, Conteuse Algérienne (1876–1940)." *Revue de l'Occident Musulman et de la Méditerranée* 37, no. 1 (1984): 47–79.

———. *Image de l'étrangère : unions mixtes franco-maghrébines*. Paris: La Boîte à documents, 1989.

Favre, Lucienne. *Tout l'inconnu de la Casbah d'Alger*. Illustrations by Charles Brouty. Alger: Baconnier, 1933.

Garber, Marjorie. *Vested Interests: Cross-Dressing and Cultural Anxiety*. London: Routledge, 1992.

Hathaway, Jane. *The Chief Eunuch of the Ottoman Harem: From African Slave to Power-Broker*. Cambridge: Cambridge University Press, 2018.

Hayes, Jarrod. *Queer Nations: Marginal Sexualities in the Maghreb*. Chicago: University of Chicago Press, 2000.

Iancu, Carol. "Les Juifs d'Algérie et de France pendant la crise antijuive algérienne (1897–1898). Correspondance inédite de Simon Kanoui." In *Les relations intercommunautaires juives en méditerranée occidentale, XIIIᵉ-XXᵉ siècles*, edited by Institut d'études africaines, 187–202. Paris: C.N.R.S. Editions, 1984.

Jacobus X. *L'Amour aux colonies*. Paris: Isidore Liseux, 1893.

Katz, Jonathan G. "Conversion, Intermarriage and the Legal Status of Jews in French Protectorate Morocco." *Journal of North African Studies* 23, no. 4 (2018): 648–74.

Khatibi, Abdelkebir. *La Blessure Du Nom Propre*. Les Lettres nouvelles, 1974.

Kocher, Adolphe. *De la criminalité chez les Arabes au point de vue de la pratique médico-judiciaire en Algérie*, vol. 19. JB Baillière & fils, 1884.

Kooijman, Jaap. "Pleasures of the Orient: Cadinot's Maghreb as Gay Male Pornotopia." *Thamyris/Intersecting: Place, Sex and Race* 22 (2011): 97–111.

Kozma, Liat. "Colonial and Post-Colonial Casablanca." In *Selling Sex in the City: A Global History of Prostitution*, edited by Magaly Rodríguez García, Lex Heerma van Voss, and Elise van Nederveen Meerkerk, 261–77. Leide: Brill, 2017.

Laskier, Michael M. "The Alliance Israélite Universelle and the Jewish Communities of Morocco, 1862–1962." Albany: State University of New York Press, 1984.

Lee, Daniel. "Prostitution in Tunis." In *Trafficking in Women (1924–1926): The Paul Kinsie Reports for the League of Nations, Vol. 2*, edited by J. Chaumont, M. Rodríguez García, and P. Servais, 228–31. Geneva: United Nations, 2017.

Lorcin, Patricia. *Imperial Identities: Stereotyping, Prejudice and Race in Colonial Algeria*. Lincoln: University of Nebraska Press, 2014.

———. "Manipulating Elissa: The Uses and Abuses of Elissa Rhaïs and Her Works." *Journal of North African Studies* 17, no. 5 (2012): 903–22.

———. "Mediating Gender, Mediating Race: Women Writers in Colonial Algeria." *Culture, Theory and Critique* 45, no. 1 (2004): 45–61.

Malino, Frances. "'Institutrices' in the Metropole and the Maghreb: A Comparative Perspective." *Historical Reflections / Réflexions Historiques* 32, no. 1 (2006): 129–42.

Massad, Joseph. "Edward W. Said and Joseph Boone's *The Homoerotics of Orientalism*." *Cultural Critique*, no. 98 (2018): 237–61.

Memmi, Albert. *Portrait du colonisé, précédé de portrait du colonisateur*. Paris: Gallimard, 1985.

Mouliéras, Auguste. *Le Maroc inconnu: étude géographique et sociologique*. Paris: Librairie coloniale et africaine, 1895.

Reguer, Sara. "The World of Women." In *The Jews of the Middle East and North Africa in Modern Times*, edited by Reeva S. Simon, Sara Reguer, and Michael M. Laskier. New York: Columbia University Press, 2002.

Rhaïs, Elissa. *Le mariage de Hanifa*. Paris: Plon, 1926.

Rosello, Mireille. "Elissa Rhaïs: Scandals, Impostures, Who Owns the Story?" *Research in African Literatures* 37, no. 1 (2006): 1–15.

Said, Edward. *Orientalism*. New York: Vintage Books, 2003.

Sextius, Arène. *De la criminalité des Arabes au point de vue de la pratique médico-judiciaire en Tunisie*. Valence: Imprimerie Ducros & Lombard, 1913.

Shepard, Todd. *Sex, France, and Arab Men, 1962–1979*. Chicago: University of Chicago Press, 2017.

Stora, Benjamin. *Les trois exils : Juifs d'Algérie*. Paris: Stock, 2006.

Taraud, Christelle. "Jouer avec la marginalité: le cas des filles soumises 'indigènes' au Maghreb à l'époque coloniale." *Clio* (2003): 65–86.

Toledano, Ehud R. *Kul/Harem Slavery: The Men, the Women, the Eunuchs*. Seattle: University of Washington Press, 2012.

Weil, Patrick. "Le statut des musulmans en Algérie coloniale." *Histoire de la justice* 1 (2005): 93–109.

Wilson, Stephen. "The Antisemitic Riots of 1898 in France." *Historical Journal* 16, no. 4 (1973): 789–806.

Yeazell, Ruth Bernard. "Public Baths and Private Harems: Lady Mary Wortley Montagu and the Origins of Ingres's 'Bain Turc.'" *Yale Journal of Criticism* 7, no. 1 (1994): 111–38.

3

"A Living Tableau of Queerness"

The Orient at the Crossroads of Genre and Gender in Proust's *Recherche*

Amr Kamal

I saw the light from my father's candle already creeping up the wall. . . . Instinctively I murmured, though no one heard me, "I'm done for!"[1]

Introduction

Marcel Proust begins and ends *À la recherche du temps perdu* with an allegorical Oriental sunrise and sunset. In the first volume, the readers encounter an Abraham-like father holding a candle whose light rises over the wall as he climbs the stairs, an image evoking the movement of the sun across the horizon or, perhaps even, over the Western Wall of Jerusalem.[2] In contrast, near the conclusion of the final volume, the text depicts a crescent shining over the Seine, which the narrator likens to the Bosporus. Comparing Paris to Sodom, the narrator imagines his city sometimes dominated by Jews and other times invaded by Muslim soldiers. Through this racialized and sexualized apocalyptic compounded image of Paris-Sodom-Istanbul, he announces the end of France as he knew it. Like the reflection of the father's candle and the crescent, the Orient emerges in Proust's *La Recherche* as an imminent threat. Always lurking from within, waiting to reveal a hidden aspect of French society. In this chapter, I examine the way Proust uses Orientalist imaginary as a form of queering to deconstruct French national identity and bourgeois culture. I investigate how the Orient in Proust represents a specter of the repressed, which haunts the text and constantly makes an appearance to reveal what is lying underneath the surface by "bringing the queer skeletons out of the nation's closet," to borrow Jarrod Hayes's words.[3] In the text, Orientalism plays a key role in the critique and historization of France, whereby the image of Jews and Muslims is "about Europe . . . its limits and limitations," as Gil Anidjar once put it.[4]

Throughout the novel, Proust deploys the Orient through a series of simulacra, a house of mirrors, in which scenes alluding to Muslims or Jews have multiple reflections throughout the text. These images mediate a triangulated connection between references to biblical scriptures or Abrahamic Law, European canonical art, and everyday life, wherein various characters inadvertently reenact the themes from Orientalist artworks into scenes from the everyday. In so doing, they expose a multidirectional relationship between nature and art in which art copies life and eventually life emulates art. Orientalism in *La Recherche*, then, represents a process of translation across genres, from that of the sacred text, to painting, to fiction, to the textual quasi-photographic documentation of the daily life. The Orient constantly vacillates between the mystified aesthetics of classical art and its aura-less mundane renditions. Precisely by portraying French society by means of an Orientalist iconography that is simultaneously theatrical, queer, and quotidian, the novel opens the possibility for the reinterpretation of national history.

In his study of Orientalism, Edward Said depicts the discursive power relations between Europe and the Orient as that of subject and object. The Orient was envisioned as a "static" and distant collection of images delivered to Europe in "fragment[s]" through "an amalgam" of scientific knowledge and phantasmatic imagination.[5] Orientalism blurred the distinction between the various populations in the Middle East, including Arabs, and Jews. As a particularly illustrative example, Said quotes Benjamin Disraeli's novel *Tancred* (1847), in which a character proclaims, "Arabs are simply Jews on horseback, and all are Orientals at heart."[6] The Orient was an unstable signifier charged with an intense libidinal energy ranging from disgust to fascination, from sexual desire to mystification. The Orient was a "supine" body, waiting for European exploration.[7] It was a place of adventure outside the confines of Europe in which all transgressions and fantasies can be fulfilled while maintaining the ethereal impression of a dream, without disturbing the European social order.

Orientalism in *La Recherche* shares many aspects of Said's definition. In the novel however, while the Orient appears in fragments, it does not constitute a place far away from home; it is part and parcel of the French nation. In some instances, the text highlights the interchangeability of Jews and Arabs within France, especially at the height of the Dreyfus affair. From the perspective of the bourgeoisie, both fulfill an exotic Orientalist role: "The Romanians, the Egyptians, the Turks may hate the Jews. But in a French drawing-room the differences between those peoples are not so apparent . . . an Israelite making his entry as though he were emerging from the desert . . . completely satisfies a certain taste for the oriental."[8] *La Recherche* is replete with numerous Orientalist references leading up to a dreaded breaking point in the plot when the Orientalist aesthetic comes to dominate the text, and readers encounter Muslim soldiers from the colonies roaming the streets of Paris.[9] It is at this particular moment that the narrator realizes that the France he once knew is not recognizable anymore, signaling as such the end of an era.[10] In response to this situation, the narrator concludes his story with an ambivalent image, suggesting at once fear and desire. He decides to adopt a feminine persona from the East in order to record his account of France's Belle Époque. Impersonating Scheherazade, he spends his nights documenting his memories of a bygone era. In this context, the queer conclusion of the novel itself marks the beginning of writing and documenting French history.

A Queer Abraham

Going back to *La Recherche*, we can trace one of the first queer accounts of the Orient when the narrator tries to persuade his mother to join him in his room. As he stands in the hallway pleading with her, he finds himself before his father, whom he compares to the figure of Abraham carrying out the law by ordering Sarah away from her son:

> He was still in front of us, a tall figure in his white nightshirt, crowned with the pink and violet cashmere scarf which he used to wrap around his head since he had begun to suffer from neuralgia, standing like Abraham in the engraving after Benozzo Gozzoli which M. Swann had given me, telling Sarah that she must tear herself away from Isaac.[11]

Cast as an Abrahamic figure, Marcel's father is expected to uphold the law by separating mother and son. Before that critical moment, the father's arrival is signaled in a quasi-cinematic style. The phallic image of the candle rising slowly up the stairs serves as a double for the father's image and introduces the specter of the symbolic. Finally, the readers meet the ominous father as he reaches the top of the stairs only to realize that he bears little resemblance to Abraham. He is instead, as the narrator suggests, an incarnation of Gozzoli's artistic interpretation of the biblical story. Proust's depiction bestows neither the aura of the scriptures nor that of the canonical painting on this paternal figure. The narrator's father wears a white dressing gown and ties a violet and pink scarf around his head because of his recurring headaches. He is an imitation of an imitation, a pale copy in a chain of simulacra, a campy Abrahamic version sketched by means of disparate elements from French Orientalist material culture. The readers therefore find themselves not before an Orientalist biblical image but rather before an excessively Orientalized one, which better fits Edward Said's description: "a living tableau of queerness."[12] The passage creates this queer picture by juxtaposing three representations: the biblical reference of Isaac, Gozzoli's classical painting depicting the same theme, and the actual memory of the narrator's quotidian, which translates Sarah and Isaac's experience into an everyday modern situation.[13]

By means of this Orientalized depiction of the father, the text effects a power shift. This queer image comes at the moment when the symbolic order is about to be transgressed. The scene begins with the young narrator soliciting his mother's attention. Yet the act of interpellation is seldom solely a double accord between interpellator and interpellated. It rather includes a series of multidirectional and intersubjective relations also called by the symbolic order.[14] When the young narrator calls his mother, he is also interpellating the father. Through that triangulated interaction (between child, mother, and father) the image of the phallic father recedes to give way to the persona of the mother. The maternal figure is what Jean Laplanche and J. B. Pontalis would call "a phallic mother."[15] The "phallic woman" represents a strong female character who occupies an ambiguous, gender role, both masculine and feminine, since she wields a significant power within the patriarchal order.[16] This charged and potentially disparaging term, "phallic woman," which almost denies this figure's womanhood, best exemplifies heteronormative anxiety; it exposes the threat that she could cause to the symbolic order. This term underscores the ambivalent, if not phobic, masculine perception of this figure.[17] The phallic mother is an archetype typically represented in paintings such as that of the Madonna and child, mother and son. As Craig Owens indicates, "The Virgin is a regressive figure [who] suspends . . . the incest prohibition (in medieval tradition, the Virgin is both mother and bride of Christ)."[18] While still being the product of its own time, *La Recherche* offers a more complex representation of influential female characters than the reductive notion of the "phallic woman." As the narrator's father permits the mother to join the child. Both, mother and child, spend the night reading George Sand's novels, such as *François le Champi*, a story about incest, written by another gender-nonconforming figure who uses a male penname.[19] In this instance, the Abrahamic Law recedes to allow a transgressive complicit moment between mother and son, reflected in the text as a game of doubles, or a theater within a theater: that of the reunion of Marcel and his mother reading in their turn Sand's incestuous texts.

Notably, the figure of Abraham enters the scene as a specter of the symbolic, which the father fails to enact. As Judith Butler indicates, while performance remains under the control of the actor who can manipulate their representation to convey, or hide, a particular message, "performativity . . . consists in a reiteration of norms which precede, constrain, and exceed the performer's will or 'choice'; . . . what is performed works to conceal, if not to disavow, what remains opaque, unconscious, unperformable."[20] The power of the performative then stems from a double-edged nature that can either elevate the utterers or destabilize them. Every utterance serves to subjugate not only those who are addressed but also those who invoked it in the first place since their act betrays their vulnerability to the same laws and norms. By the same token, the narrator's father, who is meant to uphold the Law, reveals his own subjugation to the norms, once his stern demeanor exposes a caricatural effeminized Orientalized side. The reflection of the father's candle, then, becomes part of a farce where a large ominous shadow on the wall turns out to be that of a tiny mouse: an eroticized Abraham in pink and violet silk.

By superimposing these images, the narrator queers the father. The campy image of the father insinuates that the father *n'est pas* (is not) Abraham, rather *il en est*. Namely, he is "of that kind." I borrow here a turn-of-the-century description for queerness used by the narrator elsewhere in the novel, which roughly translates as being of it (namely of that group). The French expression *en être*, dating back to the mid-seventeenth century, encapsulates at once the theatricality of heteronormative living and its disciplinary corrective dimension. The term was used to refer to same-sex desire in nineteenth-century police reports. It also denotes the individual's effort to mask his desire in order to publicly conform to social norms, while consciously identifying with a covert group. In this respect, the scene exposes the father's strict demeanor as a mere performance. He plays the enactor of laws and norms, while concealing, or perhaps not being aware of, his own subjugation to them. In contrast to simply *être* (being) or *ne pas être* (not being)—which places the subject with or in opposition to the normative, respectively—the pronoun *en* in *en être* (implying of that kind), referring to homosexuality, functions as an ambiguous signifier that defers meaning. Hayes suggests that the term *en être* exposes an "epistemological instability."[21] "The adverbial pronoun hides its antecedent—homosexuals, usually—in a sort of linguistic closet. Who can know for sure whether the intended antecedent is not something else?"[22] The expression suggests that what is queer belongs to the realm of neither being nor not being. It is not shunned altogether but rather located in parallel to, or alongside, a heteronormative order. Precisely, this dynamic of queer suspension is key to the consolidation of a heteronormative order. As Butler reminds us, heteronormative subject formation "requires the simultaneous production of a domain of abject beings, those who are not yet 'subjects' but who form the constitutive outside to the domain of the subject."[23] In that sense the term *en être* suspends Others in the parallel space of not yet subjects, where their being is constituted as mimicry. As Homi Bhabha points out: "In mimicry, the representation of identity and meaning is rearticulated along the axis of metonymy."[24] Similarly, the pronoun *en* establishes a metonymic relationship with existence. Bearing the mark of difference and *différance*, *en être* casts the individual in a simulacrum of an ontological order.[25] Later in the novel, the narrator uses the terms *être* and *en être* to depict gay French culture as an underground form of queer Zionism.[26] Playing on iconographic and linguistic ambiguities, the text produces a multiplicity of categorical closets.

More importantly, queering the Abrahamic father opens a space for another transgression, that of Proust's novel, which concludes with the narrator becoming Scheherazade. In fact, when the narrator at the end of the text compares himself to Scheherazade, he mentions specifically his early memory of his parents on the stairs.[27] From the beginning of the text, then, the narrative places itself against, and in competition with, the patriarchal order. Proust's narrative often leads us into a house of mirrors. *La Recherche* is a novel with several beginnings and several endings, several iterations of the same theme, each reflected in the other (the scriptures, the canonical paintings, and the everyday). Before the influx of memories triggered by the famous madeleine, there was the symbolic queering of the Abrahamic father, which led the path to remembering.

A Queer Life: When the Everyday Imitates Orientalist Art

The triangulated connection between the representations of quotidian life, the scriptures, and canonical art, exemplified in the Abrahamic father's scene, unfolds throughout Proust's literary project. In documenting the history of the Third Republic before World War I, Proust, like Baudelaire before him, attempts to capture modern life through the materiality of the everyday, by focusing on its "transitory, fugitive element," which contrasts with the "eternal and immutable" characteristic of art.[28] Similarly, *La Recherche* records the mundane side of the Third Republic by pitting it against canonical art. In many incidents, the narrator sketches a tableau vivant of everyday life outlining people's behaviors and actions in their typical costumes and décor and then makes a biblical reference, followed by an ekphrasis of a renowned painting that expresses a similar theme. The scene with the Abrahamic father is a case in point. In his rendition of Abraham, Proust blurs the lines between the sacred and the profane to produce a comic version of the story of Isaac. The narrator begins with a minute detailing of a vivid memory, which he compares to the biblical reference of Isaac as well as Gozzoli's canonical painting. Yet unlike the biblical reference recreated in the painting, the actual living situation exposes the failure, rather than the apotheosis, of the symbolic. As if the text is asking, what if we could imagine the biblical narrative not as part of a divine or artistic realm? What happens if we strip history of its mythological and iconographic aura and see it as an actual lived experience?

Such process of translation from the sacred to the mundane mediated by Orientalist aesthetics eventually serves as a strategy of subversion.

For instance, in "Acting Out Orientalism," Emily Apter investigates the potential of the Orientalist stereotypes in the quotidian as a tactic to destabilize heteronormative notions of gender by coding the representation of same-sex desire, a process that straddles the fine line between "being" and "doing," performance and performativity. Actors and writers dressed in excessively Orientalized costumes and staging their bodies against equally hyperbolic Orientalist décor participated in a playful theatricality that destabilized the scripted limits of heteronormative sexuality.[29] This theatrical extravaganza involves the celebration of strong biblical and historical female figures often associated with ambiguous sexuality (such as Cleopatra, Salomé, and Semiramis). Apter suggests that "acting 'Oriental' becomes a form of outing, and outing is revealed to be thoroughly consonant with putting on an act (each flips into the other unpredictably)."[30] The calculated reenactment of Orientalist themes with all their flaws, ambiguities, and incongruities produces a space for subversion that escapes the heteronormative eye, precisely due to the potential of the stereotype to circulate as an excessive image that "eliminates the need for decoding."[31] Caught within the interstices between art and reality, the viewers lose their assumed grasp over where the theatrical ends and the real (or in this case the queer gesture) begins.

In *La Recherche*, Orientalism is also part of a tactic of performative negotiation of daily social and national norms. But before turning to this point, I would like to revisit a passage from the novel that underscores Proust's exceptional attention to the question of performativity as a subversive queer act that is able to hold a mirror to French society and accordingly crafts a space for marginalized subjects. In *Le Côté de Guermantes*, the narrator watches a play with his friend Saint-Loup and Rachel, a Jewish prostitute. At the theater, the narrator meditates on the double life of actors who shine for a few moments while playing a character and then revert to their ordinary existence after leaving the stage and wiping their face "powder."[32] His reflection suggests initially that theatrical performance is constricted to the space of the theater, where the difference between being and doing is foreclosed by the borders of the fourth wall. In other words, everything within the confines of the stage demands the withholding of the spectator's judgment since it represents a fiction or a simulacrum of the real. Nevertheless, the narrative later blurs the strict distinction between the theatrical and the everyday. In the same scene, Rachel expresses her admiration of the elegant feminine movements of a male dancer. She intimates that the dancer outshines her with his feminine performance: "Isn't he too wonderful with his hands! I couldn't do the things he's doing there, even though I'm a woman."[33] The dancer responds by playfully repeating his hand movements to please Rachel:

> The dancer turned his head towards her, and his human person appeared beneath the sylph that he was endeavouring to be, the clear grey jelly of his eyes trembled and sparkled between eyelashes stiff with paint, and a smile extended the corners of his mouth in a face plastered with rouge; then, to amuse the young woman . . . he began to repeat the movement of his hands, counterfeiting himself with the subtlety of a mime and the good humour of a child. "Oh, it's too lovely, the way he mimics himself," cried Rachel, clapping her hands.[34]

The text creates a chain of representations and mirror images in which real life becomes a theatrical act. The actor frames himself as an object under examination and mimics his earlier movements. Both the actor and Rachel share a queer moment. Both are aware of the fact that he is mimicking the theatrical role that he played on stage, while implicitly showcasing his feminine side (once again we are in Proust's house of mirrors). Through this calculated reiteration of his movements, the dancer moves from performance to performativity, a process where, as Apter and Owen suggest, "a subject . . . makes it-self be by enacting [its own] objectification."[35] Performance, here, opens a place in which the dancer finds new ways of self-representation through theatricality, whereby his feminine movements are deemed a skillful talent central to a normative bourgeois notion of art rather than a sign of emasculation.

The encounter between Rachel and the dancer marks a key technique in *La Recherche*, hinging on the reversal of the role between life and art, to underscore the underlining French performance of gender, nationality, and class. As life comes to mimic the theater, the novel exposes everyday life as a continuous performative act, which in turn sheds a new light on the theatricality of the quotidian during the Belle Époque. In reenacting his own gesture, the dancer holds a mirror to Rachel in which she sees the reflection of her own subjective and objective position within the symbolic and national orders. Rachel is the dancer's double. Her interaction with the dancer in costumes produces a moment of mutual recognition at the crossroad of performance and performativity. Rachel's comments expose the fine line between the theatricality of femininity and the materiality of sex and gender. By reiterating his movements offstage to Rachel, the dancer exposes the artifice of gender performance. The dancer's playful gest highlights the elusive power of gender performativity in which "the ritualized repetition . . . produce[s] and stabilize[s] not only the effects of gender but the materiality of sex."[36] Like the dancer, Rachel, as a sex worker, belongs to a marginalized sexuality, whose exclusion plays a central role in founding heteronormativity. Her power within the patriarchal society stems from a theatrical performance of desire and femininity. As Joan Riviere suggests, "Womanliness . . . could be assumed and worn as a mask, both to hide possession of masculinity and to avert the reprisals expected if she was found to possess it—much as a thief will turn out his pockets."[37] Rachel considers femininity as a part of scripted patriarchal masquerade. Like "a thief turning out [her] pockets" (to borrow Riviere's words), she denies her mastery of a feminine performativity that soothes the male angst. Elsewhere, she is described as "an enigma . . . a regular sphinx."[38] The narrator considers her a skillful seductive actress with many faces and many roles, who considers the entire world her own theater:

> Rachel had scarcely more than a walking-on part in the little play. But seen thus, she was another woman. She had one of those faces to which distance—and not necessarily that between stalls and stage, the world being merely a larger theatre—gives form and outline and which, seen from close to, crumble to dust.[39]

Rachel's face which crumbles like dust resembles the face powder used by actors to create their stage persona. Rachel's seductive power relies on the outright performative disavowal of her own skills in mimicking gender roles. Her fascination with the dancer may be motivated by a narcissistic recognition of the uncanny resemblance between her performance of scripted femininity within a patriarchal system and that of the dancer.

In addition to gender, Rachel performs a national identity that fits the political climate in which she lives. As a Jewish woman witnessing the Dreyfus affair, she attempts to suppress her ethnic origins by disavowing her lover, Saint-Loup, as Jewish, who acquired this label because of his

"A Living Tableau of Queerness" 85

political views and his association with her: "It's just what they say: Marsantes, Mater Semita, it smells of the race."[40] The narrator highlights the irony in this situation where a Jewish woman employs antisemitic expressions to attack non-Jewish French individuals.[41] Rachel's attitude toward the dancer and Saint-Loup exposes a theatrical performance that operates and exists beyond the limits of the stage. Beneath the heavy layers of makeup covering the dancer's face, Rachel recognizes a mutual experience: that of the quotidian masquerade necessary for navigating a heteronormative and antisemitic web of social relations.

A Queer Orientalist History of French Bourgeoisie

Like Rachel's performance, Orientalism is intertwined within the theatricality of the everyday. Through the lens of Orientalism and its exaggerated manifestations, Proust brings to light the intricate and hidden dynamics of life in France, including the history of the bourgeoisie and interclass relationships. For instance, Proust traces Odette's (Swann's lover) rise from her humble beginnings as a "cocotte" (a courtesan) to an established bourgeois woman. In the beginning of Odette and Swann's relationship, Odette welcomes him in her small apartment, where Swann is taken aback by her excessive Orientalist decoration:

> He had climbed a staircase that went straight up between dark painted walls hung with Oriental draperies, strings of Turkish beads, and a huge Japanese lantern suspended by a silken cord (which last, however, so that her visitors should not be deprived of the latest comforts of Western civilisation, was lighted by a gas-jet inside). . . . Odette had received him in a pink silk dressing-gown, which left her neck and arms bare.[42]

Odette sets up her apartment as a stage that frames her as an exotic character. In her décor, the Orient as a totality, from the Far East to the Near East, collapses with no distinction into one single space specifically constructed for a Western audience, whose comfort is greatly valued and sought after, such as the case of a first-class traveler who seeks to take a tour around the world. Odette constructs, or rather mimics, the Orient by means of a collection of cheap bric-a-brac that she considers of high artistic value. Although the space gives a vague impression of the Orient, it does not indicate any place in particular. Through her décor, Odette deterritorializes, or disorients, her visitors, taking them away from the comfort of familiarity. The only sign of familiar comfort that Odette has kept is that of the gas light, which itself is a deception since it enhances the theatricality of her act by giving it an ethereal quality, transforming her house into a stage.

In manipulating the language of fashion, Odette manages to camouflage her social origins. The fashion system, Roland Barthes posits, is a multi-discursive and representational process, located at the crosscurrent between semiology and sociology. He posits, "The sociology of fashion . . . seeks to systematize certain actions and to relate them to social conditions, standards of living, and roles. Semiology does not follow the same path at all . . . The sociology of Fashion is entirely directed toward real clothing; the semiology of Fashion is directed toward a set of collective representations."[43] Likewise, Odette's Orientalist mimicry activates the tension between the sociology and semiology of fashion. Whereas French contemporary fashion, with its double focus on the iconic (semiotic) and the social, could root Odette in present-day France and place her at the bottom of an unescapable social ladder, her Oriental dress and décor connect her metonymically to a collection of distant Orientalist iconic clichés devoid of social reference. As she impairs the social signification of fashion, she situates herself within a distant map that eludes the bourgeois taxonomy of class and taste. In mobilizing the semiology of fashion, hinging on its iconographic quality, Odette extricates herself from the map of French patriarchal social hierarchy. By appropriating the semiotics of empire, Odette takes on the qualities of the Orient, an incomprehensible, indefinable signifier. In Odette's Orientalist salon, Swann loses himself in a foreign map that challenges his control. Swann's obsession with Odette resembles the desire of the colonist who strives to comprehend and dominate a continuously elusive East. Swann sinks into one of Odette's Oriental seating areas and loses himself amid the bric-a-brac. In this theatrical setting, by means of her association with an ambiguous and phantasmatic Orient, Odette succeeds in dissimulating her humble origins. She becomes an incomprehensible, indefinable signifier, a character out of time and out of the confines of the French metropolis. Odette takes on the qualities of a stereotypical fetishized, elusive Orient.

In his effort to regain control over Odette, Swann attempts to restore the object of his desire to a familiar bourgeois domain by comparing her to canonical art, Zipporah from Botticelli's fresco "The Trials of Moses" (1482), located at the Sistine Chapel.[44] Just like Gozzoli's painting of Abraham, Botticelli's painting introduces the specter of the symbolic into the scene. In so doing, Swann detaches Odette from her orchestrated Orientalist theater and places her in the familiar safeguarded realm of bourgeois cultural capital: that of classical paintings. The fresco of Zipporah, Jacques Derrida suggests, recounts both the founding and the failure of patriarchal order.[45] In the biblical narrative, it is Zipporah who circumcises Moses's eldest son to uphold the patriarchal law. Zipporah's act, Hayes suggests, exposes and "provides a matrilineal alternative to the genealogy inscribed onto the Jewish penis, which connects men to their fathers, circumcised, like them, in a chain leading all the way back to Abraham."[46] As the narrator of Albert Memmi's *The Pillar of Salt* once put it: "[Circumcision] was indeed the act that bound [Jewish men] within the great and sacred chain which, throughout the centuries, went all the way back to God."[47] In the painting, Zipporah and her sister feature as fragile virginal women dressed in white. Zipporah's innocent figure recalls Botticelli's other painting "The Birth of Venus" (ca. 1484–86). The sisters attempt to make their way in a world of men. Zipporah cedes her agency to Moses, in contrast to Odette, who is in full control of her theatrical space, almost treating Swann as another object among her Oriental bric-a-brac. In the painting, Zipporah's eyes are directed toward her sister while Moses looks downward and actively fills a bucket from the well to give water to the sheep. Interestingly, whereas Moses is the one expected to assume the leading role, both sisters carry a shepherd staff (a phallic object but also a religious token often associated with prophets). In contrast, Moses, the shepherd of the people, carries none. On one level, the representation of Zipporah/Venus holding a phallic staff portends a gender ambiguity, leading the spectator to wonder who actually holds the power in the painting, Zipporah or Moses. Like in the case of Gozzoli's painting, Swann's attempt to seize control of Odette by comparing her to Botticelli's fresco announces the failure of the symbolic. It instead heightens his infatuation and seals Odette's power grip.

After marrying Swann, Odette secures her social ascension and redefines her ties to the French bourgeoisie. At the height of the Dreyfus affair, she poses as a patriot and anti-Dreyfusard. She expresses this new position symbolically by distancing herself from her Orientalist theater and redecorating her house in a strictly French taste:

> The Far East was retreating more and more before the invading forces of the eighteenth century. . . . Nowadays, it was rarely in Japanese kimonos that Odette received her intimates, but rather in the bright and billowing silk of a Watteau housecoat.[48]

Resorting to her usual theatrical tactics, Odette copies French material culture to locate herself within the echelons of French bourgeoisie as a rich married woman. Her French décor is just as hyperbolic as was her Orientalist abode. Like Rachel, Odette confirms her new taste and political position through a preemptive and overt expression of xenophobia. She intimates that she cannot live in the midst of anything "pompous" or "hostile."[49] By rejecting Orientalist aesthetics and taking an antisemitic stance, Odette, whose own daughter would later become the duchess of Guermantes, mobilizes what Pierre Bourdieu calls the bourgeoisie's "genesis amnesia," the final process of erasing one's origins after ascending the social ladder.[50] Ironically, Swann, Odette's husband, who started as an aristocratic French spectator watching Odette in her campy exotic décor, is now cast as an Oriental who can no longer repress his Semitic traits: "Swann's Punchinello nose, absorbed for long years into an agreeable face, seemed now enormous, tumid, crimson, the nose of an old Hebrew rather than of a dilettante Valois."[51] Like the light of the Abrahamic father's candle, Swann's Semitic traits emerge to expose a secret. As Odette and Swann exchange positions, the Orient, which betrayed Odette's humble beginnings, now reveals (or outs) Swann's Jewishness. Swann's looks do not recall any figure of classical painting but rather the racialized images of Jewish men in the caricatures of the era. At the end of this aesthetic simulacra that highlights Odette's humble beginning, the aristocracy, the same object of the narrator's fascination, turns into an empty signifier, suggesting that perhaps all exalted aristocratic origins lead to another Odette.

Queer Zionism: The Enemy from Within

Just as the Orient became a way to "out" Odette's origins and Swann's Jewishness, it became the lens to "out" and bring to the surface underground same-sex culture in Paris. Using Zion as a trope for Sodom, the narrator takes upon himself the responsibility of being the readers' guide in order to warn them about the "Sodomites," who dream of rebuilding their fallen promised city.

> These descendants of the Sodomites, so numerous that we may apply to them that other verse of Genesis: "If a man can number the dust of the earth, then shall thy seed also be numbered," have established themselves throughout the entire world . . . Certainly they form in every land an oriental colony, cultured, musical, malicious, which has charming qualities and intolerable defects. We shall study them with greater thoroughness in the course of the following pages; but I have thought it as well to utter here a provisional warning against the lamentable error of proposing (just as people have encouraged a Zionist movement) to create a Sodomist movement and to rebuild Sodom.[52]

This scene is one of the most intriguing uses of Orientalism as a performative act in the novel. Distancing himself from homosexuality, the narrator poses as an Orientalist who guides his European audience through the alleys of Zion/Sodom. In the same volume, in a conversation between the narrator and Saint-Loup on the sexuality of Charlus, Saint-Loup uses the expression *en être*, used by the police but also marking homosexuality as a coded theatrical act that simultaneously passes as heteronormative while consciously forging a clandestine organized community with its own codes:

> These are milieus where people become part of a tribe and a congregation. Don't tell me it is not a small sect on its own, where one is fond of those who are in it and full of disdain for those who are not. The question is not, like in Hamlet, to be not to be, rather to *be of it* or not to *be of it*.[53]

The Orientalist imagery in *Sodome et Gomorrhe* intertwines the discourse of Zionism with that of antisemitism and homophobia, by mixing

Orientalism with the religious, legal, and scientific discourse on sexuality. The narrator's stance corresponds with Said's claim that the Orient was seen as in need of "corrective study by the West" and was framed in the language of "the classroom," "the criminal court," "the prison," and "the illustrated manual."[54] Collapsing Sodom and Zion, the narrator surprisingly renders queerness a form of Zionism but also turns Zionism queer. The Orientalist image of Sodom constructs what Eve Sedgwick calls "the spectacle of the closet," by depicting the different epistemological binaries that have produced the modern image of homosexuality.[55] Some of these binaries include "secrecy/disclosure," "private/public," "masculine/feminine," "majority/minority," "natural/artificial," "discipline/terrorism," "health/illness," "art/kitsch," and "utopia/ apocalypse."[56] These binaries are played out throughout the novel and are often framed within an East/West dialectic. In so doing, the narrator casts his entire narrative, and by extension the portrait of the French nation, as a spectacle of the closet, in which the various characters struggle to hide a latent queer side. The kitsch representation of the narrator's father sketched against Gozzoli's painting marks the beginning of that discursive style. The text suggests that the process of national integration involves a similar queer tension. Just as the homosexual characters Charlus, Jupien, and Morel make the effort to hide their homosexuality from society while sharing a common code to identify with, and express their belonging to, a larger community, the two Jewish characters in the novel, Swann and Bloch, strive to become part of the French elite by hiding their Jewish heritage. The image of the sickly effeminate Jew/Oriental who tries to dissimulate his traits and to blend within French society enhances most of the binaries that make up the closet spectacle. Such an image, as Hayes indicates, echoes a Eurocentric gendered discourse of Zionism, whereby "the promised land . . . is not merely a revival of the past or a return to roots; it is also a narrative of progress, of gendered progress, one that requires the masculinization of its men in relation to (other) European nations."[57] The novel, then, suggests that French nationalism shares a queer origin that it seeks to erase through a repressive process of symbolic masculinization.

The Other Semite: An Enemy from Without

As the novel proceeds, Orientalist aesthetics gradually take over the text to announce the end of an era. In so doing, the novel metaphorically outs the entire nation. Proust sets the trajectory for Orientalism to become inversely proportional with that of the Belle Époque, where the epitome of Orientalism marks the nadir of the era. In the final tome, *Le Temps retrouvé*, Proust concludes the novel with scenes from World War I, in which the narrator reiterates the same biblical imagery by depicting the siege of Paris as the fall of Sodom. Ironically, the fall of Sodom serves as a foundational moment of the narrative since it signals the beginning of writing, that is, the recovery of lost time. Proust's narrative of France, then, is rooted in Sodom. One can say even that the narrative intimates its queer origins. The act of rewriting consists thus of reliving, and reveling in, Sodom. As Jarrod Hayes points out, "The paradise regained by Proustian memory, could thus be Sodom."[58]

In the Proustian narrative, France of the Belle Époque, that lost Paradise/Sodom to which the narrator longs, abounds with African and North African soldiers. In contrast to the earlier Zionist imagery, the narrator imagines a Muslim France, living under the sign of the crescent. France is not simply Orientalized but also converted.[59] The narrator describes another ominous image of Paris invaded by the Orient:

> It was a transparent and breathless night; I imagined that the Seine, flowing between the twin semicircles of the span and the reflection of its bridges, must look like the Bosporus. And—a symbol perhaps of the invasion foretold by the defeatism of M. de Charlus, or else of the cooperation of our Muslim brothers with the armies of France—the moon, narrow and curved like a sequin, seemed to have placed the sky of Paris beneath the oriental sign of the crescent.[60]

Proust weaves into his narrative a classical image of the Muslim invasion of France, what Said calls a "textual attitude" toward the integration and reference of the Orient in literature.[61] As Said once noted, the epistemological dilemma that the Orient posed for European writers, such as Gustave Flaubert, was often displaced into a complex psychosexual dynamic, in which the Orient and Orientals feature as hypersexual invaders preying over a beleaguered Europe.[62] For instance, in *The Homoerotics of Orientalism*,

Joseph Boone suggests that Orientalists at once feared the impact of an encroaching Orient and projected their intellectual crises as a threat of emasculation, "of being 'unmanned' by the allure of a polymorphous [Oriental] sexuality that seems to exceed representation."[63] In response to this claim, Joseph Massad astutely pinpoints the reversal within that imaginary of invasion in which, ironically, an imperialist, yet vulnerable, Europe falls under the control of an aggressive hypersexual colonized Orient.[64] The threat of Oriental encroachment in this case serves as one of the foundational tropes for European identity and imaginary that reaches back to classical Greek texts and later permeates French literature.[65] In Proust's novel, the megalomaniac colonial expansion is projected into a paranoiac reverse narrative of invasion carried out by the colonized.

Such themes remain popular and operative within contemporary culture, especially in relation to a sexualized migrant North African Muslim population that still occupies the center of French political debates on national identity in a global context.[66] For instance, writing in 2015, a time witnessing various terrorist attacks but also a rising conservative xenophobic political movement, Michel Houellebecq pictures France under the control of a radical Muslim government. Houellebecq's book cover features the Eiffel Tower topped by a crescent, which recalls Proust's imaginary of Paris during World War I. In the novel, the protagonist, François, a professor of literature, specialized in the writings of Huysmans. Houellebecq's narrative switches back and forth between the dystopian world of Huysmans following the fall of the Second Empire (1871) and a contemporary French Muslim dystopia.

Similarly, the narrator of *La Recherche* guides the readers through the apocalyptic streets of modern Sodom: the decadent and doomed city of Paris. He witnesses the destruction of his familiar places now reduced to ashes, which he likens to the monuments of Pompeii.[67] In contrast to previous scenes, where the text references Abraham (Gozzoli's painting) and Moses (Botticelli's "The Trials of Moses"), the narrator uses a Muslim reference to represent the specter of the symbolic law. The Occident and the Orient exchange roles; the effeminized passive Orient now materializes as the sexualized masculine Other or the invader who executes revenge and restores the symbolic order: Paris lies supine under the sign of the crescent.

Whereas Charlus overlaps the image of the city with the paintings of Alexandre Decamps and Eugène Delacroix, the narrator offers another contesting Orientalist version inspired by *The Thousand and One Nights.*[68]

Retracing the Abrahamic journey, the narrator locates his Orient in Meso-potamia rather than North Africa. Expressing his feeling of estrangement and loss in Paris, he imagines himself in the Muslim Orient, as the Arab king Harun al-Rashid roaming the streets of Baghdad. Accepting his own fate, he decides to record the bygone memories of Paris of his youth by embodying the figures of the historian Saint-Simon and Scheherazade from *The Nights*, who narrates her stories at night fearing the king's wrath.[69]

As Benhaïm suggests, by deciding to become Scheherazade, the author moves "from odalisque to story-teller, from object of the gaze to subject of the writing, from passive model to the mistress of the text, the writer foreign to his own sex becomes an absolute—and freed—stranger."[70] In fact, Scheherazade the storyteller, a daughter of a vizier, is not con-sidered an odalisque in the Arab imaginary.[71] She rather represents the anti-odalisque, whose talent as narrator directed at the patriarchal phal-lic order is sharper than the executor's sword. In *The Thousand and One Nights*, Scheherazade assumes her role to protect other women, whereby storytelling serves as an apotropaic act to shield women from patriar-chal wrath. Perhaps she represents a Medusa figure of some sort within a masculinist imaginary.[72] Scheherazade is another reflection of the var-ious gender-nonconforming women in Proust's novel who also disarm their male opponents: the narrator's mother (likened to George Sand), Zipporah (holding the shepherd staff and performing Moses's role of circumcising his son), Odette, Gilberte, and Albertine. They destabilize the text by restoring its gendered ambiguity, which in turn casts doubt on the narrative's heteronormative foundational origins.

Conclusion

In *La Recherche*, Proust constructs a house of mirrors with playful reflec-tions of East and West, Muslims and Jews. The narrator decides to tell the story of modern France, by means of an ambiguous Orientalist persona. In announcing that he will embody at once Saint-Simon and Schehe-razade, the narrator of *La Recherche* chooses to become a historian in drag. The narrator—perhaps Proust as well, whose novel constantly blurs the line between art and reality—cunningly announces to his readers his adoption of an androgynous and queer voice to reconstruct the history

94 Amr Kamal

of his nation. Just as the young dancer reenacts his own movements before Rachel, the narrator in Oriental drag reenacts his life before the reader. One can even say that it is not only the narrator who will be in drag but also France as a nation that will be contemplating itself in Orientalist fashion. Dressed in Orientalist garb, Marcel retraces the beginnings of an era. Yet as the readers realize, the end of the novel marks the beginning of writing, signaling that from the start of the book, the narrator had already assumed the role of Scheherazade. He had told his entire narrative of France in drag. Like Scheherazade and the many women in *La Recherche*, Proust disarms the readers of the novel, who only learn of his queer impersonation of the protagonist from *The Nights* at the conclusion of the text. Akin to Scheherazade, a woman who dreads her own execution at dawn, the narrator writes during the night at the end of his life.[73] He prolongs through his narrative the memory of his bygone youth one night at a time. The narrator awaits the curtains to fall slowly on the Belle Époque just like Shehryar's sword is expected to fall on Scheherazade's neck: a patriarchal threat that the king never manages to enact. Proust concludes his masterpiece with the words "—in Time." trapped between an Em dash and a period. As a visual sign, the phallic Em dash itself recalls the father's candle and the king's sword.[74] Learning from Scheherazade, Proust masters the art of the apotropaic narrative: in the text, the memory of the Belle Époque like that of *The Thousand and One Nights* is forever suspended between life and death.

Notes

In the chapter title, I borrow the words "a living tableau of queerness" from Edward Said's depiction of the Orient through the eyes of nineteenth-century European travelers; see *Orientalism* (103). I would like to thank Jarrod Hayes for his generous feedback and comments on earlier drafts of this chapter. I would also like to thank Bettina Lerner, Maxime Blanchard, Brian Martin, and Vincent Sallé.

1 Proust, *In Search of Lost Time*, volume I, 47. "Le reflet de la bougie de mon père s'élevait déjà sur le mur. . . . Sans le vouloir, je murmurai ces mots que personne n'entendit : 'Je suis perdu !'" (Proust, *À la recherche du temps perdu*, 38).

"A Living Tableau of Queerness" 95

2 I owe the idea of the Western Wall to Vincent Sallé. In the French text, Proust uses the word "mur" first, then "muraille" two passages later, when he evokes Gozzoli's painting of Abraham. The word "muraille" often refers to a fortified wall, a rampart, such as the Western Wall of Jerusalem (Proust, *À la recherche du temps perdu*, 38).

3 Hayes, *Queer Nations*, 97.

4 Anidjar, *The Jew, the Arab*, xi.

5 Said, *Orientalism*, 177.

6 Said, *Orientalism*, 102.

7 Said, *Orientalism*, 220.

8 *In Search of Lost Time*, volume III, 253. "Les Roumains, les Égyptiens et les Turcs peuvent détester les juifs. Mais dans un salon français les différences entre ces peuples ne sont pas si perceptibles . . . un Israélite faisant son entrée comme s'il sortait du fond du désert . . . contente parfaitement un goût d'orientalisme" (Proust, *À la recherche du temps perdu*, 891).

9 Proust, *In Search of Lost Time*, volume VI, 172. Proust, *À la recherche du temps perdu*, 2218.

10 The novel exudes references to material culture from both the Middle East and the Far East. For *le japonisme* in Proust, see Hokenson, "Proust's Japonisme"; and Everman, *Lilies and Sesame*.

11 Proust, *In Search of Lost Time*, volume I, 49. 115–17. Proust, *À la recherche du temps perdu*, 38.

12 Said, *Orientalism*, 103.

13 For a detailed content of paintings in *La Recherche*, see Karpeles, *Paintings in Proust*.

14 On the performative aspect of interpellation, see also Butler, *Bodies That Matter*, 224–26.

15 Laplanche and Pontalis, *The Language of Psychoanalysis*, 312. In *The Language of Psychoanalysis*, Jean Laplanche and J. B. Pontalis define "phallic woman" and "phallic mother" as "woman endowed, in phantasy, with a phallus. This image has two main forms: the woman is represented either as having an external phallus or phallic attribute, or else as having preserved the male's phallus inside herself." See also Apter, "Acting Out Orientalism," 115n12.

16 Laplanche and Pontalis, *The Language of Psychoanalysis*, 312.

17 In referring to the potential of the term "phallic woman" in denying a person's womanhood, I seek to underscore how this word strictly relies on a binary that marks difference as a potential danger to heteronormativity. I am aligning with Monique Wittig's claim in "The Straight Mind," wherein for a long time, womanhood "was a political constraint,

and those who resisted it were accused of not being 'real' women.... To refuse to be a woman, however, does not mean that one has to become a man" (*The Straight Mind and Other Essays*, 12).

18 Owens, "Posing," 206.

19 As Kristeva points out, *François le Champi*'s plot centers on Madeleine, who marries her adoptive son. Although the name of the protagonist was erased from Proust's final draft, the reference to the story might be still considered an avowal of incestuous feelings (Kristeva, *Time and Sense*).

20 Butler, *Bodies That Matter*, 234.

21 Hayes, "Proust in the Tearoom," 999.

22 Hayes, "Proust in the Tearoom," 997.

23 Butler, *Bodies That Matter*, 3.

24 Bhabha, *The Location of Culture*, 129.

25 Hayes, "Proust in the Tearoom," 998. See also Derrida, *Writing and Difference*.

26 For the history of the expression *en être* and examples of Proust's uses of the term in *La Recherche*, see "en être" in Claude Courouve's *Dictionnaire Français de l'homosexualité masculine*. See also Hayes, "Proust in the Tearoom."

27 Proust, *In Search of Lost Time*, volume VI, 522–26.

28 Baudelaire, "The Painter of Modern Life," 796–97.

29 Apter, "Acting Out Orientalism," 102–5.

30 Apter, "Acting Out Orientalism," 106.

31 Apter, "Acting Out Orientalism," 103. See also Owens, "The Medusa Effect, or, The Specular Ruse."

32 Proust, *In Search of Lost Time*, volume III, 228 "Those robust if ephemeral, and rather captivating, personalities which are the characters in a play ... who by that time have already disintegrated into an actor who is no longer in the situation which was his in the play, ... into a coloured powder which a handkerchief wipes off." "Ces individualités éphémères et vivaces que sont les personnages d'une pièce ... qui déjà se sont désagrégées en un comédien qui n'a plus la condition qu'il avait dans la pièce, ... en une poudre colorée qu'efface le mouchoir" (Proust, *À la recherche du temps perdu*, 878).

33 Proust, *In Search of Lost Time*, volume III, 238. "Ah ! Vraiment il est épatant avec ses mains. Moi qui suis une femme, je ne pourrais pas faire ce qu'il fait là" (Proust, *À la recherche du temps perdu*, 883).

34 Proust, *In Search of Lost Time*, volume III, 236. "Le danseur tourna la tête vers elle, et sa personne humaine apparaissant sous le sylphe qu'il s'exerçait à être, la gelée droite et grise de ses yeux trembla et brilla

entre ses cils raidis et peints, et un sourire prolongea des deux côtés sa bouche dans sa face pastellisée de rouge ; puis, pour amuser la jeune femme, . . . il se mit à refaire le mouvement de ses paumes, en se contrefaisant lui-même avec une finesse de pasticheur et une bonne humeur d'enfant.—Oh ! c'est trop gentil, ce coup de s'imiter soi-même, s'écria-t-elle en battant des mains" (Proust, *À la recherche du temps perdu*, 882).

35 Apter, "Acting Out Orientalism," 104. Apter refers to Owen. See Owens, "The Medusa Effect, or, The Specular Ruse," 215.

36 Butler, *Bodies That Matter*, x.

37 Quoted by Owens, "Posing," 212.

38 Proust, *In Search of Lost Time*, volume III, 382.

39 Proust, *In Search of Lost Time*, volume III, 231. "Rachel jouait un rôle presque de simple figurante, dans la petite pièce. Mais vue ainsi, c'était une autre femme. Rachel avait un de ces visages que l'éloignement—et pas nécessairement celui de la salle à la scène, le monde n'étant pour cela qu'un plus grand théâtre—dessine et qui, vus de près, retombent en poussière." (Proust, *À la recherche du temps perdu*, 879).

40 Proust, *In Search of Lost Time*, volume III, 237.

41 Proust, *In Search of Lost Time*, volume III, 237.

42 Proust, *In Search of Lost Time*, volume I, 310–11. "Un escalier droit entre des murs sombres et d'où tombaient des étoffes orientales, des fils de chapelets turcs et une grande lanterne japonaise suspendue à une cordelette de soie (mais qui, pour ne pas priver les visiteurs des derniers conforts de la civilisation occidentale, s'éclairait au gaz) . . . Odette l'avait reçue en robe de chambre de soie rose, le cou et les bras nus" (Proust, *À la recherche du temps perdu*, 182).

43 Barthes, *The Fashion System*, 9–10.

44 Proust, *In Search of Lost Time*, volume I, 314–15. Proust, *À la recherche du temps perdu*, 184.

45 Bennington and Derrida, *Jacques Derrida*, 68.

46 Hayes, *Queer Roots of the Diaspora*, 192.

47 Memmi, *The Pillar of Salt*, 171; Hayes, *Queer Roots of the Diaspora*, 171.

48 Proust, *In Search of Lost Time*, volume II, 261–62. "L'Extrême-Orient reculait de plus en plus devant l'invasion du XVIIIe siècle. . . . Maintenant c'était plus rarement dans des robes de chambre japonaises qu'Odette recevait ses intimes, mais plutôt dans les soies claires et mousseuses de peignoirs Watteau" (Proust, *À la recherche du temps perdu*, 487–88).

49 Proust, *In Search of Lost Time*, volume II, 262. Proust, *À la recherche du temps perdu*, 487–8.

50 Bourdieu, *Outline of a Theory of Practice*, 78–79.

98 Amr Kamal

51 Proust, *In Search of Lost Time*, volume IV, 121. "Le nez de polichinelle de Swann, longtemps résorbé dans un visage agréable, semblait maintenant énorme, tuméfié, cramoisie, plutôt celui d'un vieil Hébreu que d'un curieux Valois." (Proust, *À la recherche du temps perdu*, 1277.)

52 Proust, *In Search of Lost Time*, volume IV, 43–4. "Ces descendants des Sodomistes . . . se sont fixés sur toute la terre. . . . Certes ils forment dans tous les pays une colonie orientale, cultivée, musicienne, médisante, qui a des qualités charmantes et d'insupportables défauts. On le verra d'une façon plus profonde plus approfondie au cours des pages qui suivront ; mais on a voulu provisoirement prévenir l'erreur funeste qui consisterait, de même qu'on a encouragé un mouvement sioniste, à créer un mouvement Sodomiste et à rebâtir Sodome" (Proust, *À la recherche du temps perdu*, 1232).

53 My translation; my emphasis. "Ce sont des milieux, me dit-il, où on fait tribu, où on fait congrégation et chapelle. Tu ne me diras pas que ce n'est pas une petite secte ; on est tout miel pour les gens qui en sont, on n'a pas assez de dédain pour les gens qui n'en sont pas. La question n'est pas, comme pour Hamlet, d'être ou de ne pas être, mais d'en être ou de ne pas en être." (Proust, *À la recherche du temps perdu*, 1299).

54 Said, *Orientalism*, 41.

55 Sedgwick, *Epistemology of the Closet*, 213–51.

56 Sedgwick, *Epistemology of the Closet*, 11.

57 Hayes, *Queer Roots of the Diaspora*, 178.

58 Hayes, "Proust in the Tearoom," 1003.

59 See Benhaïm, "From Baalbek to Baghdad and Beyond," 99, for a discussion on the persistence of this image in contemporary French politics.

60 Proust, *In Search of Lost Time*, volume VI, 172. "Il faisait une nuit transparente et sans souffle; j'imaginais que la Seine coule entre ses ponts circulaires, faits de leur plateau et de son reflet, devait ressembler au Bosphore. Et, symbole soit de cette invasion que prédisait le défaitisme de M. de Charlus, soit de la coopération de nos frères musulmans avec les armées de la France, la lune étroite et recourbée comme un sequin semblait mettre le ciel parisien sous le signe oriental du croissant" (Proust, *À la recherche du temps perdu*, 2218). In a personal correspondence with the writer Anton Shammas (April 2021), Shammas suggested that the crescent (croissant) over the scene could be an unconscious Orientalist visual recreation of the madeleine suspended over the teacup. In this case, I add, the madeleine represents personal involuntary memory experience that is still under the control of the narrator, while the other

expresses a paranoia of engulfment and losing control over memory altogether.

61 Said, *Orientalism*, 92.

62 Said, *Orientalism*, 188.

63 Boone, *The Homoerotics of Orientalism*, 17.

64 Massad, "Edward W. Said and Joseph Boone's *The Homoerotics of Orientalism*," 244.

65 Said, *Orientalism*, 51–110.

66 For examples of the imaginary of psychosexual paranoia of invasion in contemporary French political discourse of immigration, see, for instance, Todd Shepard, *Sex, France, and Arab Men*; Mehammed Mack, *Sexagon*; and Joan Scott, *The Politics of the Veil*.

67 Proust, *In Search of Lost Time*, volume VI, 207–8. For more on Proust's depiction of the brothel, see Everman, *Lilies and Sesame*, 150.

68 Proust, *In Search of Lost Time*, volume VI, 173.

69 Proust, *In Search of Lost Time*, volume VI, 524–25.

70 Benhaïm, "From Baalbek to Baghdad and Beyond," 96. Odalisque, a slave or a chambermaid in a harem, is often depicted in Orientalist paintings, such as the works of Jean Auguste Dominique Ingres (1760–1867). In his study of *La Recherche*, Benhaïm posits that in documenting the memory of the Belle Époque, Proust "unveils and reinscribes an oriental origin (imaginary but present) for France. He also envisions an oriental origin for the narrator" (87).

71 Mernissi, *Dreams of Trespass*, 15; Steiner, "Scheherazade's Achievement(s)," 122.

72 For the initial depiction of Scheherazade in *The Thousand and One Nights*, see the "Prologue" of *The Arabian Nights* (Haddawy, *The Arabian Nights*, 5–14).

73 Proust, *In Search of Lost Time*, volume VI, 524–25.

74 Proust, *In Search of Lost Time*, volume VI, 532. "—dans le Temps" (Proust, *À la recherche du temps perdu*, 2401.)

Works Cited

Anidjar, Gil. *The Jew, the Arab: A History of the Enemy*. Stanford: Stanford University Press, 2003.

Apter, Emily. "Acting Out Orientalism: Sapphic Theatricality in Turn-of-the-Century Paris." *L'Esprit créateur* 34, no. 2 (1994): 102–16.

Barthes, Roland. *The Fashion System.* Translated by Matthew Ward and Richard Howard. New York: Hill and Wang, 1983.

Baudelaire, Charles. "The Painter of Modern Life." In *The Norton Anthology of Literary Theory,* edited by Vincent B. Leitch, William B. Caine, Laurie A. Finke, John McGowan, and Jeffrey J. Williams. New York: W.W. Norton, 2001.

Benhaïm, André. "From Baalbek to Baghdad and Beyond: Marcel Proust's Foreign Memories of France." *Journal of European Studies* 35, no. 1 (2005): 87–101.

Benjamin, Walter. "The Work of Art in the Age of Mechanical Reproduction." In *Illuminations,* edited by Hannah Arendt. Berlin: Schocken Books, 2007.

Bennington, Geoffrey, and Jacques Derrida. *Jacques Derrida.* Translated by Geoffrey Bennington. Chicago: University of Chicago Press, 1993.

Bhabha, Homi. *The Location of Culture.* London: Routledge, 1994.

Boone, Joseph Allen. *The Homoerotics of Orientalism.* New York: Columbia University Press, 2014.

Bourdieu, Pierre. *Outline of a Theory of Practice.* Cambridge: Cambridge University Press, 1977.

Butler, Judith. *Bodies That Matter: On the Discursive Limits of Sex.* New York: Routledge, 1993.

Courouve, Claude. *Dictionnaire Français de l'homosexualité masculine.* Paris: Payot, 1985.

Derrida, Jacques. *Writing and Difference.* Translated and introduction by Alan Bass. Chicago: University of Chicago Press, 1978.

Everman, Anthony Albert. *Lilies and Sesame: The Orient, Inversion, and Artistic Creation in "À la recherche du temps perdu."* New York: Lang, 1998.

Haddawy, Hussein, trans. *The Arabian Nights.* New York: W.W. Norton, 1990.

Hayes, Jarrod. "Proust in the Tearoom." *PMLA: Publications of the Modern Language Association of America* 110, no. 5 (1995): 992–1005.

———. *Queer Nations: Marginal Sexualities in the Maghreb.* Chicago: University of Chicago Press, 2000.

———. *Queer Roots of the Diaspora: Ghosts in the Family Tree.* Ann Arbor: University of Michigan, 2016.

Hokenson, Jan. "Proust's *Japonisme*: Contrastive Aesthetics." *Modern Language Studies* 29, no. 1 (1999.): 17–37.

Houellebecq, Michel. *La Soumission.* Paris: J'ai lu, 2015.

Karpeles, Eric. *Paintings in Proust: A Visual Companion to "In Search of Lost Time."* London: Thames & Hudson, 2008.

Kristeva, Julia. *Time and Sense: Proust and the Experience of Literature*. Translated by Ross Guberman. New York: Columbia University Press, 1996.

Laplanche, J., and J. B. Pontalis. *The Language of Psychoanalysis*. Translated by Donald Nicholson Smith. London: Karnac Books, 1988.

Mack, Mehammed. *Sexagon: Muslims, France, and the Sexualization of National Culture*. New York: Fordham University Press, 2017.

Massad, Joseph. "Edward W. Said and Joseph Boone's *The Homoerotics of Orientalism*." *Cultural Critique* 98 (2018): 237–61.

Memmi, Albert. *The Pillar of Salt*. Boston: Beacon Press, 1955.

Mernissi, Fatima. *Dreams of Trespass: Tales of a Harem Girlhood*. New York: Basic Books, 1994.

Owens, Craig. "The Medusa Effect, or, The Specular Ruse." In *Beyond Recognition: Representation, Power and Culture*, edited by Scott Bryson, Barbara Kruger, Lynne Tillman, and Jane Weinstock. Berkeley: University of California Press, 1992.

———. "Posing." In *Beyond Recognition: Representation, Power and Culture*, edited by Scott Bryson, Barbara Kruger, Lynne Tillman, and Jane Weinstock. Berkeley: University of California Press, 1992.

Proust, Marcel. *À la recherche du temps perdu*. Paris: Quarto Gallimard, 1999.

———. *In Search of Lost Time*. Translated by C. K. Scott Moncrieff and Terence Kilmartin. Revised by D. J. Enright. New York: Modern Library, 2003.

Said, Edward W. *Orientalism*. New York: Vintage, 1978.

Scott, Joan Wallach. *The Politics of the Veil*. Princeton: Princeton University Press, 2007.

Sedgwick, Eve Kosofsky. *Epistemology of the Closet*. Berkeley: University of California Press, 1990.

Sheppard, Todd. *Sex, France, and Arab Men, 1962–1979*. Chicago. University of Chicago Press, 2017.

Steiner, Tina. "Scheherazade's Achievement(s): Practices of Care in Fatema Mernissi's Memoir, Dreams of Trespass: Tales of a Harem Girlhood, and Her Creative Non-Fiction, Scheherazade Goes West." *English in Africa* 47, no. 3 (2020): 121–54.

Wittig, Monique. *The Straight Mind and Other Essays*. Boston: Beacon Press, 1992.

Part II

PUBLIC DISCOURSE AND IDENTITY

4

Queering the Abrahamic Scriptures

Shanon Shah

Introduction

There is a burgeoning body of popular and scholarly work that showcases the experiences of queer Muslims in response to the premise that Islam is hostile toward homosexuality.[1] One significant strand explores the ways in which queer identity can be harmonized with Islamic teachings. Early manifestations of this approach were catalyzed by the advent of online forums in the late 1990s.[2] These online environments provided new, anonymous, and (therefore) safer spaces for queer Muslims to explore queer-sensitive interpretations of Islam. From their inception, however, these forums were also subjected to abuse and threats of violence from defenders of traditionalist Islamic viewpoints of gender and sexuality.

Still, the genie could no longer be put back into the bottle. The pioneering work of Scott Siraj al-Haqq Kugle, professor of South Asian and Islamic Studies at Emory University, must be understood in this context. Kugle's contribution to the volume *Progressive Muslims* (2003) employed semantic and thematic analysis that challenged anti-queer readings of the Qur'an and provided a template for queer-sensitive interpretations of Islam. He revisited the key verses used by traditionalist Muslims to condemn homosexuality to argue that these passages were actually about aggression, oppression, and male-on-male sexual violence rather than consensual and loving same-sex relations.

Kugle developed these arguments further in *Homosexuality in Islam* (2010), which connected his observations about the Qur'an with an analysis of the corpus of hadith (recorded traditions of the Prophet Muhammad) and their knock-on effects on historical constructions of *fiqh* (Islamic jurisprudence). In *Living Out Islam* (2014), Kugle showcased the lived experiences of queer Muslims in different parts of the world, many of whom were not traditionally trained religious experts. These and other publications focusing on queer-sensitive Islamic perspectives are part of Kugle's more activist strand of scholarship—he also researches and publishes widely on Islam and Sufism in South Asia. In his scholar-activist writings, Kugle acknowledges the influence of Islamic feminism and progressive Muslim scholarship.[3] His work has inspired the scholarship and activism of newer generations of queer Muslims—including mine—but it has also been subjected to numerous criticisms.[4]

Two interrelated and recurring criticisms of Kugle are that, first, his work feeds into Orientalist or Islamophobic stereotypes about Islam and, second, that he has a distorted or mistaken understanding of Islam's sacred texts. The first charge—of providing fodder for Orientalist propaganda by selectively highlighting Westernized or elitist experiences of queer Muslims—largely follows the argument developed by Joseph Massad. Massad argues that histories of European colonialism, Orientalism, and Islamophobia have partly led to an obsession by Western gay rights groups—which he labels the "Gay International"—in "rescuing" Arab, and by extension Muslim, homosexuals.[5] According to Massad, Arabs or Muslims who identify as "gay" are Westernized elites who form a "minuscule minority among . . . men who engage in same-sex relations and who do not identify as 'gay' nor express a need for gay politics." The implication is therefore that openly gay Muslim scholar-activists such as Kugle are proxies or collaborators with the Gay International. Kugle has rebutted this perspective, but it remains a recurring motif in later criticisms of his work.[6] The second charge—that Kugle's Qur'anic revisionism relies on marginal, inaccurate sources that he misunderstands and that he has an incorrect understanding of the hadith relating to homosexuality—is aimed personally at him and more generally to discredit queer-sensitive approaches to Islam.[7]

In this chapter, I explore one of the main differences between Kugle and his more traditionalist critics: Kugle draws upon the lived experiences of queer Muslims to reinterpret Islam's sacred texts and key concepts. As a gay Muslim himself, he acknowledges and affirms queer Muslim experiences of exclusion, violent threats, depression, fear, and romantic desires as valid sources of textual interpretation. Kugle's traditionalist critics do not consider these valid reasons to revisit or reinterpret Islam's central teachings.

How might we deal with this impasse? While I owe a debt to Kugle for my spiritual and intellectual formation, this chapter is not a one-sided defense of his work. Neither do I stick within the bounds of Islamic argumentation about gender and sexuality. Instead, I expand on one aspect of the debate—the role of queer lived experience in the formation of authoritative knowledge within Islam. This chapter illustrates the ways in which this queer-sensitive counternarrative of what Islam "says" about queerness could benefit from an intertextual reading of the Abrahamic scriptures.

How Do We Know What the Scriptures Really Say about Homosexuality?

The concept of *'ilm*—often glossed as "knowledge"—occupies a central place in Islamic thought. The Qur'an (39:9) identifies it as a "marker of privilege," while Islamic teachings have always enjoined Muslims "to seek knowledge 'from the cradle to the grave.'"[8] Hundreds of Qur'anic verses "explicitly deal with the issue of knowledge" or "related terms such as observation, reason, reflection, [and the] study of natural and social phenomenon."[9]

The centrality of *'ilm*, according to some commentators, is what sets Islam apart from Christianity, its Abrahamic older sibling. According to this perspective, Christian answers to the "big questions" largely follow the "nexus of sin-redemption-salvation (or living in a state of grace), while the corresponding Muslim nexus is ignorance-guidance-success (in this world and the next)."[10] This perspective is reinforced by the ways that Muslims mark the advent of Islam by referring to the pre-Islamic era as the *Jahiliyyah*—the Age of Ignorance.

The charge of Orientalist complicity and willful ignorance on the part of Kugle and other queer-sensitive Muslims must therefore be seen in the light of this dualistic conception of *'ilm* and *jahiliyyah*. The implication is that wisdom is salvific and that the only interpretations of Islam's sacred texts that can be trusted are those provided by Muslims who possess "true" *'ilm.* Accusing someone, no matter how well-intentioned, of being deficient in *'ilm* is a highly discrediting act.

Yet Muslim thinkers have been careful to point out that *'ilm* cannot be reduced to mere "knowledge." *'Ilm* is presented as "an all-embracing term covering theory, action, education, natural science etc." and that encompasses religious and secular realms.[11] According to Islamic scholars, *'ilm* not only challenges the religious-secular dichotomy; it also synthesizes the relationship between knowledge, wisdom, and action, and it connects epistemology with ethics.[12] This positive conception of *'ilm* is also used by many writers to explain the decline of Muslim political power—modern Muslims are now paying the price of neglecting the holistic significance of *'ilm.*[13]

This more expansive definition of *'ilm* means that it should not only cover strictly religious topics. In other words, "religious" knowledge can be defined more broadly and inclusively from an Islamic perspective. The natural and social sciences, for example, count as *'ilm* as much as the study of jurisprudence or Qur'anic interpretation. But, with reference to Kugle, is there room to incorporate lived experience as a basis for *'ilm*? Answering this question entails dissecting the dynamics of power in the production, distribution, and application of knowledge and other building blocks of *'ilm.*

Knowledge, after all, does not exist in a vacuum. There are "validation processes" that produce what we come to recognize as "legitimate knowledge."[14] These are constrained by two criteria—first, the experts who evaluate particular knowledge claims bring with them "a host of sedimented experiences that reflect their group location," and, second, each expert's credibility is defined by the "larger population in which it is situated and from which it draws its basic, taken-for-granted knowledge."[15] As a result, authoritative knowledge claims often exclude, dismiss, or suppress competing claims to knowledge—for example, by an ethnic majority toward ethnic minorities, by men toward women, and so on. Therefore, seemingly objective bodies of knowledge often not only are a product of unequal social relations but also serve to mask these inequalities or normalize them. Uncovering and correcting these inequalities would require what the Brazilian philosopher Paulo Freire refers to as *conscientização.*[16] This is a twofold process involving learning "to perceive social, political and economic contradictions" and then taking action "against the oppressive elements of reality."

Kugle focuses on the experiences of queer Muslims to expose and transform the contradictions and inequalities in dominant understandings of Islam. His strategy furthermore involves drawing upon other realms of knowledge, including from academic social science and the perspectives of grassroots human rights activists. This multilayered approach does not necessarily dismiss or ignore the corpus of *'ilm*, but it does subject many traditionally accepted understandings of Islam to critical inquiry. And, like the Islamic feminists who have inspired him, such as amina wadud, Riffat Hassan, and Fatima Mernissi, Kugle sometimes bypasses or breaks away from dominant Islamic tradition to draw new conclusions and insights.[17] This way of being Muslim and doing Islam very much reflects what sociologists of religion refer to as "everyday religion" or "lived religion," in which the contributions of religious nonexperts or nontraditional experts are privileged, albeit without dismissing the viewpoints of conventional religious institutions and authorities.[18]

This chapter explores how "everyday religion" or "lived religion" contributes to understandings of homosexuality and queerness that continue to unfold in Muslim tradition. It probes the relationship between the Qur'an and Hebrew scriptures and illustrates the impacts of their intertextuality on my personal experience as a queer Muslim and scholar of religion, and vice versa. Before this exploration, however, some context on what the Qur'an and the Bible "say" about homosexuality is needed.

Queering "Homosexuality" Intertextually

Justifications for Islam's supposedly blanket condemnation of "homosexuality"—a modern concept with no direct equivalent in the Qur'an—rely on paradigmatic passages such as this:

> We sent Lut and he said to his people, "How can you practice this outrage? No other people has done so before. You lust after men rather than women! You transgress all bounds!" The only response his people gave was to say [to one another], "Drive them out of your town! These men want to keep themselves chaste!" We saved him and his kinsfolk—apart from his wife who stayed behind. (Qur'an 7:80–83)

This passage is characteristic of the Qur'an's less detailed, more anecdotal summaries of passages from the Hebrew scriptures. The Qur'an often refers to figures and passages in the Jewish and Christian scriptures with the assumption that its audience will have some degree of familiarity with them. The story of the patriarch Noah and the Great Flood narrated in the book of Genesis, for example, is presented in bite-sized summaries as the story of Nuh—regarded in Islam as a prophet and messenger—in different parts of the Qur'an. The Qur'an's mention of the prophet Lut basically corresponds with the Old Testament story of the biblical Lot and the destruction of Sodom and Gomorrah in Genesis 19. Many Muslim interpreters surmised that Lut's people were punished primarily because they condoned anal sex between men, coining the term *liwat* to label this act. Kugle, however, argues that these interpretations did not go unchallenged.[19] For example, the eleventh-century Andalusian jurist Ibn Hazm maintained that Lut's tribe received punishment mainly for a host of other transgressions, including hostility toward strangers and highway robbery—not *liwat* per se.

Ibn Hazm's interpretation of the Qur'anic Lut story accords to a large extent with interpretations of Sodom and Gomorrah in many Jewish commentaries that also do not see it as referring to "homosexuality." In fact, when Sodom and Gomorrah are mentioned in prophetic books such as Isaiah, Jeremiah, and Ezekiel, they are not singled out for the "abomination" of homosexuality.[20] Rather, they are mentioned alongside other cities that breached the divine covenant by allowing insolence and injustice to fester. Moreover, in the rabbinic literature, Lot is conceptualized as the archetype of a weak, wealth- and status-conscious urbanite in contrast with the more upright, humble, and pastoral Abraham.[21] Yet, according to rabbinical commentaries, the divine plan also works through lesser and flawed figures such as Lot—even though he is not the ideal role model.

Jewish commentaries, however, are not devoid of passages that have been interpreted as anti-homosexual. According to Leviticus 18:22, "You shall not lie with a male as with a woman; it is an abomination," while Leviticus 20:13 is even more explicit: "If a man lies with a male as with a woman, both of them have committed an abomination; they shall be put to death; their blood is upon them." Legalistic passages like these find resonance in Muslim tradition through examples such as this popular hadith: "The Prophet said, 'Whoever you find doing the act of the people of Lot, kill the one doing and the one done-to.'" According to Kugle, the bulk of anti-*liwat* hadith reports, such as this one, were most likely fabricated by politically motivated groups or factions in the early history of Islam.[22] They grew alongside numerous other forgeries attributed to the Prophet, leading early Muslim scholars to develop a system to verify the validity of individual hadith reports. Under this verification system, many of the anti-*liwat* hadith reports that circulate widely among Muslims today were actually rejected. Kugle argues that the hadith cited above fails this traditional verification system both for its dubious *isnad* (chain of transmission) and for the uncharacteristic language used in its *matn* (substantive content).[23]

At the same time, patriarchal and heteronormative assumptions did get entrenched within formulations of Islamic law. *Liwat*, alongside other illicit sexual activity, was thus considered a crime punishable by the political authorities, but it was also subjected to restrictive and meticulous definition. Islamic legal rulings prohibited only sexual intercourse between men, while nonsexual expressions of same-sex affection were permitted publicly and privately.[24] Even then, the prohibitions on sexual relations followed a hierarchy, with penetrative anal sex (*liwat*, in its strictest definition) subjected to the severest punishment while "kissing, fondling, and non-anal intercourse" were considered "less serious transgressions."[25] These legalistic minutiae around what counts as *liwat* resemble contestations within Judaism on what "a man [lying] with a male as with a woman" actually describes. For more than two millennia, biblical commentators have struggled to conclude whether the Levitical laws prohibit "specifically the insertive role in anal intercourse," "the insertive and receptive roles," or "all sex acts between males."[26]

Understanding how the restricted definition of *liwat* transformed into a catchall contemporary concept of "homosexuality" requires a brief comparison with the term "sodomy." On one level, *liwat* and sodomy are often seen as synonymous. And just as the word *liwat* does not occur in the Qur'an, neither does the word "sodomy" occur in the Bible. "Sodomy" in Christendom was coined to refer to the sins of the inhabitants of Sodom just as Islamic jurists coined *liwat* to refer to the sins of the people of Lut.

On the other hand, the two terms emerged in distinctive cultural contexts and evolved along different political and legal trajectories. While classical Islamic jurists restricted their view of what counted as *liwat*, the concept of "sodomy" was eventually stretched to cover different varieties of sexual immorality. Examples include the catchall provisions criminalizing "carnal intercourse against the order of nature" in the British Empire's anti-sodomy laws or incidents such as the massacre of "sodomites" in the New World, that is, indigenous peoples engaging in "cross-dressing and presumably same-sex relations."[27] This partly explains why many Victorian travelers to the Orient found themselves scandalized by highly visible and socially accepted expressions of same-sex affection between men.[28] Meanwhile, Middle Eastern Muslim travelers to the West were struck by the lack of romantic courting of male youths by respectable European men.[29] At the same time, the situation in Muslim contexts was not that of complete tolerance. In 1807, for example, two young men were executed by being thrown off one of the minarets of the Umayyad mosque for repeatedly committing *liwat*.[30] Generally, however, behavior that natives of the Orient found acceptable because it did not technically constitute *liwat* was effectively reviled by horrified Occidentals as evidence of sodomy.

This broad conception of sodomy finds some basis in Pauline theology within Christianity. Yet Paul's conversion as a Jew to the nascent community of followers of Jesus Christ suggests that his was an "identity in flux" or "transition."[31] The impacts of his identity issues on the theology of the early church therefore need to be seen in this light. For the purposes of this chapter, it suffices to note that Paul's context provides critical background for the evolution of Christian conceptions of "sexual immorality." Paul's references to marriage and sexual morality were very much part of his mission to reconcile justification by faith and the continuing relevance of Jewish religious law. A recurring theme in Pauline theology is the need to find congruence between people's external acts and behaviors and their inner intentions (or the core of their personhood). "Immoral" sexual behavior, such as sodomy, thus ceases to become simply an aberrant "act." It is also a form of corruption of the mind and soul, of "the root not just the fruit."[32] Yet even this Pauline perspective has been challenged by queer-sensitive Christians, even while acknowledging that "there is no Christianity without Paul."[33]

The question is what potential (if any) does this intertextual queering of the Abrahamic scriptures in regard to homosexuality hold for Muslims and non-Muslims? And can it form the basis for legitimate inquiry in the pursuit of *'ilm* for Muslims? The next section explores these questions by introducing some perspectives on the intertextuality of the Abrahamic scriptures.

Beyond Homosexuality and the Qur'an

The starting point for discussions among Muslims about gender and sexuality is what the Qur'an "says," because of its status as sacred text within Islam. The traditional Islamic narrative is that the Qur'an is the literal Word of God, revealed to the Prophet Muhammad through the angel Jibril, or Gabriel. Muhammad was believed to be illiterate—these revealed passages were later dictated by him and written down by various scribes. While the Qur'an survived as an oral text, its written fragments were compiled and ordered into a single codex after Muhammad's death under the leadership of the third caliph, Uthman ibn Affan.

This verbatim-dictation model of scriptural revelation underlines teachings about the Qur'an's miraculous nature and its incorruptibility and inviolability. The Qur'an's sacred status, therefore, contains parallels both with the divinity of Jesus Christ as the living Word—for example, visual depictions of the Qur'anic revelation to Muhammad have striking similarities with representations of the Annunciation of the Virgin Mary—and with the status of the Torah as the Word of God in Judaism.

These resonances, however, have not always been regarded positively by Jews, Christians, or Muslims. In the early days of Islam, for example, the Syriac Church Fathers came to regard Arabs and Muslims as the Antichrist.[34] Christian authorities eventually dismissed Muslims as the "New Jews," and early anti-Muslim rhetoric borrowed heavily from the growing stock of antisemitism within Christianity.[35] Church leaders increasingly engaged in hostile readings of the Qur'an to point out its mistakes, inaccuracies, and distortions of the "true" message of the scriptures. This body of anti-Muslim polemic provided the basis for the recurring motif of the Qur'an as a derivative, error-laden text, a perspective that shaped Orientalist—and eventually European imperialist—attitudes toward Islam.

Jewish reactions to early Islam were more mixed. Amid the eschatological expectations circulating in the seventh century, Muslims were initially seen as potential liberators or at least Jewish allies against the growing antisemitism in Christendom.[36] This initially positive assessment of Islam was mirrored by many political and religious overtures by Muslims to gain the support of Jewish communities. But such hopes crumbled once Muslim military might and imperial power grew and came into conflict with Jewish messianic expectations.[37]

This religio-political context of Islam's emergence amid Christianity and Judaism, in turn, inspired Islamic polemics about not only the Qur'an but also the Jewish and Christian scriptures. Muslims developed the concept of *tahrif* (distortion) by Jews and Christians of their sacred texts. The mechanisms of *tahrif* that were criticized by Muslim scholars included quoting Bible passages out of context, hiding or omitting key phrases, "twisting the tongue" or deliberately mispronouncing to change the meaning of parts of the text, and willfully misrepresenting the text's true meaning. In its early forms, the concept of *tahrif* was used to address different manifestations of opposition or hostility by Jews and Christians toward Islam. Against Jews, *tahrif* explained and condemned the refusal to recognize Muhammad's prophethood and political authority.[38] Against Christians, it provided a psychological weapon against more sophisticated theological defenses of the doctrine of the Trinity and sonship of Jesus.[39] In the modern era, *tahrif* is overwhelmingly understood by lay Muslims as a wholesale dismissal of the textual content *and* interpretations of the Jewish and Christian scriptures.

Another genre that developed within the Muslim canon became known as the *Isra'iliyyat*, a label for Jewish exegetical material that made its way into Qur'anic commentaries and other Islamic texts. Earlier Muslim thinkers were ambivalent about these sources, using caution when quoting them and only avoiding their more "extravagant" versions.[40] On some level, it seems that they were accepted as a by-product of Jewish conversions to Islam. By the fourteenth century CE, this material began being viewed suspiciously, as accretions or distortions of the true Muslim canon by scholars such as Ibn Taymiyya (d. 1328) and Ibn Kathir (d. 1373).[41] In the nineteenth century, the concept was revived by Muhammad Abduh (1849–1905), eventually acquiring new political and anti-Zionist sting in response to the establishment of the modern state of Israel.[42] There was thus a renewed zeal in the twentieth century to purify Muslim sources of Jewish and Christian references that went hand in hand with anti-colonial politics and the hardening of social boundaries between Muslims, Jews, and Christians. For many Muslims, the early polemics that characterized the mutually hostile readings of Jewish, Christian, and Muslim scriptures have thus evolved into a full-blown doctrine of absolute and ultimate supersession of the Qur'an.

There are, of course, different ways of piecing together the emergence of early Islam based on the available sources. It can be argued that the

Qur'an includes diverse and eclectic groupings of monotheists in its audience, including Jews and Christians, which it addresses under the collective banner of *mu'minun*—"Believers."[43] This term's frequency in the Qur'an far exceeds references to *muslimun*, which can be rendered as "those who submit." The scholar of early Islamic history Fred Donner argues that this community was fiercely monotheistic but also "ecumenical"—"some of the early Believers were Christians or Jews—although surely not all were."[44] But what about the Qur'anic passages that are more explicitly critical or condemnatory toward Jewish and Christian beliefs and practices? According to Donner, because the Qur'an was revealed, transmitted, and recited in fragments as an oral text, these verses were probably less familiar to the Jews and Christians in this new community of Believers.[45] Whether Donner is right is beside the point—what is relevant is that the Qur'an contains the potential for dialogue *and* conflict with Jewish and Christian scriptures and communities.

This line of thought departs from both the conception of the Qur'an as verbatim Divine Speech and blanket dismissals of it as an erroneous, derivative product of the Jewish and Christian scriptures. Instead, the Qur'an synthesizes and improvises key passages from Jewish and Christian scriptures—canonical and noncanonical—to argue certain points with its audience. The Qur'an engaged with versions of Christianity and Judaism that were alive and evolving at the time, and it took an active stake in key doctrinal developments within these traditions. Supposed "discrepancies"—for example, between the Qur'anic narratives of the birth of Jesus and the canonical New Testament accounts—are therefore not arbitrary mistakes. Qur'anic elements that do not appear in the canonical gospels—Mary's withdrawal after learning of her pregnancy, her labor pains under the palm tree, and the baby Jesus's ability to speak and later bring clay birds to life—are neither fanciful Qur'anic inventions nor deficiencies. Rather, these are references to passages in some apocryphal Christian texts, including the Gospel of Pseudo-Matthew, the Protoevangelium of James, and the Gospel of Thomas.[46]

Other instances—such as the identification of Mary, the mother of Jesus, and Mary, the sister of Aaron, as the same person (Qur'an 19:28, 66:12, 3:35–36)—are similarly not mistakes or misunderstandings of the Bible. Rather, the Qur'an in these instances is plausibly echoing a method found in the rabbinic literature, in which such equivalences are made with a particular hermeneutical aim. The Targum (the Aramaic translation of the Hebrew Bible), for example, equates certain figures such as Shem with Melchizedek or Jobab with Job, but this is not due to confusion.[47] Furthermore, in the Qur'an (as with the Talmud), this exegetical strategy extends to apocryphal or noncanonical texts, too. For example, Qur'an 18:60–65 and the Babylonian Talmud, *Tamid*, 31b–32a draw upon the same passage from the *Romance of Alexander*—on the search for the water of life eternal—as something to meditate on.[48]

In fact, the Qur'an itself acknowledges its engagement with the "scriptures of Abraham and Moses" (53:32–41), the "previous scriptures" (20:133), or the "earlier scriptures" (87:16–19). It has been argued that these are not merely references to canonical books in the Hebrew Bible but include at least three apocryphal Old Testament writings—the *Testament of Abraham*; the *Testament and Death of Moses*, chapter 19 of the *Book of Biblical Antiquities*; and the *Apocalypse of Abraham*.[49]

The Qur'an's content, therefore, significantly consists of highly sophisticated intertextual references to Jewish *and* Christian texts, both canonical *and* apocryphal. This complicates the picture of mutual hostility embedded in the DNA of Islam vis-à-vis its Abrahamic siblings. It also paints a more complex picture of the religio-political influences in the construction of canonical texts that we now recognize as "Jewish," "Christian," or "Islamic."

This is why the overlap between Ibn Hazm's perspective and rabbinical commentaries on Sodom and Gomorrah cannot be ignored. Moreover, given the existence of genres such as *Isra'iliyyat* and the intertextuality between the Qur'an, the Hebrew Bible, and the New Testament within Islam, this overlap should come as no surprise. At the same time, the potential for intertextual exegesis remains underexplored by many Muslims because doctrines such as *tahrif* foreclose any curiosity or need to refer to Jewish and Christian commentaries. Yet this analytical juxtaposition of the Abrahamic scriptures does contain the seeds of an intertextual counternarrative of what Islam—or Judaism or Christianity—"says" about homosexuality. But can this counternarrative ever achieve "legitimate status" as authoritative knowledge for Muslims (or Christians and Jews)? The following section attempts to address this question by probing the connection between lived experiences of religion and religious innovation, including the construction and reception of religious knowledge.

Text, Context, and Experience

This section explores the subjective role of my "knowing self" in developing my twofold analysis so far—of the intertextuality between the Qur'an and the Bible and of passages within them that are commonly interpreted as condemning homosexuality.[50] I am an academic sociologist of religion as well as someone who identifies as gay and Muslim. My civil partner is an openly gay Anglican priest. Reflecting on the relationship between the Qur'an and the Bible—and the implications of this on understandings of queerness in Judaism, Christianity, and Islam—is not solely an academic project for me. It is how I live my life and has involved a complex, often painful, but ultimately rewarding journey of learning and unlearning to arrive at my current conclusions. It is no coincidence that a significant part of my journey has also involved the pursuit of a doctorate in the sociology of religion. In my own way, I have internalized a hadith that is fundamental for the self-formation of so many Muslims throughout history around the world: "Seek knowledge even if you have to travel to China." My endeavors before, during, and after doctoral study have thus involved questioning the status of authoritative knowledge, including conceptions of *'ilm* from a Muslim perspective.

Growing up in my native Malaysia, the compulsory Islamic Studies education I received drummed into me the foundational and enduring belief that homosexuality was an abomination—that *I* was an abomination and deserved the severest punishment. I also come from a mixed-race and multireligious background, with an extended family that includes Muslims, Catholic and Protestant Christians, Sikhs, atheists, and followers of the triangle of Buddhism, Taoism, and Confucianism (a common phenomenon among Chinese communities). My closest friendship circles have always been equally diverse. Teachings on the punishments awaiting non-Muslims—the word often used in my Islamic Studies lessons was *kafir*, or "infidel"—in the afterlife also filled me with horror.

I spent most of my teenage years asking for Allah's forgiveness—for being gay and for not being a "real" Muslim—and tried my best to be a "good" Muslim. But in my early twenties, something snapped. By this time, I was studying at a university in Australia and was being subjected to Islamophobia and racism, on the one hand, and, on the other hand, within Muslim spaces, to extreme homophobia, antisemitism, and diatribes

118 Shanon Shah

against *kafirs*. The stress was too great, and I contemplated renouncing Islam altogether.

The events of 9/11 occurred in the midst of my growing spiritual crisis. But I discovered a lifeline through the work of progressive Muslim writers and activists, including Kugle. They exposed me to knowledge and perspectives of Islam I never knew existed. This new intellectual and spiritual worldview coincided with my burgeoning human rights activism and independent journalism in Malaysia. By the time I arrived in London in 2010 for postgraduate study, I had already unlearned much of what passed as "Islam" before my spiritual crisis and cobbled together a new, progressive understanding that would probably have been seen by many other Muslims as bordering on heterodox.

Then I met and fell in love with my partner.

If my journey into a new understanding of Islam involved hugging the margins of orthodoxy, my growing engagement with Christianity propelled me beyond them. I now attend my partner's liberal Anglican church and participate in Christian worship just as frequently as, if not more often than, I observe Islam. I read the Bible and Christian sacred writings as much as I do the Qur'an and Islamic writings. New friendships have also exposed me to different Jewish perspectives of spirituality, sexuality, and social justice. As a spiritual omnivore, I am also happy to learn and absorb insights from many other traditions, including Hinduism, Buddhism, Sikhism, and pagan traditions. These choices are not arbitrary—the traditions I am curious about are the ones that I realize the people I care about hold dear. At the same time, I do not take any established story of any particular "tradition" at face value. I am equally skeptical and critical of several claims made on behalf of Christianity, whether "conservative" or "liberal," as I am of so-called Islamic claims.

As an academic scholar, I have often wondered how exactly my background and my version of religious commitment play a role in my analysis. As a sociologist of religion, for example, I have sometimes found myself at a loss for words whenever I have come across strong proponents of the secularization thesis—that religion is losing or has lost its social significance—or strong opponents who maintain that religion is making a comeback or that it never lost its vitality to begin with. It is more than being nervous about putting one's analytical wager on the wrong side of the thesis, which is an enduring paradigm in this subdiscipline. Rather, I find that my own story does not fit very satisfyingly within these grand theories of religious decline or religious resurgence.

Instead, concepts such as "everyday religion" and "lived religion" open up new ways for me to incorporate my experiences and the role of my "knowing self" in my wider research. They allow me to reconcile how, on the one hand, a particular variant of Islam has permanently lost social and personal significance for me but, on the other hand, how my religious and spiritual commitment is now more fervent, albeit fluid, than ever. My subjective position thus tells a story of how I have *received* as well as *produced* the different perspectives of scriptural exegesis and sexuality that I have explored above.

In other words, my personal story is an integral part of my own "validation process" of knowledge that I engage with as a scholar. My story also involves a significant degree of self-conscientization, or *conscientização*, to transform what I perceive as social injustice and inequality. Neither am I unique—this is what Kugle and many others like him engage in as well. Our understanding and appreciation of the sacred texts we cherish are enriched by our lived experience. Moreover, we are both producing *'ilm*, in the holistic and justice-oriented sense in which it has been conceptualized in many classical and contemporary Islamic sources.

What stops this incorporation of lived experience from being validated as legitimate *'ilm* is power. Yet it can be argued that the understandings of Islam espoused by Kugle's traditionalist critics are also shaped by their lived experiences—as cisgender, heterosexual Muslim men. But because of the dynamics of power, these experiences never need to be defended or even made explicit to a Muslim audience. At the same time, Kugle's critics speak up for Muslims in minority positions who lack power and are subjected to persistent Islamophobia in the West. They, too, can claim to advance a counternarrative of Islam against prevailing social injustices in their contexts. It is not my place to arbitrate on the cumulative privilege or oppression suffered by any of these parties. Instead, I have illustrated how lived experience and scholarly analysis can combine to make, unmake, and remake queer-sensitive interpretations of Islam through an intertextual reading of the Abrahamic scriptures.

Conclusion

This chapter has attempted to get out of the dead end of what the Qur'an "says" about homosexuality by unpacking what counts as authoritative knowledge in the interpretation of sacred texts. It explored the intertextuality of the Qur'an and the Bible and investigated the implications of this relationship on interconnected attitudes toward homosexuality in Judaism, Christianity, and Islam. At the same time, I acknowledged the role of my subjective position as a gay Muslim in my reception and production of particular narratives of interfaith intertextuality. Moreover, my lived experience of multiculturalism and spiritual fluidity has made me particularly receptive to interpretations that go beyond the grain of dominant understandings of religion more generally. But neither am I unique—in many ways, my path shares a lot with that taken by scholar-activists such as Scott Siraj al-Haqq Kugle. Furthermore, I have argued that our endeavors exemplify the holistic conception of *'ilm*, often glossed as knowledge, within Islam. In putting these outer and inner dimensions of knowledge production together, this chapter illustrates the connection between lived religion, religious innovation, and trends within the academic study of religion and sexuality.

Notes

1 Apart from the works of Scott Siraj al-Haqq Kugle cited in this chapter, some other examples include the volume edited by Samar Habib, *Islam and Homosexuality*; the contributions by Vanja Hamzic, "The Resistance from an Alterspace: Pakistani and Indonesian Muslims beyond the Dominant Sexual and Gender Norms," 17–35, and Wim Peumans and Christiane Stallaert, "Queering Conversion: Exploring New Theoretical Pathways to Understand Religious Conversion in a Western Context," 109–24, both in *Religion, Gender and Sexuality in Everyday Life*, edited by Peter Nynas and Andrew Kam-Tuck Yip; Momin Rahman's *Homosexuality, Muslim Cultures and Modernity*; Dervla Shannahan's "Textual Queerings: Contesting Islam as Heteronormative Inheritance"; Shanon Shah's *The Making of a Gay Muslim: Religion, Sexuality and Identity in Malaysia and Britain*; and Ludovic-Mohamed Zahed's *Homosexuality, Transidentity, and Islam*.

2 See Faris Malik, *Queer Jihad*, accessed March 30, 2021, https://people.well.com/user/queerjhd/.

3 Kugle, "Sexuality, Diversity and Ethics in the Agenda of Progressive Muslims," 194; Kugle, *Homosexuality in Islam*, 3.

4 See Shah, *The Making of a Gay Muslim*.

5 Massad, *Desiring Arabs*, 173–74.

6 Kugle, *Living Out Islam*, 4–5; see Anjum, "Editorial: Elements of a Prophetic Voice of Dissent and Engagement."

7 Vaid, "Can Islam Accommodate Homosexual Acts?"; Brown, "A Pre-Modern Defense of the Hadiths on Sodomy," 10–11.

8 Mir, "Multiplicity of Knowledge Forms," 100.

9 Mir, "Multiplicity of Knowledge Forms," 105.

10 Zebiri, *Muslims and Christians Face to Face*, 8.

11 Ahmad Dass, "Epistemological Paradigms of Islamic Knowledge," 38.

12 Ahmad Dass, "Epistemological Paradigms of Islamic Knowledge," 38–41.

13 Anees, "Illuminating Ilm," 19.

14 Collins, *Black Feminist Thought*, 271.

15 Collins, *Black Feminist Thought*, 271.

16 Freire, *Pedagogy of the Oppressed*, 17.

17 Kugle, "Sexuality, Diversity and Ethics in the Agenda of Progressive Muslims," 203.

18 Ammerman, "Introduction: Observing Modern Religious Lives," 5; McGuire, *Lived Religion*, 4.

19 Kugle, *Homosexuality in Islam*, 50–53.

20 Loader, "The Prophets and Sodom," 16–23.

21 Loader, "The Sin of Sodom in the Talmud and Midrash," 233; Loader, "The Prophets and Sodom," 22.

22 Kugle, *Homosexuality in Islam*, 86–87.

23 Kugle, *Homosexuality in Islam*, 102.

24 El-Rouayheb, *Before Homosexuality in the Arab-Islamic World*, 3.

25 El-Rouayheb, *Before Homosexuality in the Arab-Islamic World*, 6.

26 Olyan "'And with a Male You Shall Not Lie the Lying Down of a Woman,'" 180–81.

27 Human Rights Watch, "This Alien Legacy," 86; Tonstad, *Queer Theology*, 86.

28 El-Rouayheb, *Before Homosexuality in the Arab-Islamic World*, 1.

29 El-Rouayheb, *Before Homosexuality in the Arab-Islamic World*, 2.

30 El-Rouayheb, *Before Homosexuality in the Arab-Islamic World*, 151.

31 Dunn, "Who Did Paul Think He Was?" 193.

32 Loader, "Reading Romans 1 on Homosexuality in the Light of Biblical/Jewish and Greco-Roman Perspectives of Its Time," 130.

33 Tonstad, *Queer Theology*, 28.

34 Hoyland, *Seeing Islam as Others Saw It*, 533.

35 Hoyland, *Seeing Islam as Others Saw It*, 539.

36 Hoyland, *Seeing Islam as Others Saw It*, 526.

37 Hoyland, *Seeing Islam as Others Saw It*, 530.

38 Reynolds, "On the Qur'anic Accusation of Scriptural Falsification (Taḥrīf) and Christian Anti-Jewish Polemic," 191–92; Saeed, "The Charge of Distortion of Jewish and Christian Scriptures," 427.

39 Reynolds, "On the Qur'anic Accusation of Scriptural Falsification (Taḥrīf) and Christian Anti-Jewish Polemic," 190; Saeed, "The Charge of Distortion of Jewish and Christian Scriptures," 433.

40 Tottoli, "Origin and Use of the Term Isrā'īliyyāt in Muslim Literature," 194.

41 Tottoli, "Origin and Use of the Term Isrā'īliyyāt in Muslim Literature," 201–6.

42 Tottoli, "Origin and Use of the Term Isrā'īliyyāt in Muslim Literature," 208–10.

43 Donner, *Muhammad and the Believers*, 57.

44 Donner, *Muhammad and the Believers*, 69.

45 Donner, *Muhammad and the Believers*, 77.

46 Kuschel, *Christmas and the Qur'an*, 79, 86, 113.

47 Gobillot, "Qur'an and Torah," 613.

48 Gobillot, "Qur'an and Torah," 614.

49 Gobillot, "Qur'an and Torah," 614.

50 Davidman, "Truth, Subjectivity, and Ethnographic Research," 20.

Works Cited

Ahmad Dass, Muddasir. "Epistemological Paradigms of Islamic Knowledge: An Overview." *Hazara Islamicus* 4, no. 2 (2015): 37–50.

Ammerman, Nancy T. "Introduction: Observing Modern Religious Lives." In *Everyday Religion: Observing Modern Religious Lives*, edited by Nancy T. Ammerman, 3–18. Oxford: Oxford University Press, 2007.

Anees, Munawar Ahmad. "Illuminating Ilm." In *How We Know: Ilm and the Revival of Knowledge*, edited by Ziauddin Sardar, 10–23. London: Grey Seal Books, 1991.

Anjum, Ovamir. "Editorial: Elements of a Prophetic Voice of Dissent and Engagement." *American Journal of Islamic Social Sciences* 34, no. 3 (2017): v–xxii.

Brown, Jonathan. "A Pre-Modern Defense of the Hadiths on Sodomy: An Annotated Translation and Analysis of al-Suyuti's Attaining the Hoped-for in Service of the Messenger (s)." *American Journal of Islamic Social Sciences* 34, no. 3 (2017): 1–44.

Collins, Patricia Hill. *Black Feminist Thought*. New York: Routledge Classics, 2009.

Davidman, Lynn. "Truth, Subjectivity, and Ethnographic Research." In *Personal Knowledge and Beyond: Reshaping the Ethnography of Religion*, 17–26. New York: New York University Press, 2002.

Donner, Fred M. *Muhammad and the Believers*. Cambridge, MA: Belknap Press of Harvard University Press, 2010.

Dunn, James D. G. "Who Did Paul Think He Was? A Study of Jewish-Christian Identity." *New Testament Studies* 45, no. 2 (1999): 174–93.

El-Rouayheb, Khaled. *Before Homosexuality in the Arab-Islamic World, 1500–1800*. Chicago: University of Chicago Press, 2009.

Freire, Paulo. *Pedagogy of the Oppressed*. London: Penguin, 1996.

Gobillot, Genevieve. "Qur'an and Torah: The Foundations of Intertextuality." In *A History of Jewish-Muslim Relations: From the Origins to Present Day*, edited by Abdelwahab Meddeb and Benjamin Stora, 611–27. Princeton: Princeton University Press, 2013.

Habib, Samar, ed. *Homosexuality and Islam*. Santa Barbara, CA: Praeger, 2009.

Hamzić, Vanja. "The Resistance from an Alterspace: Pakistani and Indonesian Muslims Beyond the Dominant Sexual and Gender Norms." In *Religion, Gender and Sexuality in Everyday Life*, edited by Peter Nynas and Andrew Kam-Tuck Yip. Farnham, UK: Ashgate, 2012.

Hoyland, Robert G. *Seeing Islam as Others Saw It: A Survey and Evaluation of Christian, Jewish and Zoroastrian Writings on Early Islam*. Princeton: Darwin Press, 1997.

Human Rights Watch. "This Alien Legacy: The Origins of 'Sodomy' Laws in British Colonialism." In *Human Rights, Sexual Orientation and Gender Identity in the Commonwealth: Struggles for Decriminalisation and Change*, edited by Corinne Lennox and Matthew Waites, 83–124. London: Institute of Commonwealth Studies, School of Advanced Study, University of London, 2013.

Kugle, Scott Siraj al-Haqq. *Homosexuality in Islam: Critical Reflection on Gay, Lesbian, and Transgender Muslims*. Oxford: Oneworld, 2010.

———. *Living Out Islam: Voices of Gay, Lesbian, and Transgender Muslims*. New York: New York University Press, 2014.

———. "Sexuality, Diversity and Ethics in the Agenda of Progressive Muslims." In *Progressive Muslims: On Justice, Gender, and Pluralism*, edited by Omid Safi, 190–234. Oxford: Oneworld, 2003.

Kuschel, Karl-Josef. *Christmas and the Qur'an*. London: Gingko Library, 2017.

Loader, J. A. "The Prophets and Sodom: The Prophetic Use of the Sodom and Gomorrah Theme." *HTS Theological Studies* 47, no. 1 (1991): 5–25.

———. "The Sin of Sodom in the Talmud and Midrash." *Old Testament Essays* 3 (1990): 231–45.

Loader, William. "Reading Romans 1 on Homosexuality in the Light of Biblical/Jewish and Greco-Roman Perspectives of Its Time." *Zeitschrift Für Die Neutestamentliche Wissenschaft* 108, no. 1 (2017): 119–49.

Massad, Joseph. *Desiring Arabs*. Chicago: University of Chicago Press, 2007.

McGuire, Meredith B. *Lived Religion: Faith and Practice in Everyday Life*. Oxford: Oxford University Press, 2008.

Mir, Ali Raza. "Multiplicity of Knowledge Forms: Lessons from Islamic Epistemology." *American Journal of Islamic Social Sciences* 16, no. 3 (1999): 99–106.

Olyan, Saul M. "'And with a Male You Shall Not Lie the Lying Down of a Woman': On the Meaning and Significance of Leviticus 18:22 and 20:13." *Journal of the History of Sexuality* 5, no. 2 (1994): 179–206.

Peumans, Wim, and Christiane Stallaert. "Queering Conversion: Exploring New Theoretical Pathways to Understand Religious Conversion in a Western Context." In *Religion, Gender and Sexuality in Everyday Life*, edited by Peter Nynas and Andrew Kam-Tuck Yip. Farnham, UK: Ashgate, 2012.

Rahman, Momin. *Homosexuality, Muslim Cultures and Modernity*. Basingstoke, UK: Palgrave Macmillan, 2014.

Reynolds, Gabriel Said. "On the Qur'anic Accusation of Scriptural Falsification (Taḥrīf) and Christian Anti-Jewish Polemic." *Journal of the American Oriental Society* 130, no. 2 (2010): 189–202.

Saeed, Abdullah. "The Charge of Distortion of Jewish and Christian Scriptures." *Muslim World* 92 (Fall 2002): 419–36.

Shah, Shanon. *The Making of a Gay Muslim: Religion, Sexuality and Identity in Malaysia and Britain*. Basingstoke, UK: Palgrave Macmillan, 2018.

Shannahan, Dervla. "Textual Queerings: Contesting Islam as Heteronormative Inheritance." In *The Ashgate Research Companion to Contemporary Religion and Sexuality*, edited by Stephen J. Hunt and Andrew Kam-Tuck Yip, 107–21. Ashgate Research Companions. Farnham, UK: Ashgate, 2012.

Tonstad, Linn Marie. *Queer Theology: Beyond Apologetics*. Eugene, OR: Cascade Books, 2018.

Tottoli, Roberto. "Origin and Use of the Term Isrāʾīliyyāt in Muslim Literature." *Arabica* 46, no. 2 (1999): 193–210.

Vaid, Mobeen. "Can Islam Accommodate Homosexual Acts? Quranic Revisionism and the Case of Scott Kugle." *Muslim Matters* (blog), July 11, 2016. muslimmatters.org/2016/07/11/can-islam-accommodate-homosexual-acts-quranic-revisionism-and-the-case-of-scott-kugle/.

Zahed, Ludovic-Mohamed. *Homosexuality, Transidentity, and Islam: A Study of Scripture Confronting the Politics of Gender and Sexuality*. Translated by Adi S. Bharat. Amsterdam: Amsterdam University Press, 2019.

Zebiri, Kate. *Muslims and Christians Face to Face*. Oxford: Oneworld, 1997.

5

A Corpus-Assisted Analysis of the Discursive Construction of LGBT Muslims and Jews in UK Media

Robert Phillips

Introduction

According to the *Jewish Chronicle*, on December 1, 2021, a group of Jewish bus passengers on their way to celebrate Chanukkah in London were attacked by a mob, spit upon, verbally abused, and subjected to Nazi salutes.[1] Similarly, the monitoring group Tell MAMA reported that in the week after the *Daily Telegraph* published a column written by the then prime minister Boris Johnson, in which he compared Muslim women to "letterboxes" and "bank robbers," Islamophobic incidents in the United Kingdom rose by 375 percent.[2] In December 2019, a fourteen-year-old Muslim girl was violently attacked on her way home from school. The same month, a rabbi waiting in the Stamford Hill overground station was beaten by two men who shouted, "fucking Jew, dirty Jew" and "kill the Jews"; a month earlier a Jewish father and his two young sons were the targets of antisemitic abuse on the London Underground.[3] While these forms of generalized Islamophobia and antisemitism have unfortunately become commonplace in the United Kingdom, there exists a largely unexamined form of antisemitic/Islamophobic violence perpetuated against LGBT Muslims and Jews—double minorities. In this chapter, I examine discourses present in the British print media that may contribute to a framing of LGBT Muslims and Jews in ways that can lead to the demonization of members of both communities.

My focus here is in the collective representation of double minorities by the British press. In choosing this focus, I should point out that those minorities who are the targets of harassment are targeted largely due to the saliency of their difference. As noted above, women wearing head or body coverings of any degree and men and boys wearing what are perceived to be "Muslim" or "Jewish" clothing or hairstyle (head coverings/payot) are often targeted. This includes Sikh men and boys wearing turbans, in that some may incorrectly identify them as Muslims. Because of outward appearance, many of the victims of these crimes may also be perceived to be observant in their faith and perhaps even threatening to national security and identity.[4]

This chapter is concerned with members of these communities who also identify as LGBT, positioning them as double minorities. As with members of other diasporic communities around the globe, LGBT Muslims and Jews have assumed unique types of identity forged through a combination of factors brought about by, among other things, processes of transnational migration. As both Muslims and Jews form some of the smallest ethnic communities in Britain, they are far outnumbered by more dominant Anglo groups and share a type of liminal subjectivity. Gay Muslim and Jewish men are both an ethnic and a sexual minority, further complicating this relationship. This dual-minority status has had a distinctive effect on how nonminority British view these individuals. For instance, Yip focuses on kin relations when examining the narratives of nonheterosexual British Muslims and suggests that within these communities, there is a perception of homosexuality as a "Western" disease that did not exist in the family's community of origin.[5] They also point out the fraught negotiations between parents and children, complicated further by sociocultural and religious factors, when it comes time to marry and the subsequent strategies employed by the children. In terms of how the nation views Muslims in Britain, Jaspal and Cinnirella position such subjects as a hybridized threat—British Muslims are positioned solidly as "other" while simultaneously being framed as a threat to the survival of the "in-group."[6]

Method and Data

The method used in this study features critical discourse analysis combined with corpus linguistics, in which any number of "everyday" texts are compiled into an electronic, machine-readable format (a corpus) and analyzed to expose patterns related to grammatical or lexical features of the texts. This is typically done by comparing the corpus under investigation (the focus corpus) to a corpus of text that is representative of a given language (the reference corpus), allowing for the comparison of the patterns between corpora. Underlying this methodology is the notion that individual words do not carry meaning themselves but rather do so through their analysis as part of a larger sequence of words.[7] While this method has been employed for decades, its use has increased greatly in recent years due to the widespread availability of many computer programs capable of natural language processing, such as AntConc and Sketch Engine.[8]

As such, critical discourse analysis and corpus linguistics methods have been used often in recent years to examine issues of language and sexuality/gender in the British media in a variety of contexts. Zottola and Baker, for instance, looked at how the British press portrayed transgender individuals.[9] Partington used modern diachronic corpus-assisted discourse studies to examine, among other things, a seeming resurgence of antisemitism in the United Kingdom.[10] Similarly, Becker and Bolton employed corpus linguistics to look at antisemitic comments on the Facebook pages of major news outlets in the United Kingdom and Western Europe.[11]

This chapter, as with the works noted above, involves a quantitative analysis of the data followed by qualitative interpretation. The qualitative aspect is significant in that knowledge of a particular culture or issue is necessary for the researcher to unravel and interpret the patterns that emerge. For the current study, this empirical method is especially relevant in that it focuses the attention on "real world" speech patterns from various segments of British society from which attitudes and patterns can be extrapolated. In this case, the attitudes are extracted from differing sets of discourse surrounding LGBT Muslims and Jews.

Through the use of corpus linguistics, we are able to manipulate large bodies of text so that they reveal, among other things, keywords, concordances, and collocation patterns. Keywords are words that appear more frequently in the focus corpus than in the reference corpus. Significantly, according to Stubbs, keywords are "pointers to complex lexical objects which represent the shared beliefs and values of a culture."[12] Concordance allows for keywords and phrases to be displayed in context; through the use of software such as Sketch Engine, the researcher is able to sort these in a way that reveals underlying patterns. In the current study, the concordance tool was employed with selected keywords, which were sorted by the left context (words that precede the keyword) and the right context (words that follow the keyword), further deepening and reinforcing the analysis. Finally, corpus linguistics allows the researcher to access collocation and semantic preferences (or semantic prosody), defined by Bondi as "the tendency of the word to co-occur with other words and with words belonging to a specific semantic category or field."[13] Take, for example, my recent study of language used in the debates within Singaporean media over gay male law reform.[14] Here, it was found that within state-owned media the term "homosexuality" collocated with phrases such as *morally repugnant, protest against, looming threat*, and *consequences of*, demonstrating that these connections to the word "homosexuality" show a semantic preference for negative associations.

The method employed here follows the outline of possible steps compiled by Baker et al. in corpus-assisted critical discourse analysis.[15] In stage 1, preliminary research was carried out to formulate research questions through a thorough reading of five years' worth (2016–20) of news and other stories related to discrimination faced by Muslims and Jews in the United Kingdom. This was followed by a similar reading of sources produced by non-news outlets including blogs and Jewish/Muslim websites. These and other readings were used to inform the creation of research questions. In focusing on the discursive construction of LGBT Muslims and Jews in the British press, the following research questions were developed:

1. What are the most frequent and significant keywords and semantic themes communicated in each of the three corpora? What do these reveal about how the UK press has portrayed LGBT Muslims and Jews?

2. What does the concordance analysis of the words *Muslim* and *Jewish* in each corpus reveal? What might this concordance reveal about how the UK press has portrayed these double minorities from 2016 to 2020?

Stage 2 involved selecting the appropriate materials from which to build the corpus. The three sub-corpora created represent varying media perspectives on gay Muslims and Jews in Britain. The corpora were assembled using the search phrase "LGBT" AND "Muslim" OR "Jewish" in the Nexis Uni database, which allowed access to full articles, opinion pieces, and letters to the editor. Taking a cue from Jones and Collins, I created three separate corpora corresponding to the perceived political leanings of different mainstream news publications.[16] Jones and Collins consider the correspondence between the representation of PrEP users and the editorial stance of the paper.[17] As with these authors, I use corpus linguistics methods to suggest that there is also a correlation here between the stance of the newspaper and the representation of LGBT Muslims and Jews. The first corpus compiled was from the left-leaning *Guardian*; the total size of the unedited corpus was 53,819 words.[18] A second corpus was compiled from the centrist *Independent*; the total size of the unedited corpus was 57,882 words. A third corpus was compiled using the right-leaning *Telegraph*. However, because of the small size of the corpus generated, I decided to add another right-leaning publication, the *Daily Mail*. The combined size of this composite corpus was 23,806 words. The disparity between the center/left publications and the right-leaning publications is striking and appears to provide an initial insight that there may indeed be a difference in attitudes and editorial stance between news outlets.

In stage 3, the Sketch Engine platform was employed to see the "big picture" in each corpus, including frequencies, keywords, clusters, and so forth. Keywords are identified by comparing the focus corpora to a "benchmark" corpus, in this case the British National Corpus, consisting of approximately 100 million words. Stage 4 involved locating repeating lexical patterns via frequency and keyword extraction. Stage 5 used concordance analysis to qualitatively investigate these common themes. In the final stage, the research questions were revisited and findings were outlined.

Analysis

Keywords

As noted above, the first research question asks the rather broad question of how the press is portraying LGBT Muslims and Jews. To begin to accomplish this, lists were generated for each corpus of the most frequently used nouns. These are reported below in table 1. Also included is the number of occurrences (#) as well as the relative frequency (RF) of the term per one million words. Relative frequency can help to account for the discordant size of the three corpora. The three corpora share many of the same terms, which refer to Islam (mosque, religion, Friday [prayer services]), kinship/relationships (family, woman, man, parent, marriage, child, community), and sexuality (LGBT, homosexuality, sexuality, same sex). The number one term for each corpus was the word "people."

The Guardian and *The Independent* have their first four terms in common; they are even in the same order—"people," "year," "Muslim," and "community." This indicates, at least initially, that there is likely a stronger correspondence between these two corpora than between them and *The Telegraph / Daily Mail* corpus. Similarly, the noun "right" was 8th on *The Guardian* list while coming in at 431st on *The Telegraph / Daily Mail*, signaling

Table 1. The Most Frequent Nouns to Appear in Each Corpus

	The Guardian	#	RF	*The Independent*	#	RF	*The Telegraph / Daily Mail*	#	RF
1	people	201	3,178	people	154	2,279	people	62	2,222
2	year	119	1,882	year	134	1,983	year	48	1,720
3	Muslim	107	1,692	Muslim	124	1,835	man	46	1,649
4	community	102	1,613	community	110	1,628	Mr.	43	1,541
5	Trump	96	1,518	student	108	1,598	opera	42	1,505
6	man	92	1,455	LGBT	105	1,554	marriage	40	1,433
7	school	90	1,423	university	97	1,436	woman	34	1,218
8	right	88	1,391	Trump	87	1,287	BBC	34	1,218
9	LGBT	82	1,296	man	87	1,244	ISIL	32	1,147
10	time	76	1,201	marriage	84	1,170	thing	32	1,147

another possible correlation. While *The Telegraph / Daily Mail* shared three out of the top ten keywords ("people," "year," and "man") with the other two corpora, the remaining shared keywords were scattered throughout the top forty keywords in its corpus. Preliminary findings underline a difference in the representation depicted by the three corpora, specifically in the descriptors.

All three publications contain references to Islam via the terms "Muslim," "Muslims," "Islam," "Islamic," "ISIL," and "Islamophobia." For both *The Guardian* and *The Independent*, "Muslim" is the third most prevalent term. For *The Telegraph / Daily Mail*, the term "ISIL" appears in ninth place. In this instance, I suggest that "ISIL" serves as a placeholder for "Islam," with stories telling of Muslims coming to Britain to recruit for the organization or highlighting the fear of returning British ISIL soldiers. Only one story connects the terms "gay" and "ISIL," and it appears in a story dealing with the Eurovision song contest being used to recruit fighters for the organization. In some instances, "gay" is also used as an adjective to describe ISIL. Table 2 below outlines the appearance of variations on "Muslim."

Of note here is the strong correlation between the inclusion of "Islam" and the stance of the newspaper. *The Guardian* and *The Independent* each have, respectively, 163 and 178 references of "Muslim/Muslims," whereas *The Telegraph / Daily Mail* has a mere 28. The same holds true for the term "Islam"; each of the left- and central-leaning publications contains around 50 references to "Islam," whereas the right-leaning *Telegraph / Daily Mail* only has 6. There are no mentions of the term "ISIS/ISIL" in *The Guardian* and *The Independent*, and *The Telegraph / Daily Mail* uses the term

Table 2. Terms Related to "Islam"

	The Guardian	*The Independent*	*The Telegraph / Daily Mail*
Muslim	107	124	18
Muslims	56	52	10
Islam	46	34	6
Islamic	10	17	3
Islamophobia	6	15	0
ISIL/ISIS	0	0	32

134 Robert Phillips

32 times. Together, the presence and absence of "Islam" and related terms in these corpora are telling. Even a short glance at the data makes it clear that *The Telegraph / Daily Mail* has a different stance on Muslims and their faith than *The Guardian* and *The Independent*.

Table 3 outlines the appearance of terms related to Judaism. As with table 2, we can tell a good deal with a look at the distribution of terms. "Jew/Jews" appears often in all three corpora, but in comparison to the Islamic terms, there is a discernable lack. *The Guardian* contains 38 mentions of "Jew/Jews" in its corpus and 163 mentions of "Muslim/Muslims." This trend has made the analysis of the discourse surrounding LGBT Jews that more difficult due to the lack of data.

The appearance of "Trump" is also telling; I interpret his position on the list as an indicator of each newspaper's level of concern regarding his presidency, with the left-leaning *Guardian* the most concerned, with nearly 100 appearances, and *The Telegraph / Daily Mail* the least, coming in at 27 appearances. *The Independent* led with the number of appearances of the term "community," which would imply notions of "caring." For instance, the term appears 102 times in *The Guardian*, 110 times in *The Independent*, but only 17 times in *The Telegraph / Daily Mail*. While not directly related to issues of hate crimes, the lack of discourse surrounding community could be perceived as discouraging interaction with others not from one's own group. The right-leaning *Telegraph / Daily Mail* corpus has several instances of the terms "LGBT" and "Muslim," and many refer to Tan France, a gay Muslim cast member of the reboot of the American television program *Queer Eye for the Straight Guy*. France is known by many as the "most famous gay Muslim in the world." His appearance in

Table 3. Terms Related to "Judaism"

	The Guardian	*The Independent*	*The Telegraph / Daily Mail*
Jew	21	14	8
Jews	17	0	4
Jewish	4	1	0
anti-Semite	4	2	2
anti-Semitism	4	3	9

Analysis of the Discursive Construction of LGBT Muslims and Jews   135

the corpus is due to a series of articles that claim that he is not part of the world of "woke" LGBT politics and that he lives in Utah, rather than an east-coast LGBT community.

Multiword Keywords and Semantic Mapping

As noted above, Sketch Engine software was used for a preliminary analysis of each corpus; the first step was generating keywords. While single-word keywords were certainly useful, as noted above, they do present an incomplete picture. Multiword terms (table 4) also generated some interesting findings.

A close reading of these multiword phrases facilitated the construction of semantic categories. The top one hundred phrases from each corpus were reviewed, codes were developed based on thematic repetition, and the phrases were grouped into categories. Knowledge of sociopolitical and historical aspects of British media culture and the LGBT rights movements in Britain aided in the mapping of the semantic categories listed in tables 5, 6, and 7.

Overall, all three corpora have numerous references to "drag" culture; "Muslim drag," "drag queen," and "drag scene" dominate the top spots in the multiword keywords. I suggest that it is through the lens of popular culture that the British press is influencing public perceptions of LGBT

Table 4. Top Ten Multiword Keywords

	The Guardian	*The Independent*	*The Telegraph / Daily Mail*
1	gay Muslim	gay Muslim	NHS doctor
2	Muslim drag	Muslim drag	drag scene
3	conversion therapy	online abuse	gay marriage
4	marriage equality	drag queen	same-sex marriage
5	gay Jew	gay Muslim wedding	upper chamber
6	drag queen	Muslim wedding	draft legislation
7	Anglican communion	sex scene	gay Jew
8	white supremacist	free-thinking journalism	gay Muslim
9	same-sex marriage	gay sex	Jewish conversion
10	Muslim community	bad sex	strong endorsement

Table 5. Semantic Mapping of *The Guardian* Corpus

Semantic category	Multiword examples
marriage	marriage equality, same-sex marriage, equal marriage
hatred	white supremacist, online abuse, hate crime, American hate, anti-gay Muslim clerics
organized religion	Anglican communion, Muslim cleric, Chief Rabbi, Sharia law, Islamic law, national faith forum

Table 6. Semantic Mapping of *The Independent* Corpus

Semantic category	Multiword examples
marriage	gay Muslim wedding, Muslim wedding, Muslim marriage, same-sex marriage, physicist husband, gay marriage, Muslim same-sex
hatred	online abuse, hate crime, offensive thing, rape culture
drag culture	drag queen, Muslim drag queen, drag performer, first Muslim drag performer
sex/sexuality	sex scene, gay sex, bad sex, gay sex scene, sexual description, sexual orientation, pornographic gay sex scene

Table 7. Semantic Mapping of *The Telegraph / Daily Mail* Corpus

Semantic category	Multiword examples
national politics	upper chamber, draft legislation, gay Muslim peer, peer leading opposition, far-right revival, new Tory MP, grass-roots game, first Tory, Muslim peer, serious politician, leading opposition, protest vote, Tory MP
marriage	gay marriage, same-sex marriage, opposing gay marriage
organized religion	Jewish conversion, only Diocesan Bishop, senior Anglican Bishop, God-given order, Anglican Bishop

Jews and Muslims. For instance, in *The Guardian* corpus, the term "Muslim community" is used as part of a larger critique of Islam's stance on same-sex marriage. "White supremacist" was derived from US news in that it references Trump acolyte Steve Bannon. There are 9 references to "conversion therapy," a much-maligned attempt to change a patient's sexual subjectivity. "Gay Jew" appears several times, but it is in reference to right-wing Trump supporter Milo Yiannopoulos, who often talks of being Catholic but also claims Jewish identity.

The semantic categories themselves are also telling. The creation of such categories is, of course, subjective. However, they do provide a good overview of the concerns of the writers and editorial boards of each publication. *The Guardian*, the most liberal of the three publications, focuses on same-sex marriage, violence/hatred toward LGBT individuals, and the influence of organized religion. *The Independent* has similar sentiments regarding same-sex marriage and hatred, but it also focuses on drag culture and sexuality. Last, *The Telegraph* / *Daily Mail* corpus, the most conservative of the three, centers on national politics, marriage, and organized religion.

Concordance

Concordance allows for the display of keywords and phrases in context. While many of the predominant key phrases mapped out in the previous section are of interest and shed light on how the British press is framing LGBT Muslims and Jews, it is also of interest how other terms are being deployed. The terms analyzed in this section were chosen for several reasons. First, and most important, I have chosen to focus on "Muslim(s)" and "Jew(s)" because the contexts in which they appear are telling. A preliminary analysis of several terms such as "university" (referring to universities' ability to prevent terrorists from enrolling) and "opera" (referring to a gay Jewish Australian opera director) yielded interesting insights, but the context of the terms did not justify further study. Several words appeared frequently in all three corpora, yet none of them were identified as keywords. Nonetheless, analyses of these terms have provided insights into the broad feelings and sentiments expressed by competing media enterprises.

The Guardian contains 231 occurrences of "Muslim." Left modifiers of "Muslim," as might be expected, include "gay." This modifier was found 40 times in the *Guardian* corpus, and, in most instances, "gay Muslim" was referring to hardships experienced by this group due to their "intolerant" coreligionists. The other left modifier that stood out is "queer" (8 times). Right modifiers include "community" (11 times) and "countries" (11 times), both alluding to ideas of "place"; in the case of "community," it is local, whereas "Muslim countries" seems to emphasize the "foreignness" of Muslims to Britain. The term "Muslim" appears in *The Independent* 309 times and the left modifier "gay" 65 times. Here, "gay Muslim" is also given a negative connotation in that it is used often in the context of Islamic homophobia as well as the hardships that gay Muslims undergo within their own communities. "British Muslims" (11 instances) also appears in light of recent debates within British Muslim communities about non-normative sexualities. The right modifier "community" (11 instances) also speaks to this debate. In terms of *The Telegraph / Daily Mail* corpus, "Muslim" only appears 43 times, 15 of those times being modified by "gay." Rather unexpectedly, only 3 of these instances are negative, whereas the rest are positive—speaking of "gay Muslim peers" in Parliament and gay Muslim weddings. Due to the small size of this particular corpus, no correlations could be made with right modifiers.

"Jewish" appears 49 times in *The Guardian* corpus, far fewer than the 231 occurrences of "Muslim." There are 7 instances of "gay" modifying "Jewish," but there is no discernable pattern. More interesting, the term "Orthodox" is used 12 times as a left modifier and is used to point out the kindness and understanding shown by the Orthodox Jewish community toward LGBT Jews. This term occurs in *The Independent* 34 times, and "gay" in the left context modifies "Jewish" 16 times. While over half of the occurrences of "Jewish" were modified by "gay," there were no visible patterns. Finally, "Jewish" appears 37 times in *The Telegraph / Daily Mail* corpus, which includes 9 references to "gay Jewish," most of which were being used to describe a person, although there were three references to a "gay Jewish" conversion. Due to the small size of this particular corpus, no correlations could be made with right modifiers.

Conclusion

In this preliminary study, the aim was to examine discourses present in the British print media that may contribute to a framing of LGBT Muslims and Jews in ways that can lead to the demonization of members of both communities. In examining the semantic categories that were assembled, it should be clear that the three corpora represent three distinctly different points of view regarding the place of LGBT Muslims and Jews within British society. As might be expected, the discourse surrounding this group in the liberal-leaning *Guardian* newspaper focused on marriage, hatred, and organized religion. Here, the emphasis was on promoting same-sex marriage, fighting hatred, and questioning the involvement of religious figures. The centrist *Independent* included same-sex marriage and hatred, but also focused heavily on drag culture and sexuality. As with the other two corpora, *The Telegraph* / *Daily Mail* corpus centered on same-sex marriage and organized religion. Interestingly, one focus of the corpus seems to be issues related to the national government and how it is run, but it also contains references to "gay Muslim" members of Parliament.

In retrospect, there are several ways that this study could be modified to obtain a more accurate takeaway. First, the small sample size could be of concern. Previous corpus research used three corpora of around 115,000 words each and produced a good result.[19] In the present study, *The Guardian* and *The Independent* corpora each contained around 50,000 words and the combined *Telegraph* and *Daily Mail* corpus was only 23,000 words. This is due, in part, to the selection of a five-year period from which to draw data. In a future iteration of this research, the time period could be increased in order to increase the size of the corpora. Second, an alternative analysis could use the terms "gay" and "Muslim" or "Jewish" rather than "LGBT." Through data analysis, it became clear that phrasing such as "gay Jews" or "gay Muslims" was a much more natural way of speaking and writing than the rather unwieldy "LGBT." In fact, it was found in *The Guardian*, for instance, that "LGBT" appeared 83 times while "gay" appeared over 250 times.

While it will certainly take more analysis, preliminary data suggests that there are significant differences between the three corpora and, by extension, the manner by which these media portray the lives of LGBT citizens. Regardless of the intention of these publications, they all appear to be "othering" LGBT Muslims and Jews and portraying them as being fundamentally different than the rest of the population.

Notes

1 Pope, "Chanukah Bus Tour Attacked by Yobs Shouting Anti-Israel Slogans."
2 BBC, "Boris Johnson Faces Criticism over Burka 'Letter Box' Jibe"; Dearden, "Islamophobic Incidents Rose 375% after Boris Johnson Compared Muslim Women to 'Letterboxes,' Figures Show."
3 Weaver, "Police Release CCTV Images of Attack on Rabbi in North London"; Dalton, "Tube Passengers Unite to Challenge Man Hurling Antisemitic Abuse at Jewish Family."
4 Endelstein and Ryan, "Dressing Religious Bodies in Public Spaces."
5 Yip, "Religion and the Politics of Spirituality/Sexuality"; Yip, "Queering Religious Texts."
6 Jaspal and Cinnirella, "Media Representations of British Muslims and Hybridised Threats to Identity."
7 See Sinclair, *Corpus, Concordance, Collocation.*
8 See Anthony, "AntConc"; Kilgarriff et al., "Itri-04-08 The Sketch Engine"; Kilgarriff et al., "The Sketch Engine: Ten Years On."
9 Zottola, "Transgender Identity Labels in the British Press"; Baker, "'Bad Wigs and Screaming Mimis.'"
10 Partington, "The Armchair and the Machine"; Partington, "The Changing Discourses on Antisemitism in the UK Press from 1993 to 2009."
11 Becker and Bolton, "The Decoding Antisemitism Project—Reflections, Methods, and Goals."
12 Stubbs, "Three Concepts of Keywords," 23.
13 Bondi, "Perspectives on Keywords and Keyness," 3.
14 Phillips, "A Corpus-Assisted Analysis of the Discursive Construction of LGBT Singaporeans in Media Coverage of Pink Dot."
15 Baker et al., "A Useful Methodological Synergy?"
16 Jones and Collins, "PrEP in the Press."
17 PrEP (pre-exposure prophylaxis) is prescription medicine people at risk for HIV take to prevent getting HIV from sex or injection drug use.
18 In all three corpora, hyperlinks and other redundant artifacts were removed.
19 Phillips, "A Corpus-Assisted Analysis of the Discursive Construction of LGBT Singaporeans in Media Coverage of Pink Dot."

Works Cited

Anthony, L. "AntConc." Tokyo: Waseda University, 2011. www.laurenceanthony
.net/software/antconc/.

Baker, P. "'Bad Wigs and Screaming Mimis': Using Corpus-Assisted Techniques
to Carry Out Critical Discourse Analysis of the Representation of Trans People in the British Press." In *Contemporary Critical Discourse Studies*, edited by
Christopher Hart and Piotr Cap, 211–35. London: Bloomsbury, 2014.

———. "'Unnatural Acts': Discourses of Homosexuality within the House of
Lords Debates on Gay Male Law Reform." *Journal of Sociolinguistics* 8, no. 1
(2004): 88–106. https://doi.org/10.1111/j.1467-9841.2004.00252.x.

Baker, P., C. Gabrielatos, and M. Khosravinik. "A Useful Methodological
Synergy? Combining Critical Discourse Analysis and Corpus Linguistics
to Examine Discourses of Refugees and Asylum Seekers in the UK Press."
Discourse & Society 19, no. 3 (2008): 273–306. https://doi.org/10.1177/
0957926508088962.

BBC. "Boris Johnson Faces Criticism over Burka 'Letter Box' Jibe." BBC,
August 6, 2018. www.bbc.com/news/uk-politics-45083275.

Becker, M. J., and M. Bolton. "The Decoding Antisemitism
Project—Reflections, Methods, and Goals." *Journal of Contemporary
Antisemitism* 5, no. 1 (2022): 121–26.

Bondi, M. "Perspectives on Keywords and Keyness: An Introduction." In
Keyness in Texts, edited by M. Bondi and M. Scott, 1–18. Amsterdam: John
Benjamins, 2010.

Dalton, J. "Tube Passengers Unite to Challenge Man Hurling Antisemitic
Abuse at Jewish Family." *The Independent*, November 21, 2019. www
.independent.co.uk/news/uk/home-news/train-abuse-jewish-family
-antisemitism-london-tube-racist-a9214316.html.

Dearden, L. "Islamophobic Incidents Rose 375% after Boris Johnson Compared
Muslim Women to 'Letterboxes,' Figures Show." *The Independent*, September 2, 2019. www.independent.co.uk/news/uk/home-news/boris-johnson
-muslim-women-letterboxes-burqa-islamphobia-rise-a9088476.html.

Endelstein, L., and L. Ryan. "Dressing Religious Bodies in Public Spaces:
Gender, Clothing and Negotiations of Stigma among Jews in Paris and
Muslims in London." *Integrative Psychological and Behavioral Science* 47,
no. 2 (2013): 249–64.

Jaspal, R., and M. Cinnirella. "Media Representations of British Muslims and Hybridised Threats to Identity." *Contemporary Islam* 4 (2010): 289–310.

Jones, L., and L. Collins. "PrEP in the Press: A Corpus-Assisted Discourse Analysis of How Users of HIV-Prevention Treatment Are Represented in British Newspapers." *Journal of Language and Sexuality* 9, no. 2 (2020): 202–25. https://doi.org/10.1075/jls.20002.jon.

Kilgarriff, A., V. Baisa, J. Bušta, et al. "The Sketch Engine: Ten Years On." *Lexicography ASIALEX* 1 (2014): 7–36. https://doi.org/10.1007/s40607-014-0009-9.

Kilgarriff, A., P. Rychlý, P. Smrž, and D. Tugwell. "Itri-04-08 The Sketch Engine." *Information Technology* 105 (2004): 116.

Partington, A. "The Armchair and the Machine: Corpus-Assisted Discourse Research." In *Corpora for University Language Teachers*, edited by C. Taylor Torsello, K. Ackerley, and E. Castello. Bern, Switzerland: Peter Lang, 2008.

———. "The Changing Discourses on Antisemitism in the UK Press from 1993 to 2009: A Modern-Diachronic Corpus-Assisted Discourse Study." *Journal of Language and Politics* 11, no. 1 (2012): 51–76.

Phillips, R. "A Corpus-Assisted Analysis of the Discursive Construction of LGBT Singaporeans in Media Coverage of Pink Dot." *Journal of Language and Sexuality* 10, no. 2 (2021): 180–201. https://doi.org/10.1075/jls.20010.phi.

Pope, F. "Chanukah Bus Tour Attacked by Yobs Shouting Anti-Israel Slogans." *Jewish Chronicle*, December 1, 2021. www.thejc.com/news/news/chanukah-bus-tour-attacked-by-yobs-shouting-anti-israel-slogans-1.523135.

Sinclair, J. *Corpus, Concordance, Collocation*. Oxford: Oxford University Press, 1991.

Stubbs, M. "Three Concepts of Keywords." In *Keyness in Texts*, edited by M. Bondi and M. Scott, 21–42. Amsterdam: John Benjamins, 2010.

Weaver, M. "Police Release CCTV Images of Attack on Rabbi in North London." *The Guardian*, December 4, 2019. www.theguardian.com/uk-news/2019/dec/04/police-release-cctv-footage-of-attack-on-rabbi-in-north-london.

Wilkinson, M. "'Bisexual Oysters': A Diachronic Corpus-Based Critical Discourse Analysis of Critical Representation of Bisexuals in *The Times* between 1957 and 2017." *Discourse & Communication* 13, no. 2 (2019): 249–67. https://doi.org/10.1177/1750481318817624.

Yip, A. K. "Queering Religious Texts: An Exploration of British Non-Heterosexual Christians' and Muslims' Strategy of Constructing Sexuality-Affirming Hermeneutics." *Sociology* 39, no. 1 (2005): 47–65. https://doi.org/10.1177/0038038505049000.

———. "Religion and the Politics of Spirituality/Sexuality: Reflections on Researching British Lesbian, Gay, and Bisexual Christians and Muslims." *Fieldwork in Religion* 1, no. 3 (2005): 271–89. https://doi.org/10.1558/firn.v1i3.271.

Zottola, A. "Transgender Identity Labels in the British Press: A Corpus-Based Discourse Analysis." *Journal of Language and Sexuality* 7, no. 2 (2018): 237–62. https://doi.org/10.1075/jls.17017.zot.

PART III

BUILDING COMMUNITY, FORGING SOLIDARITY

6

Religious Life Is Life Together

Ritual, Liminality, and Communitas among Queer Jews in Postsecular Britain

Matthew Richardson

Introduction

For some, the early hours of the morning are a time when few are awake, the city quiet, and the streets empty. In London's East End, however, the dimly lit alleyways are teaming with late-night revelers. Historically characterized as largely working-class neighborhoods, districts like Bethnal Green, Shoreditch, and Whitechapel have undergone a rapid process of gentrification in recent years and are now synonymous with trendy clubs, pubs, and wine bars.[1] The Bethnal Green Working Men's Club, located just off Pollard Square, has been a cultural, political, and social hub of the East End since 1887. In recent years, the venue has become popular among students at the nearby Queen Mary, University of London, and a new wave of young urban professionals who are spatially segregated from the club regulars:

> Downstairs, the octogenarians still have their cards and gambling machine. But upstairs, the space is used for concerts, burlesque shows, voga (a dynamic fusion of yoga and vogueing), a pop-up Chinese restaurant and . . . "wild, unhinged good times."[2]

Now and again, the walkways crossing Weavers Fields and the A1209 from the Bethnal Green Underground Station become a threshold to the United

Kingdom's first queer Jewish club night. Organized around special and transitory dates in the Hebraic calendar, Buttmitzvah is a camp, erotic, playful, and satirical celebration of queer Jewish identities in postsecular Britain. The evening is centered around the backstory of the Rimmer family, pun intended, hosting their daughter Becky's Bat Mitzvah. Facilitated by a troupe of dedicated actors, dancers, and drag kings and queens, the night is more than just a raunchy get-together. In this chapter, I explore the Bethnal Green Buttmitzvah as an ethnographic case study to argue that the evening functions as an aspirational and motivational platform from which partygoers construct, demarcate, and celebrate an affirming identity politics.

To do so, I use Turnerian anthropology of experience as a key analytical, methodological, and theoretical heuristic tool to explore the affective, anti-structural, collectivizing, and subversive qualities of the Bethnal Green Buttmitzvah. First, I situate Buttmitzvah in the socio-cultural-geographic context of postsecular Bethnal Green and identify it as liminal space providing the ideal settings for the generation of *communitas*, a special type of ritualized space-time whereby all those present enjoy an intense sense of belonging and identification with each other. Next, I explore the ritualization needed to generate this social state of communitas by drawing on what I call the ritual complex, an intricate system involving myths, symbols, and rituals functioning as media through which selves and others are formed, mobilized, and resisted. Finally, I unpack the anti-structural qualities of communitas by characterizing Buttmitzvah as a liminoid phenomenon in a liminal space, providing those in attendance with a platform for subverting antisemitic, heterosexist, and postsecular social structures. As such, I argue that religious life is life together because it is only when people come together and generate the collective electricity of communitas that the aspirational and motivational forces for constructing, demarcating, and celebrating religious selves and others becomes possible. It is through ritual performance, in other words, that an imagined community is actualized in an intense emotional state of social belonging. I conclude this chapter by highlighting the benefits of engaging with Turnerian anthropology of experience when researching alongside minoritized religious communities in postsecular contexts.

The findings in this chapter are grounded in fifteen months of narrative ethnographic research (April 2020 to July 2021) with eighteen queer

Jews who were living, or had previously lived, in postsecular Britain (their selected profiles are included in the appendix for context). By narrative ethnographic I point to a methodology in which I focused on the stories participants told, the memories they recalled, and the worlds they painted through unstructured life story interviews ($n = 18$); semi-structured topical interviews ($n = 18$); and participant observation ($n = 4$). It is worth noting that this contribution is a critical exploration of ritual communitas in a changing urban landscape—for those interested, introductory texts on both narrative ethnography and Turnerian anthropology of experience are signposted here alongside comparative applications of both.[3]

The Bethnal Green Buttmitzvah: Liminality in London's East End

Traditionally a working-class neighborhood with strong French Protestant, Irish Catholic, and Ashkenazi Jewish histories, Bethnal Green has seen many cultural, demographic, and political shifts over the years. Daniel DeHanas, a political scientist and scholar of religion, offers an in-depth and critical urban biography of the district in his study of youth, religion, and politics in Brick Lane and Brixton.[4] According to DeHanas, immigration to London's East End, the historic core of East London located in the present-day Borough of Tower Hamlets, followed a pattern of culturally distinct successive waves.[5] This is because religion, "though not necessarily religiosity," often provided migrant communities with the apparatus for maintaining cultural stability and the social demarcation of selves and others.[6]

The first migrant group to arrive in the East End were the Huguenots, French Calvinists fleeing violent persecution from the Catholic state following the Huguenot rebellions of the early seventeenth century. The Huguenots, largely weavers by trade, were centralized around Spitalfields, their presence still reflected in the cultural landscape via the naming of streets, thoroughfares, and green spaces. Though an enclave community at first, the Huguenots assimilated into wider society due to the increased socioeconomic mobility resulting from the weaver trade and were replaced with Irish migrants fleeing *an Gorta Mór* (the Great Famine) in the mid-1800s. Though the London Irish were largely concentrated in the areas of

Kilburn, Islington, and Camden, a sizeable community did settle in the East End with their Catholic faith still manifest in the urban landscape via the high presence of Catholic schools throughout the borough.[7]

Toward the end of the 1800s, Ashkenazi Jews fleeing pogroms in the Pale of Settlement began to settle in the area, which—according to Liane (Life story interview, August 2020)—led to classed and denominational friction with the small albeit socioeconomically significant Sephardi community already residing there. By the turn of the twentieth century, the Jewish population of the East End had grown to over one hundred thousand people, leading the district to be referred to colloquially as "Little Jerusalem."[8] Indeed, nostalgic depictions of the East End's Jewish heritage were evident in participants' narratives:

> R.: We learned about some of the—the like, um, the Jews in the old East End, uh, like the working-class Jews, um, who—who helped fight fascism at that time, um, and, uh, I think my nan would've been pleased to hear about that as well, um, uh, may her memory be a blessing. She—she died in 2005, um, and she was a big old cockney. Um, just the most—the most amazing old lady you ever met.
>
> Life story interview, November 2020

Such nostalgic cultural memories of the East End have been criticized by James, who argues that collective memories of diaspora space are "appropriated across ethnic boundaries" for a myriad of political ends.[9] Following the devastation of World War II, much of the population (Jewish or otherwise) had left the East End due to extensive damage sustained during the blitz and greater socioeconomic mobility. With the Commonwealth Immigrants Act of 1962, East Pakistan's independence as Bangladesh in 1971, and the Immigration Act of 1971, a substantial population of Bangladeshi migrants settled in the East End in the latter half of the twentieth century.[10] Since then, the East End has become renowned for its British-Bengali cultural landscape and has featured prominently in representations of Bengali Muslims in recent years.[11]

These shifting ethnoreligious landscapes are reflected in demographic data. Comparing the 2001 and 2011 censuses, Islam became the largest religious group in Tower Hamlets, with 38 percent of the population (96,536 persons) identifying as Muslims in the 2011 census.[12] This reflects a population growth of 1.6 percent (25,147 persons) between the two censuses. Contrarily, Christianity, formerly the largest religious affiliation, shrank from 39 percent (75,783 persons) of the population share in 2001 to 30 percent (75,714 persons) in 2011, a percentage point change of −8.8. The Jewish population in Tower Hamlets saw the largest negative percentage point change of −23 in the same period, with a population of 1,831 persons in 2001 decreasing to 1,413 persons in 2011. Correspondingly, the largest percentage point change of +200 was seen among Hindus, with a population of 1,544 persons in 2001 growing to 4,626 in 2011.

Regarding ethnicity, the largest demographic remains white ethnic groups, decreasing from a majority of 51 percent (100,799 persons) in 2001 to 45 percent (114,189 persons) in 2011.[13] Non-white ethnic groups all saw population share growths in the same period. Significantly, Asian/Asian British groups increased their population share from 38 percent (75,380 persons) in 2001 to 41 percent (104,501 persons) in 2011, a percentage point change of +39 compared to +14 among white ethnic groups. The largest ethnic group within the Asian/Asian British category are (predominantly Muslim) Bangladeshis, who make up 32 percent (81,377 persons) of the total population of the borough.

The changing, evolving ethnoreligious landscapes have had widespread ramifications on public discourses and social structures surrounding race, religion, and ethnicity. Coaxed by racism and xenophobia, public debates surrounding the role of religion in the public sphere, demographic changes, integration, extremism, and grooming gangs have taken alarming precedence in the British public sphere.[14] These debates both cause and reflect increasing tension between religious and ethnic groups, often resulting in acts of racist violence that, in turn, shape the landscape in tangible ways. For example, Saint Mary's Park, located between Adler Street, White Church Lane, and Whitechapel Road, was renamed Altab Ali Park in 1998 after the 1978 racially motivated murder of Altab Ali, a twenty-five-year-old Bangladeshi textile worker in the same area.

The (re)emergence of (racialized) religion in public discourses has been noted by social and cultural geographers. For example, Julian Holloway forwards the idea of a "postsecularism" that recognizes "the limits of reason, rationality, and secularism, the restrictions of a liberal consensus of separate public-political and private-religious spheres, and a political pluralism that, by necessity, includes constituencies of the religious and the faithful."[15] This reflects Talal Asad's critique that secularization paradigms largely fail to contest the politicized and racialized nature of secular politics as imbued with preserving Euro-American, secular hegemony via the authoritarian categorization of religion as a purely private matter.[16] In this context, there has also been growing attention regarding the intersections between race, religion, gender, and sexuality. Such debates, according to Shanon Shah, have often settled comfortably into constructing problematic binaries between minoritized religious groups on the one hand and minoritized gender and sexual groups on the other, binaries often precluding the existence of those who find themselves having multiple, intersecting social characteristics.[17] One example of this dynamic in postsecular Britain is found among queer Jewish praxis in postsecular Bethnal Green.

The "soaring" rates of antisemitic and queerphobic incidents in postsecular Britain have received much public concern in recent years.[18] Between 2017 and 2018, the Home Office recorded an unprecedented wave of antisemitic hate crimes across England and Wales.[19] In the same period, hate crimes on the grounds of sexual, gender, and religious identities became increasingly prevalent in urban centers and public transport systems.[20] In addition to discrimination relating to social structures maintaining heterosexism and postsecularism, a perceived dichotomy between Jewish and queer identities is often seen as disrupting the full membership of queer-identifying Jews and Jewish-identifying queers into both the Jewish and queer communities.[21] As such, queer Jews are positioned as liminal personae—not quite fully queer, not quite fully Jewish, and maligned from wider British society by antisemitic and queerphobic discursive forces. The term "liminal personae" comes from British anthropologist Victor Turner and refers to both ritual performers in the liminal stage of rites of passage and persons in socially marginal positions.[22] Turner's understanding of liminality is rooted in classical ethnographer Arnold van Gennep's notion of rites of passage and the liminal stage of the ritual process.[23]

For van Gennep, human life is punctuated by environmental and psychosomatic changes (e.g., childbirth, death, seasonal changes) in constant processes of psychosocial transition.[24] These processes necessarily involve psychosocial transitions since cosmic rhythms do not occur without disturbing both collective and individual life, for example, changes in kinship ties resulting from the death of a family member, spouse, or person holding social office. Therefore, people adopt rituals to aid them in mitigating such harmful, often disruptive, effects.[25] According to van Gennep, rituals are able to fulfill this role by guiding people into new states of being that restore a sense of cosmic continuity through the processes of separation, transition, and incorporation.[26] Following this, van Gennep characterizes rites associated with the processes of separation "preliminal rites," rites associated with the transition stage "liminal rites," and rites associated with the processes of incorporation "postliminal rites."[27]

Though it will be necessary to unpack what is meant by the term "ritual" in the next section, what is important here is van Gennep's influence on Turner's notion of liminal personae. This is because Turner first explores the concept of liminality in relation to the liminal stage in rites of passage. Specifically, the liminal stage presents what Turner calls an "interstructural situation," a moment when those undergoing the psychosocial transition are between the preliminal and postliminal conditions and thus between the positions assigned to them by the socioeconomic-historical relations they participate in.[28] For Turner, social structures are intricate webs of relations between socially prescribed positions assigned and maintained by various social institutions.[29] Following Alexander, a contemporary of Turner, these social structures are at once both positive and necessary for social life, but they also have the potential to be deeply problematic via processes of alienation, distance, inequality, and exploitation.[30] Moreover, these social structures are contested, are resisted, and have multiple (often competing) meanings for all those who participate in them.[31]

Returning to the concept of liminality, liminal personae hang between the different social structures they are marginalized from. As such, Alexander argues that it is the ambiguity of social relations between liminal personae, within these interstructural spaces, that enables more direct and egalitarian exchanges between all those present.[32] Liminal spaces, therefore, become the ideal contexts for the generation of deeply affective spacetimes, suspended in an interstructural plasma, known as communitas. States of communitas are characterized by an intense emotional belonging and identification with all those also inhabiting the liminal space. The specifics of communitas, especially its subversive anti-structural character, and the ritualization needed for its generation will be explored in the latter two sections of this chapter. Here, I want to identify three reasons the Bethnal Green Buttmitzvah represents a liminal space.

Founded in 2016 by a group of queer Jews in central London, Buttmitzvah is an event that centers the experiences of liminal personae with two (and certainly not the only) minoritized social characteristics: those who are simultaneously queer and Jewish. The evening does this by branding itself as a queer and Jewish event, with the name "Buttmitzvah" representing a queer play on the Jewish rite of passage Bat Mitzvah:

> **O.K.:** So, uh, Buttmitzvah is, uh, a night in which the idea is that it's—it's centered around a fake Bat Mitzvah for a girl who's got two Jewish parents of which are both drag queens, uh, the man is in drag as—the man is in drag as the male but he's dragged up as a male, um, who play her Jewish—who play her Jewish parents and it's a night where you go and you dance to Jewish music but also like the normal, general like mainstream music. Uh, it's a club night, basically.
>
> Semi-structured interview, November 2020

By "stating very loudly" that Buttmitzvah is a queer Jewish space (T.M., Semi-structured interview, August 2020), the organizers (trans)form a mythic framing of the event that assumes a common past among the ritual performers and demarcates the event space as one that is meaningfully queer *and* Jewish.[33] For example, the tagline for the night calls Buttmitzvah "the ultimate cumming of age party," which puts the "Oy Gay! into the ancient teenage Jewish ritual, [Bat] Mitzvah."[34] This play on words is important, as it demonstrates the idea of Buttmitzvah as a liminoid phenomenon within a liminal space. Whereas Buttmitzvah is a liminal space due to the centering and presence of liminal personae, the phenomena occurring throughout the evening are liminoid as, according to Turner, they are associated primarily with play, satire, and leisure.[35] The notion of liminoid phenomena will be explored fully in the final section of this chapter, particularly in relation to its anti-structural character. What is important here is to understand that Buttmitzvah incorporates liminoid phenomena in a liminal space.

Buttmitzvah can be considered a liminal space also due to its organizational structure and timing. To reiterate, the evening is a parodical take on a teenage Jewish rite of passage featuring satirical performances of the rituals, not necessarily religiously prescribed, typically associated with a Bat Mitzvah. For example, one of the partygoers is elected to play

Buttmitzvah Becky, whom the other partygoers and performers dance the hora around and who is given a raunchy, parodical Bat Mitzvah speech to read aloud to the dance hall.[36] Consequentially, the evening mimics the transitionary period typical of a coming-of-age ceremony and allows for the creation of a satirical yet authentic liminal space. Buttmitzvah is largely organized around special and transitory dates in the Hebraic calendar (e.g., Rosh Hashanah, Pesach, Purim) and is almost always held on a Friday evening at the beginning of the Sabbath. As such, the evening is a liminal space as it occurs in those immediate hours following the transition from work to rest and in anticipation of the new week to come.

The context in which the event is held is also important. On the micro-level, liminality is spatialized in the segregation of partygoers and regulars in the working men's club. As sites traditionally associated with classed, gendered, provincialized, and racialized modes of being, working men's clubs are also "succumbing to modern life."[37] The club is thus an event space in transition between an aging form of reaction and newer highly individualized leisure activities—where, through liminality, tradition and contemporaneity brush up against one another.

On the macro-level, the rise in antisemitic and queerphobic hate crimes found in Home Office reports is also picked up on by the event's founder, Josh Cole, when he says in an interview with *Hey Alma* that Buttmitzvah has gained popularity at a time when "Anti-semitism [and queerphobia] is becoming popular again."[38] For people who are both queer and Jewish, marginalization occurs both due to the supposed dichotomy between queer and Jewish identity markers and due to wider marginalization from dominant heterosexist, postsecular British social structures. Increasingly, the evening represents a safe space for people who lie, to varying degrees, between marginalizing social structures. As such, Buttmitzvah is a liminal space because (mostly) liminal personae compose said space. Moreover, liminality is spatialized in the urban setting of Bethnal Green, a neighborhood in a process of (resisted) transition between two different states. Historically a (contested) site of transition for new immigrant populations, the area has felt the brunt of growing gentrification—something crystallized around the 2012 London Olympics social drama.[39] With property- and state-led gentrification, many East Enders are being driven out by rising housing costs and the gradual (yet contested) (re)aggregation of the area from working class to middle class.[40]

156   Matthew Richardson

Due to its liminal qualities, the Bethnal Green Buttmitzvah acts as the ideal setting for the generation of communitas—a ritual space-time characterized by great porosity and potentiality where anything is possible. Following Australian anthropologist Bruce Kapferer, liminality does not guarantee communitas, nor is communitas an accidental by-product of liminal personae gathering in liminal spaces.[41] Instead, the generation of communitas relies on the convergence of several behavioral and performative conditions and the liminal personae's ability to ritualize action within the liminal space itself. As such, it is necessary to explore what I refer to as the ritual complex, an analytical, methodological, and theoretical heuristic tool adapted from Turnerian anthropology to explore religious behavior within social action.

Buttmitzvah and the Ritual Complex

Hannah: I don't usually feel at home in the sort of queer nightlife but, actually, there's a night called Buttmitzvah, uh, which is a queer Jewish night, um, and I've been a couple of times and it's really nice, um, and it does—it's really cool to feel that intersection of both, um, and I'm not massively into dressing up but, um, I remember the last time I went, I went and I wore like a shirt and a kippah and it felt—and so it was kinda draggy in a sense, um, and it was really nice. It felt very—it was a really cool expression, um, that wasn't—yeah, that was really just like no one was really looking, um, it was just nice. Um, that was really cool. Um, it was very accepting, very inclusive, and it had—it had both—yeah, it had both things that I was just talking about in that, you know, went in and instantly, the group I was with, we all recognized different people, um, because of Jewish connections, and we were having really interesting conversations about kind of, you know, what we were expecting from the night and they did some—they did some skits and it was like we were at this Bar Mitzvah and it was kind of this quite intellectual take on things and it was like—um, it was very debatey [Matt: Mm] in that kind of Jewish like "what—what do we . . ." it wasn't kind of—it was having fun for the sake of fun but there was also commentary to it, um, which felt very Jewish, um, but then it was also just ridiculous, and people we wearing all kinda things like drag and not—and just themselves and, um, yeah, it was a real celebration of kind of—um, like someone blew like a shofar on stage, I think, and then like, um, there was like Israeli dancing and things like that but then, at the same time, we were all being so queer in that space and that was quite liberating because I'm sure so many people in that room have felt quite excluded from Jewish spaces if they grew up more ortho-dox or whatever, but like literally someone was like wielding a dildo on stage or something and it was just—yeah, it was just bizarre and whacky, um, but just, yeah, accepting.

Semi-structured interview, February 2021

During the Bethnal Green Buttmitzvah, the blowing of the shofar com-bines with the camp Europop beats on the dance floor; the Jewish intel-lectual tradition of debate with the party-like aura of the club; and the rhythmic dancing of the hora with the dildo-wielding partygoer. These are all ritual symbols with highly sensory components—components that, through their embodiment in the ritual performance, fuse the ideological with the concrete.[42] It is through this symbolic interchange that communi-tas is generated—an affective atmosphere hanging both in and out of time.

For Turner, rituals are the "prescribed formal behaviour for occasions not given over to technological routing" and have "reference to beliefs in mystical beings or powers."[43] Symbols, likewise, are the "smallest unit of ritual" and can be any empirical object, activity, relationship, event, ges-ture, or spatial unit.[44] Following van Gennep, Turner argues that symbols are indicative of social processes whereby rituals function as media for groups to adjust to internal psychosomatic and external environmental changes.[45] As such, Turner encourages scholars of religion to focus on "ritual symbols" since these symbols function as motivating factors in social actions that ultimately serve human "interests, purposes, ends, and means."[46] Therefore, when we study rituals, we must look at the symbols used in them because these symbols signify information beyond that which is transmitted through the empirical embodiments of the rite.

Importantly, Turner categorizes ritual symbols as relative to two poles, the concrete and the ideological.[47] Symbolic referents of the physi-ological kind cluster at the concrete whereas symbolic referents to moral norms and principles governing any given social structure cluster at the ideological. During ritual performance, these poles flip, melding the moral and the material in the psyches of the ritual performers.[48] The concrete pole, through its association with the ideological, becomes purged of its infantile and hedonistic character. The ideological pole, through its association with the concrete, becomes charged with the pleasurable affects. In her ethnography of the Huichol peyote hunt, Myerhoff used the term "symbol complex" to refer to the intricate web of myths, symbols, and rituals drawn upon in the hunt.[49] Commenting on Turner's symbolic interchange, Myerhoff claimed that such a process results in the highest ideals of a collectivity becoming saturated with emotion, while the more hedonistic and infantile emotions are ennobled through their proximity to lofty social values. For Myerhoff, symbols are concepts made concrete in the form of highly emotional and widely recognizable empirical things that are performed in behavioral contexts via rituals.[50] Because of this, I prefer the term "ritual complex" over "symbol complex" since the former places greater emphasis on the fact that rituals make symbols work by enabling them to achieve their purpose via performative action.

The congruence of human experiences via the media of ritual also requires processes of mythmaking. Since symbols signify information beyond that transmitted in the empirical forms of the rite, myths are used to provide the context, setting, and explanation for these ritual symbols. In this way, we can consider the parodical Bat Mitzvah for a north London, suburban Jewish girl named Becky as a mythic formula:

> **Matt:** So, in—in this context what does it [Becky] mean?
> **Blue:** It means like a very materialistic Jewish princess, like, never expects to have to work [Matt: Yeah.], normally obsessed with fashion, not very interesting or deep. That is—and Jewish, specifically [Matt: Okay.], um, from the name Rebecca like being the standard for Jewish names.
>
> Life story interview, August 2020

To reiterate, myths are "sets of conceptions" that "draw upon and reflect people's cultural environment"—shaping the "actions and perceptions of those who accept or challenge them."[51] Buttmitzvah Becky is thus a mythic character who sets the scene for the ritual performance through the inculcation of appropriate dispositions and responses.[52] Crucially, Myerhoff argues that the origins of myths, symbols, and rituals are situated in the most intimate layers of childhood, where they were first taught to us by pastoral figures.[53] Myerhoff uses the term "domestic religion" to explain this type of ethnoreligiosity acquired in early childhood; completely associated with family and the household, domestic religion blends nurture and ethnic complexities to create a hearth-based religion that endures contingency and tumult.[54] As such, it is not just rites of passage that enable us to reckon with cosmic and social changes. Instead, rituals are the media through which symbols and myths are employed to make sense of experience. Moreover, domestic religion employs well-known sensory triggers to generate deeply affective sacred spaces that evoke the ritual performer's earliest memories stored in the body and inculcated from childhood. These sacred space-times, characterized by scholar of religion Kevin O'Neill as "hair standing on the back of a neck, the warm glow of holiday festivities, the rush of enthusiasm at a political rally," are what I have identified above as communitas.[55]

Domestic religion and the ritual complex are also at work during Buttmitzvah. First, the structure of the evening draws from both ethnoreligious and queer cultural reservoirs. Both the evening's setting in a historically Jewish neighborhood and its structure around a Jewish rite of passage trigger an emotional response in the partygoers:

> O.K.: I remember the first time I went, it just felt, um, really liberating. It felt good because it had the positive—it had history, it had my history, but it also had my queer future. It—it sounds really strange. Like, there was something really nice about like, um, interacting with people who've had the same experience that I have had.
>
> Semi-structured interview, November 2020

Ritual symbols have reference to information beyond that which is empirically transmitted during the rite. The sense of a Jewish history and queer future is something that is felt or sensed, like an aura perforating the liminal space of the Working Men's Club. Unlike Myerhoff, who claimed that these sensations are more felt than rationalized, theologized, or theorized, it was clear in my interview with O.K. that participants in Buttmitzvah attempted to also theorize these feelings via the narrative and dialogical space of the interview.[56] Moreover, this demonstrates, I argue, a link between Turner's understanding of rituals as "having reference to beliefs in mystical beings or powers" and Gans's symbolic ethnicity.[57] In other words, Buttmitzvah employs ritual symbols referring to a symbolic Jewish people mobilized via the performance of rituals that pertain to collective experiences.[58]

Developing this, domestic religion emerges through rituals in forms including, though not exclusively, the hora and the Bat Mitzvah speech. Likewise, Jewish and queer symbols are employed in the jokes surrounding the event's backstories, the fancy dress and drag costumes worn by some of the partygoers (e.g., Pharaoh and the Rimmer family's *frum* cousins), and the props used throughout the night (e.g., the chair used in the hora and a Friday night dinner setup).[59] The formal strictures surrounding the Bat Mitzvah (or the Passover or Chanukkah special editions) are charged with emotion due to the emotional resonance of the ritual symbols employed. The emotional response to their "Jewish history" is then made congruent through quasi-mythmaking when partygoers link this to their "queer future[s]."

The sensory experiences of dancing in unison to queer and Jewish anthems (here linked to Europop club hits and Barbara Streisand show tunes), the erotic proximity of bodies pressed up against one another in the dimly lit dance hall, and the tipsiness of the intoxicated revelers, all fundamentally concrete and carnal symbolic triggers, thus fuse with the partygoers' Jewish histories and queer futures and generate communitas. In this moment, those participating in the series of events are unified and enjoy an intense sense of emotional belonging and identification with all those in attendance—the realization of an "imagined community."[60] Here, the collective enjoys itself as a collective, with the suspension of time enabling those enthralled in the superindividual organism of the group to make sense of their own experiences as liminal personae.[61] As such, religious life is life together since the process of collective and individual identity construction, demarcation, and celebration is not possible without the presence of other bodies that, in unison, come together to generate a special type of social electricity akin to Durkheim's notion of effervescence.[62]

These dynamics have been found also in other studies with minoritized groups. For example, Julian Holloway's study of spiritualist seances as sacred spaces highlights the way in which an affective, erotic, and sacred atmosphere is generated through the proximity of gendered and classed bodies.[63] Similarly, Lynn Davidman found that the performance of rituals by secular Jews functioned as both a cathartic method for retaining warm family memories and a politically conscious act of affirming and maintaining one's identity and well-being.[64] Likewise, Anny Bakalian's study of Armenian Americans explores the sacred and secular cultural apparatuses that Armenian Americans adopt in the construction of their symbolic ethnic identity.[65] Here, is it important to unpack the terms "community" and "identity," as neither are stable or uncontested categories. Indeed, one's reflexive sense of community and identity is fluid and in a constant process of construction, maintenance, and affirmation. For example, in her cultural geography of Edinburgh Hindu communities, Malory Nye argues that it is problematic to uncritically "use the term community to describe" a group of people that is "very loosely organized and differentiated."[66] Nevertheless, an ethereal and ineffable understanding of "community" can emerge among people who share certain social characteristics, for example, religion or sexuality, and share certain space-times together.

This links to other studies in the geography of religion exploring ethnoreligious identity movements. For example, in his study of identity formation and resistance among minoritized Muslims in Israel, Nimrod Luz argues that religious spaces act as the nexus of identity formation as they operate as metaphors for ethnic struggle and identity.[67] It is the affective quality of these spaces achieved, I argue, via that generation of communitas that makes them stand out against other sites and function as a platform to "rally people and groups that do not necessarily agree or cooperate on a daily basis" in a powerful and collective identity politics.[68] Identities, therefore, can be disparate, diverse, yet forged in relation to a collective as a means to countering experiences of marginalization. As such, Buttmitzvah is more than just a raunchy-themed club night. Following Luz, the evening functions as an emotional and motivational platform for the formation and mobilization of politicized subjectivities.[69] The political potential of communitas lies in its anti-structural qualities as it is these that provide those who experience communitas with the opportunity to enliven, regenerate, resist, and subvert hegemonic structures.

Communitas and the City: Anti-Structure and Liminoid Phenomena

Attendees at Buttmitzvah often feel a sense of liberation due to having attended the event. Participants often spoke of the "liberatory" feelings inculcated in the Buttmitzvah ritual communitas (Hannah, semi-structured interview, February 2021; O.K., semi-structured interview, November 2020). If queer Jews feel liberated by attending Buttmitzvah, then it is worth exploring what it is they feel liberated from. Part of this is done by looking at the anti-structural quality of communitas.

Turner used the term "anti-structure" to describe a unique quality to both liminality and communitas. Indeed, anti-structure refers to the

> liberation of human capacities of cognition, affect, volitions, creativity etc., from the normative constraints incumbent upon occupying a sequence of social statuses, enacting a multiplicity of social roles, and being acutely conscious of membership in some corporate group such as a family, lineage, clan, tribe, nation, etc., or of affiliation with some pervasive social category such as class, caste, sex, or age divisions.[70]

It is in liminal spaces that the opportunity for this liberation emerges. This is because liminality acts as an "interfacial region" where, mirroring O.K.'s comment about a Jewish history and a queer future, the past is momentarily suspended and the future is yet to begin.[71] In these moments of communitas, intense and aspirational potential emerges.[72] During these affective space-times, according to Kapferer, the bodies gathered within them come together "individuated, freed, and fully themselves," stripped of the attributes of structure, and confront one another directly and equally in a state of anti-structure.[73] The result of this unity is a deep understanding of the self as felt by the individuals in relation to the collective.

Similar phenomena are found also in contemporary ethnographies. In her ethnography of the Enawenê-Nawê of western Brazil, Chloe Nahum-Claudel finds that the annual fishing dam–building ritual provides the men of the village with the opportunity to experience communitas.[74] During the ritual, the men of the village are physically separated from the dualistic social structure of village life, its public ceremonialism, and spousal and kinship obligations as they travel to the site of the fishing dam.[75] Consequentially, the site of the fishing dam is a liminal space in terms of both physicality and sociality, providing the men with a "holiday from structure" that functions as a restorative cordial to psychosocial life.[76] Similarly, in his study of ritual liminality in an African American Pentecostal church, Bobby Alexander identifies possession as fostering the suspension of everyday social norms.[77] This is because the process of possession removes participants from social structures via ritual liminality and the introduction of alternative, communitarian relations generated in the mode of communitas. Specifically, Alexander argues that the demands of social structures relating to gender, race, and class are relaxed when members enter the church as they physically and symbolically separate themselves from the social context in which they are marginalized by such structures.[78]

It is in these spaces, characterized by an ecstatic sense of belonging, that the aspirational and motivational forces that are needed to regenerate, rejuvenate, resist, and/or subvert hegemonic structures emerge.[79] The radical unity experienced during communitas, according to Alexander and mirroring Durkheim, challenges the social differentiation on which social structures are based. This experience provides participants with snapshots of new modes of life and, in turn, coaxes them into political mobilizations that resist and subvert dominant social norms.[80] This phenomenon is reflected in Luz's study whereby the affective atmospheres residual in sacred spaces function as aspirational and motivational reservoirs from which minoritized peoples can draw to engage in subversive identity politics.[81]

That said, communitas does not guarantee resistance and subversion. In her ethnography of the peyote hunt, Myerhoff argues that it is the cathartic effects of communitas that inhibit the Huichol from engaging in political mobilization addressing their mistreatment by the Mexican state.[82] This mirrors wider Turnerian theory whereby communitas serves hegemonic social structures by providing marginalized peoples a legitimate avenue to vent their frustrations without threatening the stability of the hegemonic social structure. According to Alexander, this is because the sense of solidarity experienced during communitas runs underneath social structures, thus bringing communitas and social structure into mutual relation.[83] Though communitas has the potential for motivating ritual performers in political praxis, this potential rests on whether members of the communitas have vested interests in maintaining hegemonic structures and whether communitas can be institutionalized. Here, institutionalization refers to the groups' abilities to prepare the nest for the generation of communitas via the prescription of certain rites, symbols, and myths.[84]

There is an important point to raise here regarding the institutionalization of communitas and the proportion of liminal personae at Buttmitzvah.

> T.M.: Yeah, so I've been to Buttmitzvah a few times.
>
> Matt: How did you find Buttmitzvah?
>
> T.M.: Mm, yeah, I think it's got too big, um, I think it—um, it initially felt like genuinely a place which was, um—um, both genuinely queer and Jewish at the same time and I think as it got larger it starts to be both of those things kind of in name only. So, there's lots of people who are, um—yeah, so—so—so, like the first time I went, there were, yeah, lots of kind of queer Jewish people and by the time—the most recent time I went there, it was kind of a rarity to meet somebody else who was Jewish and queer and there were lots of people who were just Jewish or just queer or neither.
>
> Semi-structured interview, August 2020

Following Misgav and Johnston's take on Mary Douglas's dirt theory, the embodied presence of non-queers/non-Jews is symbolic of "ontological anxieties" concerning "order and disorder, borders and crossings, being and not being."[85] It could be argued that T.M.'s concern is that a decreasing majority of liminal personae taking part in the event may threaten the existential function of the evening as a celebration of queer Jewishness and Jewish queerness. Replying to this concern, O.K. argues that the inclusion of allies in the space is "fine" since the space remains a "celebration" and an opportunity for "other people to celebrate our culture" (Semi-structured interview, November 2020).

As such, it is the inclusive and welcoming space of Buttmitzvah, filled with liminal personae, that represents a threshold between the outside world as characterized by social structures relating to antisemitism, heterosexism, and postsecularism and the inside space where queer Jews can participate fully as themselves without having to bifurcate their identities in a politically radical act of identity affirmation. Buttmitzvah, then, is a space where attendees do not have to fear "walking home from synagogue with [their] yarmulke on" or "leaving a gay club wearing [their] high heels and [their] wig," since it is in these spaces that they are safe to celebrate both parts of their identity.[86] There are three important points to explore here: first, the fact that communitas is an ephemeral, temporary state; second, that the structures present in ordinary space-times still mold states of communitas; and, third, the anti-structural and subversive qualities of liminoid phenomena.

Communitas is sporadic and temporary by nature. The liminal state conducive to the generation of communitas is always followed by processes of reincorporation due to the anti-structural characteristic of the interstructural state. According to Myerhoff in her discussion of the Woodstock generation, when communitas is sought as a replacement to social structure rather than as a part of it, it becomes a structural end in itself and evacuates the phenomenon of any substantial significance.[87] As such, it is the liminal personae's ability to integrate communitas into a dialogical relationship with structure (whether preexisting, renewed, or subversive) that enshrines communitas's affective and political potential. In the case of Buttmitzvah, it is the sporadic and temporary hosting of the event that successfully preserves the evening's potential to engender a sense of communitas. This is not to say, however, that the fleeting nature of communitas precludes the persistence of its effects outside the space-times in which it occurs. Indeed, the identity congruence experienced during communitas can have lasting influence as it provides participants with an enduring reservoir for identity affirmation.

The sporadic and temporary nature of communitas also relates to a dynamic whereby hegemonic social structures still shape spaces of anti-structure. The residual effects of social structure persist in states of anti-structure since they condition who can experience anti-structure in the first place. In her study of female pilgrimage to Lord Ayyapan's shrine in Sabarimala, Vadakkiniyil argues that the social structures relating to gender, religion, and sex act as vortexes discharging space-times of communitas that, in turn, act as sites of conflict, renewal, and the subversion of gender and religious norms.[88] It is the incorporation of sexed and gendered bodies, molded by and in resistance to heterosexist social structures, that acts as a "catalytic vortex" in the generation of communitas.[89] The persistence of structure within the Buttmitzvah communitas is also evident in Abby's experience as the "queer unwanted":

> **Abby**: Oh, yeah, like queer Jewish spaces like Buttmitzvah is really fun but it's also like just so—so like, um—it's just very like gay. Like, it's very gay not queer energy and very like male-dominated [Matt: Mm.], um, which is really sad. Um, like the first time I went it was really fun and it was Halloween, and it was great and then the second time I went I was like—I just had that feeling that I was like "ah, like, I need to be next to someone who like is—is—maybe reads more as queer [Matt: Mm] so that I can feel like I have a place here." Basically, it was misogynistic like *Laughs* is the long-winded way of saying that.
>
> Life story interview, February 2021

Liminality and communitas are never fully cleaved off from structure.[90] For Abby, Buttmitzvah remains a ritual space-time that is "male-dominated"— (trans)forming her femme subjectivity through a feeling of out-of-placeness and a "yearning for belonging."[91] We can then argue that if one is privileged within a certain social structure (here gendered heteronormativity), then they may not be aware of their persistent subjectifying power within moments they perceive as anti-structural.

Whereas T.M. made no mention of the gendered structures operating within the Buttmitzvah communitas (Semi-structured interview, August 2020), Abby was unable to overlook them since they remained subjectified as a femme queer Jew within the liminal event space. This does not take away from the liberatory experience of communitas felt by selves and others but shows how the effects of communitas are felt insofar that one is free from the regulatory structures that persist within its realization. Buttmitzvah thus adds empirical weight to recent theorizations of the "staggered" and "uneven" nature of communitas.[92] Likewise, though the evening generates a space-time characterized by anti-structure, it does so via processes of late-stage capitalism and the night-time economy.

The working men's club, steeped in left-wing, working-class history, exists nevertheless due to capitalist modes of production via the processes of commercial exchange, for example, ticket and alcohol sales. Though Buttmitzvah generates a space-time characterized by anti-structure, it is never wholly independent of structure since it is embedded in the market institutions of the late-night hospitality industry. This reflects Lugosi's study of communitas in queer venues whereby commercial environments latent in hegemonic social structures of capitalism are appropriated and adapted in queer contexts to provide an inclusive liminoid space.[93] Buttmitzvah thus represents a "rival, mimetic structure" dependent on commercial processes of exchange *and* outside the heteronormative, postsecular regulations of ordinary space-time.[94] In this way, Buttmitzvah reflects local style—a form of resistance "understood more in the frictional than the opposi-tional sense: a rub against the rules, rather than a breaking of them."[95]

Finally, the notion of Buttmitzvah as a liminoid phenomenon is important as it highlights the anti-structural and subversive qualities of celebration and play. Mirroring anti-structure's relationship with structural capitalism, the liminoid differs from the liminal since the former, according to Turner, is "more like a commodity" that one "selects and pays for."[96] The liminoid is felt to be more liberating than the liminal since it is a matter of choice, not obligation, and since it is intrinsically tied to the phenomenon of play. It is within these moments of play that the creative qualities of communitas emerge and enable participants to playfully experiment with alternative modes of living that can resist and subvert hegemonic social structures. This is encouraged by the voluntary nature of Buttmitzvah. Since attendance is a deliberate and voluntary act, those in attendance become bound by reciprocal contractual relations, thus fostering a liminoid phe-nomenon in a liminal space and generating the ideal settings for commu-nitas. Moreover, Turner argues that the presence of liminoid phenomena in social critiques and revolutionary movements is expressed via creative products, for example, plays, paintings, songs, films, dress, and so forth.[97]

As such, Buttmitzvah is a liminoid phenomenon because it functions specifically as a celebration of queer Jewish identities. The Jewish and queer jokes seen in the double entendres of "cumming of age," "Oy Gay," and the "Rimmer family" signify, like all ritual symbols do, something greater than a witty play on words. They signify a radical celebration of queer Jewish identities as formed in relation to the collective that generates this sense of identity in the first place. Similar arguments have been drawn by Jeffrey Rubenstein in his discussion of Purim, liminality, and communitas.[98] Like Buttmitzvah, Rubenstein argues that communitas, ritual, play, and other "phenomena of liminality" are "readily recognizable during Purim celebra-tions."[99] Since social differentiation is suspended in communitas, religious life can be seen as life together since those participating in the gener-ation of this sacred space-time come to recognize the "core humanity" they share; relationships become more spontaneous as the group reminds itself that all its members are human and equal, despite emergent social and hierarchical differences, at the most fundamental level.[100] Buttmitzvah, therefore, is a queer Jewish rite of passage—a moment of great (trans) formative potential for "living more fully as empowered selves within and beyond [the] ritualized experience."[101]

Conclusion

Buttmitzvah is more than just a raunchy-themed club night. It is a site of queer ritual innovation that assists in the construction, demarcation, and celebration of queer Jewish selves and others. In this chapter, I turned to Buttmitzvah as an ethnographic case study and Turnerian anthropology of experience to explore the phenomena of ritual, liminality, and communitas. I began by situating Buttmitzvah in its own sociohistorical and geographic context. This enabled me to identify Buttmitzvah as a liminal space frequented by liminal personae. This liminality operates as the ideal setting for the generation of communitas, an anti-structural space-time characterized by an emotionally intense sense of belonging and identification with all those in attendance.

That said, liminality does not automatically guarantee communitas. Instead, communitas depends on several ritualized psychosomatic conditions. Specifically, the interchange between the concrete and ideological symbolic poles is pivotal in generating communitas since it creates an emotionally powerful union between the moral and the somatic. This accounts for the affective atmospheres generated by the utilization of the ritual complex during Buttmitzvah. The liminal space of Buttmitzvah, in tandem with the ritual complex, thus created an emotionally charged landscape with the potential for the generation of communitas.

I finished this chapter by exploring the anti-structural qualities of communitas. This led to a critical reading of anti-structure as in constant oscillation with structure. This is demonstrated in both who is conditioned to experience communitas in the first place and the structural dependency of anti-structure on processes of commercial capitalism. The subversive quality of play during Buttmitzvah characterizes the evening as a liminoid phenomenon in a liminal space. The voluntary and creative work of identity celebration during Buttmitzvah signifies the event as a communitas, the platform from which queer Jews can mobilize collectively in a politically conscious act of identity construction, demarcation, and affirmation.

Turnerian anthropology of experience is just one analytical, methodological, and theoretical heuristic tool through which the events surrounding Buttmitzvah can be explored. To understand how these events manifest both among queer Jews in postsecular Britain and among other demographics is subject to further research and collaboration with heuristic tools, including but also beyond those used in this chapter. Nevertheless, Turnerian anthropology of experience is worth exploring when researching alongside queer religious minoritized groups since it enables scholars to unpack the functionality of ritual in navigating and subverting the processes of structure and anti-structure that we all participate in.

Appendix: Selected Participant Profiles

Abby (She/Her)
Abby is a queer, gay, bisexual cisgender Jewish woman in her mid-twenties. She lives in Greater London and comes from a Progressive Jewish background. She describes herself as slightly observant and religiously and culturally Jewish.

Blue (She/Her)
Blue is a cisgender, bisexual Jewish woman. She is in her mid-twenties and spends her time between university and home in London. Blue was raised Modern Orthodox and states that she is pretty observant—now attending Masorti services.

Liane (She/Her, They/Them)
Liane is a cisgender and non-binary, queer Jew living in London. Liane is from a mixed Ashkenazi-Sephardi background and is now in her early thirties. They were brought up Modern Orthodox and now describe themselves as moderately observant. They are currently affiliated with Reform Judaism.

O.K. (He/Him, They/Them)

O.K. is a gender-questioning gay Jew in his early thirties. He was raised Modern Orthodox and describes himself as religiously and culturally Jewish. They are slightly observant but are no longer affiliated with any particular branch of Judaism.

R. (They/Them)

R. is a non-binary, gender fluid, and gender queer Jew living in London. They describe themselves as lesbian and queer and were raised in a secular interreligious household. They are in their early thirties and currently attend services at a Liberal synagogue.

T.M. (He/Him)

T.M. is a cisgender bisexual Jewish man in his early thirties. He was raised Reform Jewish and describes himself as moderately observant. Like Blue, he is currently affiliated with Masorti Judaism and describes himself as religiously and culturally Jewish.

Notes

1 Watt, "'It's Not for Us,'" 100.
2 Engelhart, "Britain's Working Men's Clubs Succumb to Modern Life."
3 Bruner, "Experience and Its Expressions," 139; Richardson, "Geographic Roots, Anthropological Routes," 6; Faulkner and Hecht, "The Negotiation of Closetable Identities," 829; Myerhoff, "Life History among the Elderly," 99.
4 DeHanas, *London Youth, Religion, and Politics*, 10–14.
5 DeHanas, *London Youth, Religion, and Politics*, 10.
6 DeHanas, *London Youth, Religion, and Politics*, 11.
7 DeHanas, *London Youth, Religion, and Politics*, 11–13.
8 DeHanas, *London Youth, Religion, and Politics*, 11–13.
9 James, "Whiteness and Loss in Outer Easy London," 652.
10 DeHanas, *London Youth, Religion, and Politics*, 11–13.
11 DeHanas, *London Youth, Religion, and Politics*, 11–13.
12 Tower Hamlets Council, *Religion in Tower Hamlets*.
13 Tower Hamlets Council, *Ethnicity in Tower Hamlets*.
14 DeHanas, *London Youth, Religion, and Politics*, 1–3.
15 Holloway, "The Space That Faith Makes," 203.

16 Asad, *Formations of the Secular*, 25.

17 Shah, *The Making of a Gay Muslim*, 1–4.

18 Elks, "UK Police 'Let Down' Gay Community as Hate Crimes Soar"; Khomami, "Antisemitic Incidents in UK at All-Time High."

19 Home Office, "Hate Crime, England and Wales, 2017/2018."

20 Batchelor, "Homophobic, Religious, and Race Hate Crimes on Public Transport Are Soaring, Figures Reveal."

21 Schnoor, "Being Gay and Jewish," 43.

22 Turner, *The Ritual Process*, 108–9.

23 Van Gennep, *The Rites of Passage*, 21.

24 Van Gennep, *The Rites of Passage*, 1–4.

25 Van Gennep, *The Rites of Passage*, 13.

26 Van Gennep, *The Rites of Passage*, 21.

27 Van Gennep, *The Rites of Passage*, 21.

28 Turner, *The Forest of Symbols*, 95.

29 Turner, *The Ritual Process*, 95.

30 Alexander, "Correcting Misinterpretations of Turner's Theory," 27.

31 Alexander, "Correcting Misinterpretations of Turner's Theory," 27.

32 Alexander, "Correcting Misinterpretations of Turner's Theory," 27.

33 Bint Abdullah Sani, "Corporeal Poetics of Sacred Space," 303; Rappaport, *Ritual and Religion in the Making of Humanity*, 135.

34 Smith, "Say Hello to Buttmitzvah."

35 Turner, *From Ritual to Theatre*, 55.

36 Here the hora refers to a celebratory circle dance that is often performed at rites of passage including marriage and b'not mitzvah.

37 Engelhart, "Britain's Working Men's Clubs Succumb to Modern Life."

38 Tohill, "Buttmitzvah Is a Queer Jewish Club Night Unlike Any Other."

39 Watt, "'It's Not for Us,'" 99.

40 Watt, "'It's Not for Us,'" 100–103.

41 Kapferer, "Crisis and Communitas," 1.

42 Myerhoff, *Peyote Hunt*, 193; Turner, *The Forest of Symbols*, 54.

43 Turner, *The Forest of Symbols*, 19.

44 Turner, *The Forest of Symbols*, 19.

45 Turner, *The Forest of Symbols*, 19.

46 Turner, *The Forest of Symbols*, 20.

47 Turner, *The Forest of Symbols*, 54.

48 Turner, *The Forest of Symbols*, 54.

49 Myerhoff, *Peyote Hunt*, 193.

50 Myerhoff, *Peyote Hunt*, 196.

51 Lugosi, "Queer Consumption and Commercial Hospitality," 168.

52 Rappaport, *Ritual and Religion in the Making of Humanity*, 117.

53 Myerhoff, *Number Our Days*, 225–27.

54 Myerhoff, *Number Our Days*, 256.

55 O'Neill, "Beyond Broken," 1095.

56 Myerhoff, *Number Our Days*, 256–59.

57 Turner, *The Forest of Symbols*, 19; Gans, "Symbolic Ethnicity," 1–2; Gans, "Symbolic Ethnicity and Symbolic Religiosity," 577–78.

58 Myerhoff, *Number Our Days*, 255–57.

59 *Frum* is a word taken from Yiddish meaning "religious" or "pious." Here it refers to Becky's cousins, the Clitovichs, who are dressed in modest clothing.

60 Anderson, *Imagined Communities*, 6–7.

61 Durkheim, *The Elementary Forms of Religious Life*, 282.

62 Durkheim, *The Elementary Forms of Religious Life*, 157.

63 Holloway, "Enchanted Spaces," 185.

64 Davidman, "The New Voluntarism and the Case of the Unsynagogued Jews," 59.

65 Bakalian, *Armenian-Americans*, 164.

66 Nye, "Temple Congregations and Communities," 204.

67 Luz, "Metaphors to Live By," 58.

68 Luz, "Metaphors to Live By," 62.

69 Luz, "Metaphors to Live By," 62.

70 Turner, *From Ritual to Theatre*, 44.

71 Turner, *From Ritual to Theatre*, 44.

72 Turner, *From Ritual to Theatre*, 44.

73 Kapferer, "Crisis and Communitas," 1.

74 Nahum-Claudel, "In Permanent Transition," 11–15.

75 Nahum-Claudel, "In Permanent Transition," 11–15.

76 Nahum-Claudel, "In Permanent Transition," 11–15.

77 Alexander, "Correcting Misinterpretations of Turner's Theory," 35.

78 Alexander, "Correcting Misinterpretations of Turner's Theory," 35.

79 Alexander, "Correcting Misinterpretations of Turner's Theory," 30.

80 Alexander, "Correcting Misinterpretations of Turner's Theory," 37.

81 Luz, "Metaphors to Live By," 58–62

82 Myerhoff, *Peyote Hunt*, 65.

83 Alexander, "Correcting Misinterpretations of Turner's Theory," 29–30.

84 Turner, *The Ritual Process*, 138.

85 Misgav and Johnston, "Dirty Dancing," 732; Douglas, *Purity and Danger*, 44–45.

86 Kean, "Buttmitzvah Is a Jewish, Queer Club Night That's Held in London."

87 Myerhoff, "Organisation and Ecstasy," 60–66.

88 Vadakkiniyil, "Mahishi's Rage," 16.

89 Vadakkiniyil, "Mahishi's Rage," 16.

90 Richardson, "Geographic Roots, Anthropological Routes," 8.

91 Brettschneider, "Ritual Encounters of the Queer Kind," 32.

92 Banfield, "From Liminal Spaces to Spatialities of Liminality," 6; Richardson, "Geographic Roots, Anthropological Routes," 7.

93 Lugosi, "Queer Consumption and Commercial Hospitality," 171.

94 Wigley, "The Sunday Morning Journey to Church Considered as a Form of 'Micro-Pilgrimage,'" 710.

95 Massumi, "The Political Economy of Belonging and the Logic of Relation," 187.

96 Turner, *From Ritual to Theatre*, 55.

97 Turner, *From Ritual to Theatre*, 54.

98 Rubenstein, "Purim, Liminality, and Communitas," 247.

99 Rubenstein, "Purim, Liminality, and Communitas," 249.

100 Rubenstein, "Purim, Liminality, and Communitas," 250.

101 Brettschneider, "Ritual Encounters of the Queer Kind," 43.

Works Cited

Alexander, Bobby C. "Correcting Misinterpretations of Turner's Theory: An African-American Pentecostal Illustration." *Journal for the Scientific Study of Religion* 30, no. 1 (1991): 26–44. https://doi.org/10.2307/1387147.

Anderson, Benedict. *Imagined Communities: Reflections on the Origins and Spread of Nationalism*. New York: American Council of Learned Societies, 1991.

Asad, Talal. *Formations of the Secular: Christianity, Islam, Modernity*. Stanford: Stanford University Press, 2003.

Bakalian, Anny P. *Armenian-Americans: From Being to Feeling Armenian*. New Brunswick, NJ: Transactions, 1993.

Banfield, Janet. "From Liminal Spaces to Spatialities of Liminality." *Area* 54, no. 4 (2022): 610–17. https://doi.org/10.1111/area.12791.

Batchelor, Tom. "Homophobic, Religious, and Race Hate Crimes on Public Transport Are Soaring, Figures Reveal." *The Independent*, April 12, 2018.

www.independent.co.uk/news/uk/crime/hate-crimes-public-transport
-homophobic-religion-racist-uk-attacks-tube-train-bus-a8291761.html.

Bint Abdullah Sani, Hanisah. "Corporeal Poetics of Sacred Space: An Ethnography of *Jum'ah* in a Chapel." *Space and Culture* 18, no. 3 (2015): 298–310. https://doi.org/10.1177/1206331215579750.

Brettschneider, Marla. "Ritual Encounters of the Queer Kind: A Political Analysis of Jewish Lesbian Ritual Innovation." *Journal of Lesbian Studies* 7, no. 2 (2003): 29–48. https://doi.org/10.1300/J155v07n02_04.

Bruner, Edward. "Experience and Its Expressions." In *The Anthropology of Experience*, edited by Victor Turner and Edward Bruner, 3–30. Chicago: University of Illinois Press, 1986.

Casey, Mark. "The Queer Unwanted and Their Undesirable 'Otherness.'" In *Geographies of Sexualities: Theories, Practices, and Politics*, edited by Jason Lim and Kath Browne, 125–36. London: Routledge, 2007.

Cloke, Paul, and Justin Beaumont. "Geographies of Postsecular Rapprochement in the City." *Progress in Human Geography* 37, no. 1 (2012): 27–51. https://doi.org/10.1177/0309132512440208.

Davidman, Lynn. "The New Voluntarism and the Case of the Unsynagogued Jews." In *Everyday Religion: Observing Modern Religious Lives*, edited by Nancy T. Ammerman, 51–67. Oxford: Oxford University Press, 2007.

DeHanas, Daniel N. *London Youth, Religion, and Politics: Engagement and Activism from Brixton to Brick Lane*. Oxford: Oxford University Press, 2016.

Douglas, Mary. *Purity and Danger: An Analysis of the Concepts of Pollution and Taboo*. London: Routledge, 1966.

Durkheim, Emile. *The Elementary Forms of Religious Life*. Translated by Carol Cosman. Oxford: Oxford World Classics, [1912] 2008.

Elks, Sonia. "UK Police 'Let Down' Gay Community as Hate Crimes Soar." *Reuters*, July 19, 2018. Accessed September 17, 2018. www.reuters.com/article/us-britain-crime-lgbt/uk-police-let-down-gay-community-as-hate-crimes-soar-idUSKBN1K92JB.

Engelhart, Katie. "Britain's Working Men's Clubs Succumb to Modern Life." *New York Times*, April 15, 2014. Accessed July 25, 2022. www.nytimes.com/2014/04/20/travel/britains-working-mens-clubs-succumb-to-modern-life.html.

Faulkner, Sandra F., and Michael L. Hecht. "The Negotiation of Closetable Identities: A Narrative Analysis of Lesbian, Gay, Bisexual, Transgendered

Queer Jewish Identity." *Journal of Social and Personal Relationships* 28, no. 6 (2011): 829–47. https://doi.org/10.1177/0265407510391338.

Gans, Herbert J. "Symbolic Ethnicity: The Future of Ethnic Groups and Cultures in America." *Ethnic and Racial Studies* 2, no. 1 (1979): 1–20. https://doi.org/10.1080/01419870.1979.9993248.

———. "Symbolic Ethnicity and Symbolic Religiosity: Towards a Comparison of Ethnic and Religious Acculturation." *Ethnic and Racial Studies* 17, no. 4 (1994): 577–91. https://doi.org/10.1080/01419870.1994.9993841.

Holloway, Julian. "Enchanted Spaces: The Séance, Affect, and Geographies of Religion." *Annals of the Association of American Geographers* 96, no. 1 (2006): 182–87. https://doi.org/10.1111/j.1467-8306.2006.00507.x.

———. "The Space That Faith Makes: Towards a (Hopeful) Ethos of Engagement." In *Religion and Place: Landscape, Politics and Piety*, edited by Peter E. Hopkins, Lily Kong, and Elizabeth Olson, 203–18. New York: Springer, 2013.

Home Office. "Hate Crime, England and Wales, 2017/2018." *London: UK Statistics Authority (Statistical Bulletin 20/18)*, October 16, 2018. Accessed November 1, 2018. www.gov.uk/government/statistics/hate-crime-england -and-wales-2017-to-2018.

James, Malcolm. "Whiteness and Loss in Outer Easy London: Tracing the Collective Memories of Diaspora Space." *Ethnic and Racial Studies* 37, no. 4 (2014): 652–67. https://doi.org/10.1080/01419870.2013.808761.

Kapferer, Bruce. "Crisis and Communitas: Victor Turner and Social Process." *Anthropology Today* 35, no. 5 (2019): 1–2.

Kean, Owen. "Buttmitzvah Is a Jewish, Queer Club Night That's Held in London." BBC, October 22, 2019. Accessed September 15, 2020. www.bbc.co .uk/news/av/stories-50101360.

Khomami, Nadia. "Antisemitic Incidents in UK at All-Time High." *The Guardian*, February 1, 2018. Accessed September 17, 2018. www.theguardian .com/society/2018/feb/01/antisemitic-incidents-in-uk-at-all-time-high.

Lugosi, Peter. "Queer Consumption and Commercial Hospitality: Communitas, Myths, and the Production of Liminoid Space." *International Journal of Sociology and Social Policy* 27, no. 3–4 (2007): 163–74. https://doi.org/10 .1108/01443330710741093.

Luz, Nimrod. "Metaphors to Live By: Identity Formation and Resistance among Minority Muslims in Israel." In *Religion and Place: Landscape, Politics and Piety*, edited by Peter E. Hopkins, Lily Kong, and Elizabeth Olson, 57–74. New York: Springer, 2013.

Massumi, Brian. "The Political Economy of Belonging and the Logic of Relation." In *Anybody*, edited by Cynthia Davidson, 174–88, Cambridge, MA: MIT Press, 1997.

Misgav, Chen, and Lynda Johnston. "Dirty Dancing: The (Non)Fluid Embodied Geographies of a Queer Nightclub in Tel Aviv." *Social and Cultural Geography* 15, no. 7 (2014): 730–46. https://doi.org/10.1080/14649365.2014.916744.

Myerhoff, Barbara G. "Life History among the Elderly: Performance, Visibility, and Remembering." In *A Crack in the Mirror: Reflexive Perspectives in Anthropology*, edited by Jay Ruby, 99–118. Philadelphia: University of Pennsylvania Press, 1982.

———. *Number Our Days: A Triumph of Continuity and Culture among Jewish Old People in an Urban Ghetto*. New York: Simon and Schuster, 1978.

———. "Organisation and Ecstasy: Deliberate and Accidental Communitas among Huichol Indians and American Youth." In *Symbol and Politics in Communal Ideology: Cases and Questions*, edited by Barbara G. Myerhoff and Sally F. Moore, 33–67. Ithaca, NY: Cornell University Press, 1975.

———. *Peyote Hunt: The Sacred Journey of the Huichol Indians*. Ithaca, NY: Cornell University Press, 1974.

Nahum-Claudel, Chloe. "In Permanent Transition: Multiple Temporalities of Communitas in the Enawenê-nawê Ritual Everyday." *Anthropology Today* 35, no. 3 (2019): 11–15.

Nye, Malory. "Temple Congregations and Communities: Hindu Constructions in Edinburgh." *New Community* 19, no. 2 (1993): 201–15. https://doi.org/10.1080/1369183X.1993.9976356.

O'Neill, Kevin L. "Beyond Broken: Affective Spaces and the Study of American Religion." *Journal of the American Academy of Religion* 81, no. 4 (2013): 1093–116. https://doi.org/10.1093/jaarel/lft059.

Rappaport, Roy A. *Ritual and Religion in the Making of Humanity*. Cambridge: Cambridge University Press, 1999.

Richardson, Matthew. "Geographic Roots, Anthropological Routes: New Avenues in Geographies of Religions." *Geography Compass* 16, no. 3 (2022): 1–13. https://doi.org/10.1111/gec3.12613.

Rubenstein, Jeffrey. "Purim, Liminality, and Communitas." *Association for Jewish Studies* 17, no. 2 (1992): 247–77. https://doi.org/10.1017/S0364009400003688.

Schnoor, Randal F. "Being Gay and Jewish: Negotiating Intersecting Identities." *Sociology of Religion* 67, no. 1 (2006): 43–60. www.jstor.org/stable/3712419.

Shah, Shanon. *The Making of a Gay Muslim: Religion, Sexuality and Identity in Malaysia and Britain*. New York: Springer eBook, 2018.

Smith, Amy. "Say Hello to Buttmitzvah: London's First Queer Jewish Night." *TimeOut*, October 20, 2016. Accessed September 1, 2020. www.timeout.com/london/blog/say-hello-to-buttmitzvah-londons-first-queer-jewish-night-101916.

Tohill, Mimi K. "Buttmitzvah Is a Queer Jewish Club Night Unlike Any Other." *Hey Alma*, October 30, 2019. Accessed September 1, 2020. www.heyalma.com/buttmitzvah-is-a-queer-jewish-club-night-unlike-any-other/.

Tower Hamlets Council. *Ethnicity in Tower Hamlets: Analysis of 2011 Census Data*. London: Tower Hamlets Council, 2013. Accessed December 1, 2020. www.towerhamlets.gov.uk/Documents/Borough_statistics/Ward_profiles/Census-2011/RB-Census2011-Ethnicity-2013-01.pdf.

——. *Religion in Tower Hamlets: 2011 Census Update*. London: Tower Hamlets Council, 2015. Accessed December 1, 2020. www.towerhamlets.gov.uk/Documents/Borough_statistics/Ward_profiles/Census-2011/2015-04-21-Faith-key-facts-Revised-data.pdf.

Turner, Victor W. *The Forest of Symbols: Aspects of Ndembu Ritual*. Ithaca, NY: Cornell University Press, [1967] 1970.

——. *From Ritual to Theatre: The Human Seriousness of Play*. New York: PAJ Publications, 1982.

——. *The Ritual Process: Structure and Anti-Structure*. London: Aldine-Transaction, [1969] 2008.

Vadakkiniyil, Dinesan. "Mahishi's Rage: Communitas and Protest at Sabarimala, Kerala." *Anthropology Today* 35, no. 5 (2019): 16–20.

Van Gennep, Arnold. *The Rites of Passage: A Classic Study of Cultural Celebrations*. Translated by Monika B. Vizedom and Gabrielle L. Caffee. Chicago: Chicago University Press, [1909] 1960.

Watt, Paul. "'It's Not for Us': Regeneration, the 2012 Olympics and the Gentrification of East London." *City: Analysis of Urban Change, Theory, Action* 17, no. 1 (2013): 99–118. https://doi.org/10.1080/13604813.2012.754190.

Wigley, Edward. "The Sunday Morning Journey to Church Considered as a Form of 'Micro-Pilgrimage.'" *Social and Cultural Geography* 17, no. 5 (2016): 694–713. https://doi.org/10.1080/14649365.2016.1139168.

7

Eid Parties, Iftar Dinners, and Pride Parades

Navigating Queer Muslim Identity through Community

Elizabeth Johnstone

Introduction

This chapter explores queer Muslim identity in the United Kingdom by examining how a variety of individuals and grassroots organizations navigate queer and religious identities that are often depicted as conflictual. First, this chapter considers the processes and consequences of an oppositional understanding of queerness and Islam. Then, it presents a range of strategies employed by queer Muslims to navigate the mutually exclusive way their identities are often represented. Finally, it investigates the role of support groups and networks that are specifically targeted toward queer Muslims. I argue that targeted support groups and networks can simultaneously act as ethnoreligious spaces and queer spaces, giving them the ability to create new forms of queer Muslim citizenship within the spaces they occupy and, thus, improving the psychological well-being of queer Muslims.

Queer Muslims are doubly marginalized. Muslims and those racialized as Muslim have faced increasing levels of anti-Muslim racism in North America and Europe since September 11, 2001. This is reflected in the transnational far right's string of victories in recent years.[1] A racialized Muslim, immigrant *other* has been central to the justification of extremist positions, such as Donald Trump's and Geert Wilders's proposed "Muslim bans" and Marine Le Pen's proposed moratorium on both illegal and legal immigration. Racist, anti-Muslim, anti-immigrant discourses and policies have also been mainstreamed beyond the far right. This increasingly hostile climate impacts the everyday lives of visible minorities across the "West," with reported race- and faith-based hate crimes increasing by 23 percent across the United Kingdom in the eleven months following the EU referendum.[2]

In addition to these obstacles, queer Muslims must often navigate marginalization and rejection from other members of their ethnoreligious social groups. An analysis of the British National Survey of Sexual Attitudes and Lifestyles found that 58 percent of Black and South Asian respondents believed that same-sex relationships were "always wrong," while 12 percent of white participants agreed.[3] Religiosity also predicted acceptance of homosexuality: 60 percent of those who attended religious services weekly responded that same-sex relationships were "always wrong," compared with only 11 percent of those who did not identify as religious.[4]

While legal obstacles still exist for queer people in the United Kingdom, major legislative wins have been achieved within the last several decades, and much of the focus has shifted to issues such as economic equality and social acceptance.[5] However, much like anti-Muslim racism, discriminatory attitudes and behavior on the basis of sexual orientation and gender identity (SOGI) can manifest in violence. A study conducted in the United Kingdom found that, over the twelve months prior to being surveyed, 16 percent of lesbians, gays, and bisexuals and 41 percent of transgender people had experienced a SOGI-based hate crime.[6]

Those with intersecting queer and Muslim identities may experience exclusion nationally and locally, from the media and in the family, resulting in a multitiered rejection and leading to isolation. Qualitative studies on queer Muslim identity in the United States and Canada, France, and the United Kingdom have focused on issues and concepts such as interpretations of Islam, universal citizenship, performativity, internal processes of reconciliation, and the "coming out" experience.[7] A particularly relevant example is Jaspal and Cinnirella's qualitative sociopsychological work on young British Muslim gay men of Pakistani backgrounds.[8] The researchers examined the effect of gay affirmative social contexts and relations with other gay men on identity integration—the belief that one's identities are compatible. They noted the potential benefits, explaining:

> [Gay affirmative social contexts] may allow individuals temporary social and psychological shielding from negative social representations of homosexuality, which are prevalent in their heteronormative ethnoreligious contexts. Exposure to positive representations disseminated in these contexts is likely to benefit self-esteem.[9]

Despite this potential benefit, Jaspal and Cinnirella note that potential anti-Muslim prejudice within such contexts may position gay Muslims as "ingroup black sheep," undermining attempts to seek belonging. Discrimination and *othering* within gay affirmative social contexts can extend beyond religious affiliation and into ethnicity and color. Minwalla et al. note, "As one integrates a gay identity, color dynamics and the whiteness of gay culture can become an issue of concern."[10] In this vein, Jaspal and Cinnirella conclude that psychological well-being among their cohort might be improved through a change in social representations of homosexuality in ethnoreligious spaces and of ethnic/religious minorities in gay/queer spaces. This chapter explores alternative solutions that are available to queer Muslims in the absence of such representational shifts in dominant ethnoreligious spaces and queer spaces. Accordingly, this chapter argues that social spaces that simultaneously affirm queer, religious, and ethnic identities are the most beneficial to queer Muslims in the United Kingdom.

Methodology and Participants

I conducted my research over five months, from late May through mid-September 2018. While I was primarily based in London, I held interviews with individuals in different cities across the United Kingdom and participated in an event in Brighton and Hove.

I collected my data, in part, through participant observation. I did an online search for relevant support groups, sent out an email to three, and received a response from one within a few days. I heard back from a second group about a month later. The first group to respond is called Hidayah, which means "guidance" in Arabic. On its website, Hidayah is described as "a secular organization, however its projects and activities are developed specifically for the needs of LGBTQI+ Muslims."[11] Their mission is "to provide support and welfare for LGBTQI+ Muslims and promote social justice and education about the Muslim LGBTQI+ community to counter discrimination, prejudice and injustice."[12] Since one of Hidayah's core aims is to bring visibility and awareness to the existence of queer Muslims and the struggles they face, the board was open to meeting and working with me.

I first met Hidayah members at their Ramadan Shoebox Appeal, for which we prepared and boxed food for homeless people. Following this event, the Hidayah board asked me to join them for an Iftar gathering and invited me to march with them at Pride in London. I later attended two of their monthly "Stories Events" and marched with members of Hidayah and several other British support and activist groups in Brighton and Hove Pride. As I became more involved with Hidayah, I was added to their members' WhatsApp group. A Hidayah member also invited me to join a Kik group she manages for queer Muslims. While these online networks are not among my primary objects of analysis, they were essential in forging deeper connections with other members and understanding group dynamics.

I conducted interviews with ten individuals who identify as queer and Muslim. I structured my interviews around two primary goals. First, I sought to get a broad image of the lived, individual, subjective experiences of queer Muslims in the United Kingdom. Second, I aimed to understand how the existence of queer Muslim communities might affect these experiences.

My participants' ages ranged from nineteen to forty. While the majority of them were from London, I also interviewed individuals from Newcastle, Glasgow, and Manchester and an asylum seeker from Bangladesh. Most of my participants were second-generation immigrants and had navigated British Pakistani or British Bangladeshi identities since childhood. One interviewee, Adam, had converted to Islam as an adult and identified as white. When it comes to sexual and gender identity, table 1 displays the terminology participants used to describe themselves. While all of my participants identified as Muslim, three of them were not practicing and were skeptical of the religion. Those three separately explained to me that they continue to identify as Muslim for cultural reasons and see it as part of their ethnic identity. The rest of my participants identified as Shia or Sunni, besides Adam and Joy, who did not identify with a particular sect.

Table 1. List of Anonymized Research Participants, along with Relevant Background Information

Name	Sexual Identity	Gender Identity	Religious Identity
Zara	"Part-time lesbian"	Transgender; bigender[13]	Shia Muslim
Joy	Bisexual	Cis woman	Muslim
Participant #3[14]	Gay	Cis man	Nonreligious
Abir	Gay	Cis man	Sunni Muslim
Rafiq	Gay	Cis man	Shia Muslim
Asmara	Bisexual	Genderqueer; transgender woman	Spiritual[15]
Khaled	Gay	Cis man	Sunni Muslim
Sadiya	Lesbian	Cis woman	Sunni Muslim
Adam	Bisexual	Cis man	Muslim
Rose	Queer	Cis woman	Nonreligious

"Good" Queer Muslim Citizenship

Sexual citizenship, or intimate citizenship, *queers* citizenship studies. It looks at the relationship between queerness and the state, access to rights, and citizen responsibility and obligation. Smith theorizes that in order to maintain certain rights, "good homosexual" citizens are legally and socially obligated to confine themselves to the private sphere.[16] Richardson expands upon this idea, asking:

> When demands are centred upon *public* recognition of lesbian and gay relationships and identities, the question that arises is what are the sorts of obligations that are concomitant on the recognition of such rights? Who or what, in this political context, will be representative of responsible/good and irresponsible/bad lesbian citizenship?[17]

In this section, I explore what "good" queer Muslim citizenship looks like in the context of participants' families, larger ethnoreligious communities, and predominately white queer spaces. I discuss the ways in which participants navigate conditions of acceptance and potential consequences of coming out. Finally, I consider the mental health issues associated with a conflictual understanding of queerness and Muslimness.

Belonging and Family

To varying degrees, each of my interviewees admitted to believing that queerness and Muslimness were incompatible at some point in their lives. The most commonly reported sources of this feeling were family and larger ethnoreligious communities. Every participant besides Adam—the man who converted to Islam as an adult—mentioned that there were members of their family who viewed nonnormative sexual and gender identities negatively. This greatly affected relationships and the ways in which queerness was performed around family. One pattern that came up was a form of conditional tolerance that I began to call the *don't ask, don't tell* policy.

In 1994, the Clinton administration instituted the Don't Ask, Don't Tell (DADT) military policy. As one of the most overtly ironic pieces of legislation to date, this directive simultaneously prohibited the harassment of closeted LGB individuals in the military and outlawed openly LGB individuals from service.[18] Effectively, DADT both outlawed and legalized discrimination. The explicit message was that the true crime of having a nonnormative sexual identity was verbalizing it and acting upon it. In a similar spirit, three of my participants' families tolerated their queerness on the unwritten condition that it was not mentioned or expressed in front of them.

Joy explained that she had never officially come out to family. For her, this means that, although she had never verbally declared herself bisexual or spoken about her queerness with family, they may have had a clue due to past girlfriends they had met and Facebook posts they had seen. While Joy is queer, she married a cis man. The manifestation of her queerness at the time of our interview was able to fit well enough within the framework of her family's heteronormative expectations for it not to be a source of conflict, as long as it was not discussed.

Like Joy's situation, Sadiya and her family did not discuss her queerness. After she came out to them as a lesbian, they both decided to give each other space and stopped speaking. After some time apart, they reunited.

At the time of our interview, her family tolerated her identity. They knew her girlfriend and knew that she helped manage a queer Muslim support group. Sadiya was clear that her family avoids the topic of her queerness, but they "leave [her] alone regarding it."

Asmara also described a lack of dialogue around her queer identity within her family. Unlike Joy, Asmara had explicitly come out to her family as a transgender woman. When I asked about her parents' reaction, she explained:

> [My father] was trying to be sympathetic and supportive which is interesting because he normally blows his top and gets angry. So I was expecting that reaction, but it didn't happen. Instead, he went kind of straight to bargaining phase. Like, okay well, maybe you feel this way, but maybe you should just still do the right thing and try to suppress it. And [he tried to] you know convince me that I'm normal and all that stuff.

Asmara's father's initial sympathy and support were grounded in the belief that her transgender identity could be suppressed. She had inferred that her mother was close to accepting her, based on facial expressions during their interactions. However, she believed that her parents saw her as a gay man, as they continued to use he/him pronouns and her birth name to refer to her. A lack of communication and the linguistic erasure of Asmara's transness are some of the conditions upon which Asmara's relationship with her parents seemed to rely.

A pattern that came up while discussing family was the fear of creating a burden. Four of my participants brought up this issue, explaining that they did not want to cause "pain," "emotional pressure," "hurt feelings," or "stress." For some, this fear was linked to the fact that being queer meant they would not be able to fulfill expectations around marriage and children. One interviewee explained that the decision not to come out was rooted in respect for her family because she did not want to hurt them.

Rose's and Sadiya's concerns went beyond potential emotional distress, as they feared their families could be shunned or physically harmed. When I asked Rose about her decision not to come out to family, she said that doing so would feel "selfish." She explained:

> [I don't want] to put my family in danger or to have them ostracized and stuff. It's more about them than about me really. . . . I just want to protect them.

Sadiya felt the same responsibility. While she helps run a support group and is out to family, she is not as visible as other activists. She does not show her face in the media and withholds her last name during interviews. She admitted to worrying that a high profile as a lesbian activist might lead to vandalism of her family's home. Sadiya also echoed Rose's concern about ostracism. Recognizing that her family was also part of a marginalized community, Sadiya defended her decision to keep a low profile:

> I don't want them to be ostracized from a community. Just like I need the LGBT community and—you know—that's why my queer Muslim support network is there. They need the Bengali community. . . . It's their support group. And so who am I to say my support group is more important and everything that you've known for the last 30, 40, 50, 60 years has to now be broken because of me?

Rose's and Sadiya's fear of bringing harm to their families suggests that coming out to one's family and community—a rite of passage that legitimizes queerness in Western and predominately white queer communities—is not a realistic or even desirable goal among many of my participants. Participants demonstrated an acute awareness of the potential consequences of coming out and carefully chose the degree to which they did so, keeping in mind the well-being of themselves and their families.

Another theme that emerged with regard to family relationships and larger ethnoreligious communities was the fear of being ostracized and persecuted. Two participants told me they did not have the option of coming out to family, as they would be disowned. Four had been either verbally attacked or rejected by close friends after coming out. Asmara told me that she feared being "hunted down," explaining:

> It's not just a simple case of being cut off. You could be sort of hounded by people. I had this thought that you can't escape it.

Asmara worried that an "indoctrinated friend of a friend of a friend" might hear about her and try to do her harm. While, fortunately, she had not experienced such an attack at the time of our interview, her fear was well founded.

Abir, an asylum seeker from Bangladesh, survived persecution. He told me that he had undergone teasing, "corrective measurements," and torture in Bangladesh for being gay. After convincing his family that he was no longer gay, Abir came to the United Kingdom to study. During that time, he became more confident in his sexual identity and told his family that he was, in fact, still gay. At this point, his family and his entire community in Bangladesh ostracized him. While Abir continues to experience verbal abuse in the United Kingdom from members of his local mosque, he explained that the situation waiting for him back home is "life-threatening."

Fitting In with the Queer Community

Most participants had spent time in queer spaces that were not targeted toward ethnic or religious minorities. These included online support forums, HIV charities, student groups, "meetup" groups, activist groups, friend groups, and nightclubs. While participants reported finding acceptance in these spaces sometimes, they often found themselves negotiating their Muslimness and dealing with *othering*.

Zara found a sense of belonging in several online transgender support forums, but she felt unable to speak about religion openly. A forum she helped manage had a rule against political or religious posts. Even so, Zara decided to share an informational post, which explained that some religious groups are accepting of transgender identities. She was met with backlash from group members:

> A bunch of people just decided to chime in about how religion is all nonsense. And you know I . . . told them that I didn't post those things so they had a right to come and attack my religion, or every religion. . . . So yeah there was some intolerance there.

Zara believed that the responses she received were rooted in the group's "pro-atheist" stance, rather than anti-Muslim bigotry, in particular.

188 Elizabeth Johnstone

Nevertheless, the message was that Zara's religiosity was not welcome in the group and that she would have to keep that part of herself quiet going forward.

Participant #3, who is of South Asian descent, had experienced racial fetishization in predominately white queer spaces. He recalled that at an LGBT event, an attendee asked to take a picture of him, declaring that they had never met a brown gay person before. He had also been asked to march with organizations at Pride to show that they were diverse. Post-colonial theorists explain that the concept of fetishism, which refers to an idolization of the *other*, fits within colonial discourse, as it relies on notions of essential difference between race categories.[19] Thus, the events outlined by participant #3 position him as a novelty and an outsider to the queer community. He is reduced to his ethnicity and becomes a prop for photographs.

Adam's perspective allowed him to have a unique insight into the hate directed toward Muslims in the queer community. Born into a Christian family, Adam grew up in a predominately white town in North East England. He became very active in the queer community as an adult, working and volunteering for several HIV charities and queer rights activist groups. Adam had established deep roots in North East England's queer communities when he decided to convert to Islam following the loss of a friend to HIV. He explained that telling his family and friends he was Muslim was "like coming out a second time." To his surprise, his family was accepting of his new identity. His partner even suggested throwing an Eid party. However, when Adam announced this change on social media, he received some backlash from acquaintances within the queer community:

> I had one guy tell me, "[You]'ve joined an oppressive religion that kills gays. I can't believe you're a part of that. You're a hypocrite after all these years of LGBT campaigning and work. I can't believe that you'd affiliate yourself with a disgusting religion of psychopaths."

Adam's recollection of his social media friend's comment fits within a broader *homonationalist* narrative. Puar's *Terrorist Assemblages* (2007) proposes the concept of *homonationalism*, wherein Western nationalist discourses intentionally link the acceptance and promotion of queer rights to the national imaginary. This strategy may be used to brand non-Western countries as intolerant and "backward" in order to justify interventionism and racist or anti-Muslim domestic policy. According to this social media comment, Adam had betrayed his community, as Islam was an existential threat to the queer cause.

Mental Health Consequences

None of my planned interview questions were directly related to mental health. However, this issue came up in most of my interviews, as the majority of my participants had dealt with mental health problems. They reported that at some point in their lives they had felt "stressed," "tense," "scared," "unhappy," "guilty," "conflicted," "confused," "alone," "on edge," and "abnormal" as a result of their identities. Several had experienced "self-hatred" and a lack of confidence. Among other issues, these feelings were attributed to a lack of understanding about their sexual feelings and to the beliefs that they were displeasing Allah for being queer, that they would be disowned or persecuted, that they were alone in their identities, and that they would not be able to fulfill societal expectations, like heterosexual marriage.

Five participants said they had dealt with depression related to their identities, and two others described depressive symptoms, such as isolation, guilty feelings, a lack of confidence, and a negative self-image. Three interviewees told me they had experienced suicidal ideation, two had self-harmed, and one had survived a suicide attempt. One individual described symptoms of alcohol abuse, including alcohol-related injuries and hospitalization. Three participants explained that they were seeing a counselor to help them with issues related to identity. It is important to note that, as I did not ask directly about mental health, it is possible that more of my participants dealt with these problems. It is also worth mentioning that those who join support groups may seek them out in attempts to resolve psychological issues. In this respect, my sample is potentially biased to show more mental health problems than if I had recruited participants in a different way.

Those who were out and still in contact with family—besides Adam—were tolerated on the condition that their queerness was not displayed or discussed in their presence, to varying degrees. All others—besides Abir—were not out to family due to fears of causing them emotional or physical

190   Elizabeth Johnstone

hurt or due to fears of being shunned or persecuted. Seven participants reported living a sort of "double life," wherein they acted one way when they were with family or in Muslim contexts and acted an entirely different way when they were in nontargeted queer spaces. The notion of sexual citizenship is key here. These findings support Smith's analysis that "good" queer citizens must keep aspects of their life private in order to maintain certain rights.[20] To varying degrees, in the examples I have laid out, "good" queer Muslims in the United Kingdom must confine their queerness to the private in Muslim spaces and their Muslimness to the private in queer spaces, perpetuating the notion that one cannot be both openly queer and openly Muslim.

Dealing with Feelings of Identity Conflict

This section looks at strategies that participants used to deal with feelings of identity conflict—the belief that one's identities are incompatible. I present two broad approaches that emerged: (1) the rejection or suppression of elements of either their Muslim or queer identity and (2) the attempted reconciliation of identities. These two approaches should not be seen as neat categories with distinct boundaries. Indeed, many participants describe using strategies that fall within these two broad categories at some point in their lives, sometimes at the same time.

Distancing Oneself from Religion or Queerness
Four of my interviewees either had rejected religion in the past or were unsure about the existence of God at the time of our interview. All of them continued to identify as Muslim for cultural reasons. Participant #3 explained that holding onto this identity was a way of showing solidarity with a community that had been racialized and marginalized, saying he "would never deny [his] ethnic heritage."

Asmara told me she had distanced herself from religion for a period of time. She explained that queer Muslims sometimes go through a phase in reaction to conservative Islam, thinking that "you're going to kick me out, so I'll kick you out first." Abir had gone through a similar phase. At the time of our interview, he reported feeling hopeful that he could regain his faith by seeking out inclusive interpretations of Islam. He could fit himself into the Islam he was in the process of discovering without feeling guilty about being gay. However, his queer identity was nonnegotiable. He maintained, "If I [have] the wrong interpretation, I can't be faithful to my religion at all." These examples indicate that distancing oneself from religion can act as a method of resolving feelings of identity conflict. In my sample, participants distanced themselves from religion when they were not able to conceive of an Islam that would accept them. Unable to reconcile Islam and queerness, they left Islam.

Many participants told me they had gone through a denial stage regarding their queerness, during which they tried to convince themselves they were straight or cisgender. Participant #3 tried to convince himself he was bisexual, so he could imagine eventually marrying a woman to fulfill societal expectations. Sadiya confessed that if she had not become involved in support groups, she would probably have married a man, despite being lesbian. Marriages of convenience, or MOCs, were a topic of discussion across the queer Muslim online support groups I observed. MOCs, in this context, referred to the practice of a gay man marrying a lesbian woman. They would live together and sometimes have children together in order to placate family and fit in better with society. There typically would be some sort of understanding between the married man and woman that they were essentially just married friends and could have other romantic or sexual partners of the same sex.

While none of my interviewees had gone through with MOCs, Khaled's story comes close. Khaled married a woman despite his friends' protestations and despite being gay. This marriage was different from a MOC because his wife was not aware of his sexual identity. After some time into the marriage, Khaled realized that the situation was unsustainable, and they divorced. Like participant #3, Asmara, and Abir, Khaled was unable to reconcile his queer identity with his interpretation of Islam. But rather than reject his faith, he attempted to suppress his sexual identity—the effects of which were harmful to both him and his wife.

Reconciling Identities

A second broad strategy that participants employed to deal with feelings of identity conflict was attempting to reconcile Islam and queerness. If successful, this strategy would allow both religious belief and queer identity to coexist peacefully.

192   Elizabeth Johnstone

A theme I observed across several interviews was a stress on the importance of recognizing the effects of history, politics, economics, and culture on the privileging of certain interpretations of Islam. Asmara told me that learning about the effects of Western colonization on the acceptance of queer people in majority Muslim countries helped her begin to reconcile her identities. Zara echoed the belief that mainstream interpretations of religion are popular not necessarily for their inherent superiority but as a result of geopolitics. She brought up the effects of the spread of Salafism by Gulf states, explaining that "all of the religious texts that are funded out of Saudi Arabia—which come to this country—are all very hardcore right-wing Salafi texts." Finally, Joy asserted that while female Imams are extremely rare and tend to be looked down upon, Muslim women have been leading prayers in parts of China for hundreds of years. She attributed the lack of awareness of this practice to "institutionalized racism within Muslim communities."

A related method of accepting one's queer identity without sacrificing religiosity was the acknowledgment of the long-standing existence and tolerance of queer people in certain Muslim contexts. Adam and Zara told me about accounts in which Prophet Muhammad had interacted with transgender people and in which they guarded his grave after his death. Zara also referenced the centuries-old existence of Hijras in South Asia and the recognition of transgender rights in Iran and Pakistan.

Many participants reported seeking out or creating their own inclusive interpretations of Islam, alternative to mainstream belief. Zara made sense of her queerness from an Islamic perspective, telling me that one of the ninety-nine names of Allah in Islam is "Just." She asserted that Allah created her as a transgender person. She could not be punished for it, as it would not be just. In a similar fashion, Joy described her interpretation of a hadith in which Prophet Muhammad sends a queer person into exile:

> So, I'm thinking that prophet being a compassionate man, wary of social situations and circles, had this person exiled for their own safety, rather than actually hating this person out of religion. . . . He was only doing what was socially acceptable at that time. He couldn't actually tell this whole community, "It's perfectly okay to be queer," because you can't change an entire culture overnight.

According to Joy's reading, she might have been exiled out of "compassion" and for her own protection had she lived during the time of this story. In this way, Joy's admiration for Prophet Muhammad did not conflict with her bisexuality. Her Islam did not simply tolerate her but embraced and reaffirmed her queerness. She explained that her queer identity pushed her to look deeper into religious texts and to question doctrine. She believed that her examinations and subsequent reinterpretations of religious texts strengthened her faith.

Some interviewees looked to others, seeking out inclusive interpretations of Islam from experts. Abir's respect for Imams as figures of authority and knowledge brought him to contact one of the five openly gay Imams in the world:

> As I speak with Imam Asif,[21] he's just giving me a lot of good advice and a lot of good reference that I can still bring my faith back in Islam and I can still be a Muslim and be gay.

Abir trusted that Imam Asif's inclusive interpretation of Islamic texts was legitimate due to his status as a religious leader. As Abir did not possess this level of authority himself, this relationship was vital to his ability to reconcile religious belief and being gay.

While Abir held Imams in high regard, Adam's respect for academics led him to seek out the work of Scott Kugle. Kugle's book *Homosexuality in Islam* (2010) looks critically at the parts of the Quran and hadith that are often used to justify the condemnation of queer people. He argues that Islamic scripture can be understood as not only tolerant but also accepting of nonnormative sexual and gender identities. Adam explained that Kugle's work gave him a "liberal" interpretation of Islam:

> [His books] really opened my eyes and I thought *I can do this*. I can comfortably be myself in this religion. I can now separate what I see as the cultural views of Islam versus the religious ones.

This process was transformative to Adam's understanding of his place within Islam. As an academic himself, he respected Kugle as a researcher. Adam viewed Kugle as an expert in his field, lending legitimacy to his inclusive interpretation.

194   Elizabeth Johnstone

Targeted Support Groups and Networks

Regaining a Sense of Belonging

Earlier in this chapter, I mentioned that family, larger ethnoreligious spaces, and predominately white queer spaces were some of the main external sources of the feeling that Islam and queerness were incompatible. Support groups targeted specifically toward queer Muslims, like Hidayah, provide a counternarrative, accepting members' queer and Muslim identities simultaneously. Joy explained her motivation in joining support groups:

> I don't feel that I have to separate or choose between religion and sexuality. One thing I have noticed is within the queer community there's often this thing where you have to choose between sexual orientation and religion and it's the same with certain Muslim circles.

Indeed, the groups I studied provided physical and virtual spaces in which queer Muslims did not have to compartmentalize identities and were relatively free from judgment. Hidayah is a grassroots organization that was founded and run by queer Muslims themselves. In this way, it simultaneously offers a queer space that embraces members' Muslimness and ethnic identities and an ethnoreligious space that embraces members' queerness. In this sense, Hidayah has the authority to counteract exclusivist narratives.

A related benefit my participants commonly reported was the realization that they were not alone in their identities. Six interviewees believed that meeting other queer Muslims through support groups was pivotal to their self-acceptance, with two describing the friendships they had made as "family." Support groups decreased feelings of isolation. Sadiya described this change:

> I met others that were like me and that was an eye-opener to know that, actually, I'm not potentially the only gay Muslim in the world. That for me was my saving grace.

Indeed, meeting other queer Muslims seemed to result in a more positive self-image and improved mental health in my sample. Rafiq told me that he met queer Muslim role models through Hidayah when none existed in the media. By allowing members to be unapologetically open about their queer and Muslim identities simultaneously, Hidayah changed what it meant to be a "good" queer Muslim in the spaces they provided.

I came to realize that the support groups I observed often acted as a psychological service. When I asked Sadiya about her motivations in creating Hidayah, she replied:

> If we managed to just help one person, we'd hit our aim as an organization—in helping one person not want to kill themselves—to not want to commit suicide and stuff like that, you know?

This aim was reflected in monthly gatherings called "Stories Events." These events were open to Hidayah members and revolved around a different theme each month. I attended two of these events, the themes of which were "my community" and "love and respect." For both of these gatherings, members met up in a public place, such as a coffee shop, and discussed the experiences and challenges they faced, often offering wisdom and support to those struggling. The attendees at the Stories Events I observed ranged in their openness. Some of them spoke honestly about feelings around past relationships, rejection from family, and the ability to fit in at the workplace. Other members listened and did not contribute verbally to the group conversations. Sadiya acknowledged their reservations, explaining, "Just to be present can be a big step." After each Stories Event, attendees would go out for dinner together. This offered them the opportunity to forge friendships and strengthen bonds in a more casual setting.

The online forums I joined also acted as a mental health resource. They provided members with virtual networks of people with shared experiences, reachable at all hours of the day. Conversations mostly consisted of banter, event announcements, and discussions about news, movies, and music. Rose described how she felt about a WhatsApp group she had joined:

> Everyone's really welcoming on there. It's like a big family, really. And they're all really funny. If somebody's sad, they'll cheer them up. If somebody's lonely, there's always somebody online so you don't have to feel very lonely for long because somebody will pick up and message. It's quite nice to feel connected in that way.

196 Elizabeth Johnstone

As Rose suggested, these online groups offered light-hearted fun as well as support for those feeling sad or depressed. This was similar to Zara's vision when she created a queer Muslim support Kik group. She explained:

> The Kik group came out of a need that wasn't really being addressed in forums that I was a part of, where people were popping up and really had almost suicidal tendencies and suicidal thoughts because they didn't have anyone to really talk to.

I observed that members of online support networks could listen to and help each other effectively, as they understood the specific complexity of queer Muslim identity—a component that existing mental health services may lack.

Rose acknowledged that Hidayah helped her regain a connection to her "culture" that she had lost. She explained that it was "more of a safe link to [her] culture than [her] family." She also felt that Hidayah helped her navigate her religious identity, observing:

> Since I've been to the Hidayah meetings, I feel a bit more at peace with [Islam]. I feel like I'm more included in the umbrella of being Muslim. It hasn't rejected me completely. There are many people there. They are really happy and very devout and they have a lot of faith. It gives me a bit of hope that maybe I could get the faith back or I could be more comfortable with it in the future.

Meeting queer people who embraced Islam allowed Rose to begin to imagine an Islam that might accept her. At the same time, she did not feel pressured to perform religiosity at Hidayah events. She could regain her "cultural" identity and explore her faith relatively freely in these spaces.

Self-Representation

In addition to the services Hidayah offers internally, it also serves as a platform for queer Muslims to represent themselves publicly. Individuals like Sadiya fear that if their names and faces are attached to their activist voices, they or their families might face violence or shunning. Nevertheless, Hidayah's public platform provides the opportunity for these voices to represent queer Muslims relatively anonymously. Decisions around logos, website branding, and signage at Pride events position Hidayah and queer Muslims within the broader public.

While I was marching with Hidayah's section at Pride in London, a member of the board offered me a T-shirt and asked me to wear it during the event. The shirt was white with the organization's logo—a large cartoon image of a mosque covered in rainbows—printed in the center (see image below). Under the mosque were the words "Hidayah Gender, Sexuality & Islam." Most members wore these shirts while marching. The logo covered our section, prominent on banners and posters as well. At the front of our section, a member of Hidayah spun around and waved at onlookers. She was dressed in drag and wore an ornate blue and gold lehenga—a traditional South Asian gown. These decisions present Hidayah as unapologetically queer and unapologetically Muslim, providing a positive image of itself to both the public and their own members, for some of whom living confidently and openly is still aspirational. Moreover, the integration of queer symbolism (the rainbows and the drag queen) and Islamic and South Asian symbolism (the mosque and the lehenga) suggests that queerness is compatible with Muslimness and South Asianness, challenging Islamist, Huntingtonian, and homonationalist narratives of an unavoidable civilizational "clash" between Islam and the East and supposed Western values. The notion of hybridity is particularly relevant to this dimension of Hidayah. *Hybridity* was theorized in the 1990s by scholars such as Paul Gilroy, Homi Bhabha, Robert Young, and Stuart Hall.[22] Recognizing that representation and cultural production are both inherently expressive and constitutive, hybridity asserts the value in instances of self-representation of historically colonized people. Bhabha explains that in the hybrid moment

> the transformational value of change lies in the re-articulation, or translation, of elements that are *neither the One . . . nor the Other . . . but something else besides* which contests the terms and territories of both.[23]

These new transcultural forms challenge hegemony and colonial discourses by destabilizing notions of fixed cultural boundaries. Hidayah and other similar support groups may be read as hybrid spaces that produce representations of British (primarily South Asian) Muslims on their websites and newsletters and during events involving the public. With the

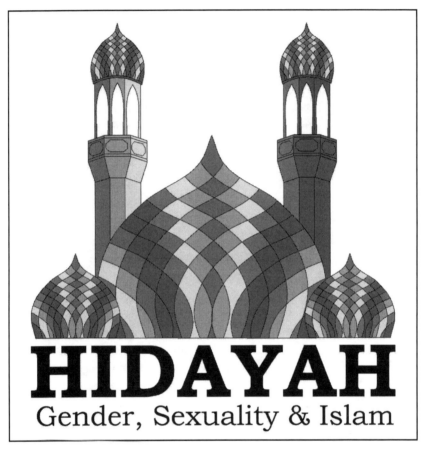

Source: Hidayah, "What Is Hidayah."

history of British colonization of South Asia and majority Muslim countries in mind, the examples laid out here may be read as instances of queer Muslim Asian subalternity coming into self-representation.

Conclusion

This chapter examined the construction of queer Muslim identities in the United Kingdom, with a focus on the role of community. I began by looking at queer Muslim citizenship. I found that participants' ethnoreligious communities played a substantial role in feelings of identity conflict and rejection. Some also had experienced racism and religious intolerance in nontargeted, predominately white queer spaces. With Smith's "good homosexual" citizen in mind, I discussed the conditions upon which the tolerance of queer Muslims relies.[24] I theorized that the "good" queer Muslim is obligated to keep their queerness private in their ethnoreligious spaces and their Muslimness private in queer spaces in order to maintain their status as a member of these groups. Then, I explored the strategies that participants employed to attempt to resolve feelings of identity conflict. I proposed two broad categories that may overlap and change over time: (1) attempts to reject or suppress elements of one's identity and (2) attempts to reconcile identities. Finally, I examined the role of queer Muslim support groups and networks within the context of my participants' experiences. I found that these spaces could take on the role of a psychological service, noting that improving members' mental health was a motivation of organizers. I also looked at Hidayah's self-representation at Pride through a postcolonial lens, reading it as a hybrid moment that challenged notions of mutual exclusivity between Muslimness/Asianness and queerness.

In the beginning of this chapter, I discussed Jaspal and Cinnirella's conclusion that well-being may be improved by more positive representations of queerness in ethnoreligious spaces and of ethnic/religious minorities in queer spaces.[25] I expressed skepticism in the feasibility of changing hegemonic prejudice in these contexts within a timeframe that would benefit my participants. The final section of this chapter responded to this issue by identifying Hidayah as both an ethnoreligious space and a queer space, citing its grassroots nature and its management by queer Muslims themselves. While Hidayah does, indeed, challenge prejudice in wider queer and ethnoreligious spaces through self-representation, it also offers an alternative inclusive space. Because Hidayah is both queer and Muslim from its members to its chair, it has the authority to create new conditions for "good" queer Muslim citizenship in the spaces it provides.

Notes

1 In 2016, the United Kingdom voted to leave the EU and Donald Trump was elected president of the United States. Shortly thereafter, the Front

National's Marine Le Pen was voted into the *second tour* of France's 2017 presidential election and Geert Wilders's Partij voor de Vrijheid reached second place in the Netherlands's 2017 general election. Most recently, two parties linked to Nazism, Freiheitliche Partei Österreichs and Alternative für Deutschland, have made major gains in Austria and Germany, respectively.

2 Bulman, "Brexit Vote Sees Highest Spike in Religious and Racial Hate Crimes Ever Recorded." Bulman, from *The Independent*, reported this statistic, which was determined based on data obtained from eleven of the thirty-two police forces in England and Wales through Freedom of Information requests.

3 Watt and Elliot, "Continuity and Change in Sexual Attitudes."

4 Watt and Elliot, "Continuity and Change in Sexual Attitudes."

5 Legal victories include marriage and adoption rights for same-sex couples, the right to serve openly in the military, and the possibility of changing one's legal gender. Discrimination protections have also been put in place requiring equal treatment in employment and public and private services, regardless of sexual orientation, gender, or transgender status. See UK Parliament, *Equality Act 2010*.

6 Stonewall, "LGBT in Britain."

7 See, e.g., Minwalla et al., "Identity Experience among Progressive Gay Muslims in North America"; Provencher, "Coming Out *à l'oriental*"; Provencher, "Ludovic-Mohamed Zahed's Performance of Universal French Citizenship and Good Muslim Brotherhood"; Yip, "Queering Religious Texts"; Jaspal and Cinnirella, "Coping with Potentially Incompatible Identities"; Jaspal and Cinnirella, "Identity Processes, Threat, and Interpersonal Relations"; Jaspal and Siraj, "Perceptions of 'Coming Out' among British Muslim Gay Men"; and Jaspal, "Non-Heterosexual British Asian Men."

8 Jaspal and Cinnirella, "Identity Processes, Threat, and Interpersonal Relations."

9 Jaspal and Cinnirella, "Identity Processes, Threat, and Interpersonal Relations," 220.

10 Minwalla et al., "Identity Experience among Progressive Gay Muslims in North America," 121.

11 Hidayah, "What Is Hidayah."

12 Hidayah, "What Is Hidayah."

13 Zara is part of the transgender community. More specifically, she is bigender. This means that she is comfortable in both male and female gender roles. She uses she/her and he/him pronouns and sometimes

presents as a man, sometimes as a woman. At the request of Zara, I use she/her pronouns when referring to her throughout this chapter.

14 Participant #3 requested not to have a pseudonym.

15 Asmara does not adhere to any particular religion or sect. She describes herself as spiritual and interested in Sufi Islam and Eastern religions.

16 Smith, *New Right Discourse on Race and Sexuality*.

17 Richardson, "Claiming Citizenship?" 269; emphasis in original.

18 Department of Defense, *DoD Directive 1304.26*.

19 Bhabha, "The Other Question . . ."

20 Smith, *New Right Discourse on Race and Sexuality*.

21 Name changed to maintain anonymity.

22 See Gilroy, *The Black Atlantic*; Bhabha, *The Location of Culture*; Young, *Colonial Desire*; and Hall, "New Ethnicities."

23 Bhabha, *The Location of Culture*, 41; emphasis in original.

24 Smith, *New Right Discourse on Race and Sexuality*.

25 Jaspal and Cinnirella, "Identity Processes, Threat, and Interpersonal Relations."

Works Cited

Bhabha, Homi. *The Location of Culture*. London: Routledge, 1994.

———. "The Other Question . . ." *Screen* 24, no. 6 (1983): 18–36.

Bulman, May. "Brexit Vote Sees Highest Spike in Religious and Racial Hate Crimes Ever Recorded." *The Independent*, July 10, 2017. Accessed March 29, 2021. www.independent.co.uk/news/uk/home-news/racist-hate-crimes -surge-record-high-after-brexit-vote-new-figures-reveal-a7829551.html.

Department of Defense. *Qualification Standards for Enlistment, Appointment, and Induction*. Washington, DC: DoD Directive 1304.26, March 4, 1994.

Gilroy, Paul. *The Black Atlantic: Modernity and Double Consciousness*. Cambridge, MA: Harvard University Press, 1993.

Hall, Stuart. "New Ethnicities." In *Stuart Hall: Critical Dialogues in Cultural Studies*, edited by David Morley and Kuan-Hsing Chen, 441–50. London: Routledge, 1996.

Hidayah. "What Is Hidayah." 2021. Accessed March 29, 2021. www.hidayahlgbt .com/about.

Jaspal, Rusi. "Non-heterosexual British Asian Men: Social Representations, Identity and Social Relations." In *International Encyclopedia of the Social and Behavioral Sciences*, 2nd ed., edited by James D. Wright, 861–66. Amsterdam: Elsevier, 2015.

Jaspal, Rusi, and Marco Cinnirella. "Coping with Potentially Incompatible Identities: Accounts of Religious, Ethnic, and Sexual Identities from British Pakistani Men Who Identify as Muslim and Gay." *British Journal of Social Psychology* 49, no. 4 (2010): 849–70.

———. "Identity Processes, Threat, and Interpersonal Relations: Accounts from British Muslim Gay Men." *Journal of Homosexuality* 59, no. 2 (2012): 215–40.

Jaspal, Rusi, and Asifa Siraj. "Perceptions of 'Coming Out' among British Muslim Gay Men." *Psychology and Sexuality* 2, no. 3 (2011): 183–97.

Kugle, Scott. *Homosexuality in Islam: Critical Reflection on Gay, Lesbian, and Transgender Muslims*. London: Oneworld Publications, 2010.

Minwalla, Omar, B. R. Simon Rosser, Jamie Feldman, and Christine Varga. "Identity Experience among Progressive Gay Muslims in North America: A Qualitative Study within Al-Fatiha." *Culture, Health, & Sexuality* 7, no. 2 (2006): 113–28.

Provencher, Denis M. "Coming Out *à l'oriental*: Maghrebi-French Performances of Gender, Sexuality, and Religion." *Journal of Homosexuality* 58, no. 6 (2011): 821–33.

———. "Ludovic-Mohamed Zahed's Performance of Universal French Citizenship and Good Muslim Brotherhood." *French Cultural Studies* 24, no. 3 (2013): 279–92.

Puar, Jasbir. *Terrorist Assemblages: Homonationalism in Queer Times*, Durham, NC: Duke University Press, 2007.

Richardson, Diane. "Claiming Citizenship? Sexuality, Citizenship and Lesbian/Feminist Theory." *Sexualities* 3, no. 2 (2000): 255–72.

Smith, Anna Marie. *New Right Discourse on Race and Sexuality*. Cambridge: Cambridge University Press, 1994.

Stonewall. "LGBT in Britain: Hate Crime and Discrimination." 2017. Accessed March 29, 2021. www.stonewall.org.uk/lgbt-britain-hate-crime-and -discrimination.

UK Parliament. *Equality Act 2010, c.15*. London: National Archives, 2010.

Watt, Laura, and Matt Elliot. "Continuity and Change in Sexual Attitudes: A Cross-Time Comparison of Tolerance Towards Non-traditional Relationships." *The Sociological Review* 65, no. 4 (2017): 832–49.

Yip, Andrew K. T. "Queering Religious Texts: An Exploration of British Non-heterosexual Christians' and Muslims' Strategy of Constructing Sexuality-Affirming Hermeneutics." *Sociology* 39, no. 1 (2005): 47–65.

Young, Robert J. C. *Colonial Desire: Hybridity in Theory, Culture and Race.* London: Routledge, 1995.

Afterword

Lessons in Historical Nominalism

David M. Halperin

The great diversity of the material contained in *Queer Jews, Queer Muslims* has prompted me to reflect a bit on the current intellectual politics of queer theory as well as on the play, or interplay, of identities.

It is now more than thirty years since "queer"—that old term of abuse and more recent activist epithet—was appropriated, redefined, and elaborated in order to suit the disciplinary needs of US academe as well as the changing worldwide demands of popular identity politics.

In the academic context, "queer" has now become a token of progressive political virtuousness so radical, and so far beyond any possible concrete or specific exemplification or instantiation, that there is almost nothing that can lay uncontested claim to it, nothing that is queer enough to qualify for the designation. Already by 2005, the contributors to a special issue of *Social Text* entitled "What's Queer about Queer Studies Now?" maintained that queerness certainly could not be reduced to anything so ordinary or banal as nonstandard varieties of sex and gender; some of those same contributors continued to promote, in a 2020 sequel to that issue, called "Left of Queer," their predecessors' notion of a "subjectless critique," predicated on a definition of queerness freed from all "fixed" reference to queer subjects—or, indeed, to any subjects or objects whatsoever.[1] That was also the argument of Maggie Nelson's celebrated memoir *The Argonauts*. According to Nelson, the last people who deserve to qualify as queer are gay men or various assorted sexual radicals.[2]

Outside the academy, by contrast, "queer" seems to mean hardly anything else *but* gay. "Queer" has largely turned into a synonym of gay, or a trendy version of gay, or a convenient global category comprising the alphabet soup of identities: LGBTQQIA+. We can judge the extent to which the word "gay" has been decommissioned by observing the recent journalistic accounts of the monkeypox epidemic, an epidemic that in Europe and the US almost entirely affected men who have sex with men. And yet, when the media, concerned understandably about stigmatizing gay men, dared at all to mention the specific demographic vectors of viral transmission, they tended to refer to the disease's spread among "members of the queer community" or "members of the LGBTQ community"—as if sexual encounters arise from community or as if lesbians were at particularly high risk of contracting monkeypox or as if there were any connection between queerness in general and the latest pandemic. Don't say gay: that seemed to be the watchword of the mainstream media. Queer, though, is fine. (The correct designation, of course, for the risk category was not an identitarian one but the forensic, epidemiological, purely descriptive one: men who have sex with men. It was used occasionally by the media, but it was too close to "gay" for comfort.)

It's much too late to do anything about the replacement of "gay" by "queer" or about the unthinking assimilation of queerness to gayness, and of course it's impossible as well as undesirable to police popular usage. But it may be worth pointing out that treating queer as equivalent to gay defeats the whole point of creating a new non-identitarian identity category called queer. The purpose, and the payoff, of talking about sex and gender deviance not in terms of gay versus straight but in terms of queer versus normal (those being the two sets of relevant oppositions) could be summed up by the observation—which I made thirty years ago—that there is nothing in particular to which queer necessarily refers. Queer is not the name of a specific kind of sexuality or gender or social status: it is, on the contrary, an identity without an essence, a marginal position, a departure from the norm, a deviation from a specific standard or convention.[3] Queer means something different from gay—or, at least, it once did. After all, there are some gay people who are not terribly queer. And there are some queer people who happen not to be gay. They are queer for other reasons or according to other criteria.

The fact that there is nothing to which queer necessarily refers turns out, as I also argued back when, to be both good and bad.[4] It is good because it frees us from dominant, reductive labels (gay, straight) that simply reconsolidate normative sexual and gender dichotomies and that are themselves the product of sexual racism. In other words, it is good because it enables us to disidentify from gayness, to refuse the label, without doing so homophobically. After all, no social identity is tolerable if it constitutes a life sentence, a final truth about who you are, the sum total of everything there is to say about you. The only kinds of identities we can bear to accept are those that allow for some leverage in relation to them, some possibility to suspend them or to resist them or to renegotiate them or to escape from them. (Even Matthew Richardson, for whom identity politics can be "affirming," remains eager to celebrate, in his contribution to this volume, "the anti-structural qualities of communitas.")

The shift from gay or lesbian to queer also makes possible strategic coalitions with social deviants of all kinds, with a large and varied group of social outcasts—those whom our society stigmatizes, demeans, and marginalizes not only on account of their sexual practices, their sexual desires, their gender practices, and their gender identities, but also on account of their bodies, their race, ethnicity, nationality, age, disability, religion, health, educational level, incarceration, drug use, homelessness, or immigration status—on account, in short, of their nonnormality or queerness. That is the very possibility that the editors of those special issues of *Social Text* seized on in order to free queerness from necessary reference to specific subjects and to enlarge its scope. So those are some of the good consequences of shifting from gay to queer.

At the same time, the queer label is bad precisely because—once again—there is nothing specific to which it necessarily refers, because queer makes no specific reference to sex or gender. It thus conduces, as the editors of those special issues of *Social Text* also illustrate, to the despecification of sexual and gender politics in the name of some broad celebration of marginality, transgressiveness, and never-to-be-achieved radicality. It licenses new expressions of homophobia and sexism, directed against women or gay people who do not measure up to the now unattainable standards of queerness. And it is the greatest favor queer people ever did for heterosexuals. Queer is now a game the whole family can play.

In US academe, training in queer theory has become an expected qualification. Which is to say that the queer theory everyone is now required to be versed in could not exactly be characterized as an insurgent intellectual movement: it has become a conventional academic discipline. Nothing could be more normal—that is, less queer—than this standardized queer theory.

In this context, it may be worth remembering how the politicized queer category came into being. Queer politics and queer identity emerged directly from the mobilization against HIV/AIDS in the 1980s, which required activists to defend everyone affected by the epidemic, especially those who suffered most from social discrimination and abjection, regardless of their sexualities, genders, or other identities. In fact, it is no accident that the retooled model of queerness we now are all familiar with makes sense only when it can be brought into relation with the vicissitudes of the HIV/AIDS pandemic.

Let us recall a few facts. AIDS has been, always and everywhere, a disease of poverty. All over the world, HIV infection has tracked inequality and social violence. It first appeared in the US among gay men, hemophiliacs, sex workers, Haitian immigrants, injecting drug users, and their infant children. As the pandemic progressed, it produced a kind of X-ray of structural inequality in society, as well as an X-ray of global inequality.[5] For women, one of the chief risk factors worldwide is heterosexual marriage.[6] The US prison population has been at exceptionally high risk for HIV infection. (The reluctance of the authorities to make condoms available to prisoners does not help.) Another example is provided by the distinguished epidemiologist Susan Buchbinder and her team of researchers in a 2005 article on risk factors for HIV infection: "On multivariate analysis," they write, "after controlling for specific sexual behaviors, the only demographic variable that remained significantly associated with HIV seroconversion was lack of private health insurance."[7] Lack of private health insurance, of course, is not itself a direct cause of HIV infection: it is not a transmission pathway for the virus. Rather, it serves here as a marker for certain social disadvantages: poverty, marginalization, unemployment or underemployment, youth, lack of access to benefits. Nearly ten years before the conference entitled "Queer Theory" at the University of California at Santa Cruz or the founding of Queer Nation, both of which took place, independently of each other, in the spring of 1990 and which launched the new discourses of queerness, HIV/AIDS had already created a highly diverse group of despised, marginalized, or disadvantaged people, branded with the stigma of sexual or social deviance, who were refused admission to the scene of social belonging in contemporary societies. They were, and they were felt to be, in that proper sense, queer.

That is where queer identity comes from. Being uninsured is not an identity. Or, if it is, it is an identity without an essence. If there was ever a queer identity without an essence, a non-identitarian identity, it is the identity of being affected in one way or another by the epidemic of HIV/AIDS.

And if "queer" names a non-identitarian identity, if it operates as a solvent of identity, that is because HIV cuts across so many identity categories as to dissolve them. Queer theorists routinely invoke "queer" as something radical—as defined so radically by its utter negativity that nothing can possibly qualify as queer. But what is queer about our lives is not that they are radical but that they are not organized by identity.

For a good illustration of this phenomenon, consider what Gayle Rubin has to say about the origins of the silicone dildo.

> About twenty years ago [Rubin was writing in 2003] there was a great dildo divide. In the 1970s, most of the dildos available in the United States were made of a particular type of relatively stiff rubber and were shaped like more or less anatomically correct penises (although they tended toward anatomically unrealistic sizes). These were sold mainly in seedy sex shops that catered mostly to a straight male clientele (or, less frequently, to gay men). The shops were thus rather intimidating and relatively inaccessible to many female customers. Moreover, the low status and marginal legality of such shops tend to make customers of all kinds feel ashamed. Shopping for dildos was thus part of the furtive and socially stigmatized world of sex shops and porn.
>
> All of this began to shift with the emergence of feminist, woman-oriented sex shops such as Good Vibrations in San Francisco and Eve's Garden in New York City. Both shops began to sell a limited supply of a new kind of dildo. These were made of silicone rubber, which had a softer feel than the older style of dildo yet sufficient stiffness to "perform" admirably. These silicone rubber dildos were also made in

210   David M. Halperin

many shapes; in addition to the realistically penile, many were available in more muted designs. These silicone rubber dildos quickly became the favorites among aficionados and standard equipment for lesbians who were interested in penetration.

What most of those who use these dildos do not realize is that the revolution of dildo design, production, and distribution began with a straight black male paraplegic. The silicone dildo was invented by a guy in a wheelchair who wanted to have a sexual relationship with his wife and who did not like the commercially available prosthetic penises. So he developed the silicone dildo and sold a few through Eve's Garden. Good Vibrations then brought the Scorpio dildo to the West Coast. When Susie Bright was managing Good Vibrations, she engaged in intensive discussions with the producer about dildo design; he made one to her specifications, which was called, in her honor, the Susie.

There are now several producers of these silicone dildos, and they come in a vast range of shapes, from dolphins to corncobs to goddesses to equipment that looks as if it belongs on the body of some kind of space alien. There is even a company called Divine Interventions that produces dildos for the blasphemous among us, including the Jackhammer Jesus, God's Rod, the Diving Nun, and the Baby Jesus butt plug. There is also the Buddha's Delight (for finding Nirvana) and the Moses (for parting the Pink Sea and getting to the Promised Land). But everyone who has ever used a silicone dildo—lesbians, bisexuals, women fucking their boyfriends—owes a great debt of gratitude to a straight black guy in a wheelchair who was trying to improve his marital sex life.

The story of the silicone dildo illustrates that much of what we assume without investigation can be wrong, that social life is infinitely complex, and that the social histories of sexual change are often full of surprising connections. This too should make us a little humble and cautious about consecrating any group as the specially anointed agents of change.[8]

Queer theorists have, or at least we ought to have, every motive for humility of the kind that Rubin recommends: we never know who our friends and allies are. Queerness is not about identity. But it is not subjectless either: the subjectivity of queer subjects counts for a lot. Not only does it flow from and contribute to the unique, specific experiences that are often formative for individuals, including the experience of rerouted sexual desire that motivated the inventiveness of the African American paraplegic cited by Rubin; such "lived experiences," as Shanon Shah argues in this volume, in a subtle exploration of the queer relations among Islamic and other Abrahamic theologies, also give rise to concrete, situated knowledges. Those knowledges, in turn, alter and refashion our perspectives: Shah contends, for example, that the resulting insights enrich "our understanding and appreciation of the sacred texts we cherish." As Shah goes on to argue, "My subjective position thus tells a story of how I have *received* as well as *produced* the different perspectives of scriptural exegesis and sexuality." Moreover, as Shah insists, the same could be said of all other theologians, conservative as well as progressive, whether or not they are conscious of their subjective position and whether or not they are willing to acknowledge it.

In sum, queerness is a solvent of identities precisely because it springs from unsystematic, happenstance personal histories and other accidents of social practice. That is why it is both annoying and frustrating to witness the way that unproblematized identities are driving us all mad, with everyone jostling to decry other people's privileges and to gain prestige or clout over others by leveraging their own supposedly radical identities, more radical than thou.

This identity preening is ultimately reactionary. For what is radical about queerness, basic queerness—the kind of queerness that is really queer in the sense of odd, bizarre, nonstandard—is its ability to defeat all our notions about who is radical and who isn't, whose identity is bad and whose is good, who is who. In this volume, Robert Phillips is able to show, through a linguistic analysis of British journalistic discourse, that queerness dissolves differences between the representations of Muslims and Jews: when it comes to LGBT folks, Muslims and Jews are spoken about in largely the same vocabulary, though the specific vocabulary employed by different publications varies according to each publication's political orientation.

Such mold breaking is the promise of queer scholarship. But it will only produce this welcome, transformative, eye-opening effect if we study the social world in all its irreducible specificity, letting its weird non-correspondence to what we take for granted about our politics and theory destabilize our own categories and demolish the specious self-evidence of our own theoretical commonplaces. When that happens, we actually learn something. The researcher must, of course, want that to happen; it has to be a deliberate scholarly project. Mere facts won't do it all by themselves.[9] When the facts are astutely, adroitly mobilized with the requisite engagement and intent, and such a research project succeeds, it proves that good scholarship, true scholarship, is also queer scholarship. The chapters collected in this volume provide a number of eloquent examples.

Let me dramatize this point in a general way by discussing one example I know something about—one, at least, I know more about than the imbricated histories of queer Muslims and Jews, for in that domain I am an admitted and helpless nonspecialist. I refer to sexual life and sexual attitudes in the ancient Mediterranean world and, more specifically, in ancient Greek society. In fact, I have long argued that the study of classical antiquity has the queer potential to disrupt and to decommission our identities.[10]

If it is examined in all its unsystematic specificity, classical antiquity will actually undo all the ideologies that have been constructed on its ostensible foundation and in its name—the Eurocentrism, the white supremacism, the various ethnonationalisms, the racisms, the chauvinisms, the parochialisms, and the many reactionary varieties of identity politics (white, male, European, elitist identity politics, even chauvinist gay and lesbian identity politics).

Consider homosexual relations in ancient Greece.

The Greeks have long been a source of lesbian and gay pride. They have seemed to provide a culturally prestigious precedent for the social approval and even the celebration of same-sex desire. Sappho, the most renowned female poet of ancient Greece, sang the praises of the beauty and desirability of women and girls. Plato's dialogues portray Socrates drooling over hunky boys who often seem to appeal to him more for their good looks than for their philosophical acuity. The gayness of the Greeks has long been something of a standing joke, and the word "Greek," at least as it once featured in personal ads, refers not to an ethnicity but to a disreputable sexual act—whence the relentless, centuries-long efforts on the part of proponents of gay pride to conscript the ancient Greeks into service as avatars of contemporary lesbian and gay identity.

When classical scholarship has not altogether avoided the issue, or bracketed it by taking the sexual peculiarities of the Greeks for granted, it has occasionally disputed the meaning of Greek homosexuality and disagreed about how much gay sex the Greeks really had. Finally, the issue was more or less settled in 1978 by the great classicist K. J. Dover—a straight married man, by the way—in a book called *Greek Homosexuality*.[11] Dover was no queer theorist, and as the title of his book makes plain, he left the modern categories of homosexuality and heterosexuality largely uninterrogated. But because he examined, without any theoretical presuppositions, the major surviving documents in all their particularity, he produced an account of sexual behavior and attitudes in classical Athens that actually destroyed the self-evidence of the notions of homosexuality and heterosexuality and prevented their unproblematic application to the ancient Greeks. For example, the evidence he presented indicated, without his making anything of it, that the only sexual relations that the Greeks viewed as ordinary and conventional were ones that featured an asymmetry between the partners in social status: so long as an adult, native-born, free Athenian male citizen had sex with a person who counted as a statutory minor, his behavior was sexually unobjectionable. ("Minor" here does not mean younger but rather socially subordinate.) It was normal and ordinary for such a fully entitled male citizen to want to have sex, under the right circumstances, with women, boys, foreigners, and slaves. But if he had sex with someone like himself, with another adult male Athenian citizen, that was really shocking and bizarre. In that sense, there was no such thing as Greek homosexuality.

Michel Foucault, reviewing the French translation of Dover's book in the newspaper *Libération* in 1982, put this point as follows:

> Of course, we'll still find easy-going souls ready to accept the notion that homosexuality has more or less always existed. . . . To such naive spirits, Dover administers a good lesson in historical nominalism. Sexual relations between two individuals of the same sex is one thing. But to love someone of the same sex, to take pleasure in one's own sex, is quite another. It's a whole experience, with its objects and their meanings, with a way of being on the part of the subject and the subject's own self-awareness. That experience is complex, it is diverse, it changes form.[12]

Foucault insists, in other words, that you can't reduce "homosexuality" to the act of same-sex sex. Sexual contact among persons of the same sex may well occur in most societies or eras, but such contact does not amount to a single phenomenon, a single concept, a consistent sexual or social form. Those people who are so naive as to think that homosexuality is a thing, outside of history, culture, and consciousness, have been rebuked by Dover, Foucault insists, insofar as Dover gives them "a good lesson in historical nominalism."

Dover did not need to be a queer theorist in order to administer that lesson. He just needed to be a good classicist, a good historian. His scholarship actually made queer theory possible, because it made it possible to undo unexamined presumptions about ancient sexuality, because his recovery of specific sexual attitudes and practices of pederasty in classical Athens exploded the specious universality of modern notions of homosexuality and heterosexuality, even though that wasn't his main intention. (Shanon Shah's scholarly analysis in this volume of the centuries-long theological bricolage that eventually gave rise to the legal category of *liwat* undertakes a similar labor of historical defamiliarization.)

It is history itself, Foucault implies, whose irreducible specificity defeats essentialist, transcendental concepts as well as the universalizing identities and identity categories grounded in them, along with all the chauvinisms, racisms, and ideologies that are forged in their name.

I want to linger for a while on Foucault's phrase "historical nominalism." It is at the heart of what I want to say about the valuable insights into queer Jews and queer Muslims that emerge from the work collected in this volume.

The greatness of (good) history lies in its nominalism. Aristotle once said that poetry is more philosophical than history.[13] He meant that remark as a compliment to poetry, but it is really an unwitting and backhanded compliment to history. Since it deals with particular facts, events, one-time occurrences—in short, with what actually happened—history cannot rise to the level of speculative, hypothetical generality achieved by poetry and required by philosophy. And that is a very good thing. The great virtue of history, in other words, is that it is *not* philosophical. Historians, to be sure, are certainly free to theorize, but (with some unfortunate exceptions) they do not deduce history from theory. It is to the immense credit of history that it defeats ideological dogma by introducing

Afterword   215

inconvenient and stubborn facts, happenstance occurrences, exceptions, counterexamples, uncategorizable relations: the Black heterosexual paraplegic who became the source of lesbian sexual pleasure; the festive parody of the female Jewish coming-of-age ritual, Bat Mitzvah, called "Buttmitzvah," celebrated at a queer club in London's Bethnal Green and described in this volume by Matthew Richardson; the support groups for queer Muslims, studied by Elizabeth Johnstone, that have sprung up in the United Kingdom. You can't make this stuff up: you have to do your research and find it out.

If you want a poetic version of history, then ideology is your baby. Ideology is a kind of political poetry, minus the aesthetics. Ideology makes a highly selective use of history and turns it into a fable that is misleading but easy to grasp. History, by contrast, precisely because of its nominalism, because of its focus on what is particular, nonrepeatable, nongeneralizable, unanticipated, and nontheoretical, is the perfect antidote to ideology. Once you know what actually happened, you can no longer believe in familiar, taken-for-granted notions based on uninformed assumptions about how things are and what they mean. You can't believe in the same way in America if you study US history, which is why right-wing ideologues today want the study of US history to be banned from schools and universities. History reveals phenomena that can't be easily sublimated into a single coherent idea and that can't be wished away. Historical specificity gives the lie to false universals; it interferes with ideology's tendency to transform concepts with a concrete history into transcendental ideas or idealizations.

In short, history baffles all efforts to turn the story of the world into the illustration of a notion.

I am not, of course, objecting to large-scale scientific theories like gravity, natural selection, or relativity, which can claim to be true only insofar as they survive empirical tests. I am not speaking of general lessons that can be drawn from history or of philosophies of history. I am speaking of the power of historical nominalism to serve, like queerness, as a solvent of identity.

If you had any doubt about that, they will have vanished by this point in your reading of the volume you are holding. It purports to be organized around identity terms: Muslim, Jew, queer. But, in fact, the work produced by the various contributors puts those identity categories under extreme pressure. Katrina Daly Thompson specifically opposes the practice that would preserve the singularity of those identity terms by separating them with commas: she prefers to join them by means of hyphens, so as to dramatize "gender-sexuality-race-religion intersections." As Elizabeth Johnstone writes, "These new transcultural forms challenge hegemony and colonial discourses by destabilizing notions of fixed cultural boundaries." The tales of ethnic, racial, national, cultural, religious, sexual, and gender hybridity invented by the women writers of the French Maghreb whom Edwige Crucifix studies provide even more flamboyant examples of such disruptions of stable identities, though the resulting figures of boundary crossing tend to be of the febrile, imaginary kind, typical of the fantasies colonialism seems to inspire in its subjects, whether dominant or oppressed.

In another analysis of cultural hybridity, Amr Kamal rereads Proust's *Recherche* and discovers its Orientalism not only in the well-known passages that evoke the fashionable décor of the youthful Odette's boudoir or the subversive underground freemasonry of "Levantine" Jews and their closeted *semblables*, the "accursed race" of inverts, but, more surprisingly, in the narrator's final identification of himself with Scheherazade, the narrator of the fables contained in the eighteenth-century Egyptian compilation *The Thousand and One Nights*. That astonishing act of gendered-cultural-religious-historical-ethnic-literary drag, which takes place at the very conclusion of the *Recherche* and for which nothing has prepared the reader (despite the earlier hints that Kamal discovers and catalogs), casts a retrospective light on Proust's entire literary project and forces us to reinterpret Proust's own understanding of it in a new and unanticipated way—not as a proto-Freudian auto-analysis, as Janet Malcolm and others have persuasively argued,[14] but as something quite different: the show-stopping performance of a desperate, death-defying diva.

Queerness, then, as the studies collected in this volume demonstrate, is much more concrete, unsystematic, unpretentious, humble, close at hand, and surprising than it is sometimes made to seem nowadays. It would be a pity, it would be a waste, to allow queer theory to conduce to a re-idealization of our categories of thought, to become a new theology or metaphysics, and to stabilize political certainties and the various hierarchies that are constructed on their basis.

What, after all, could be less queer?

Notes

1 Halberstam, Muñoz, and Eng, *What's Queer about Queer Studies Now?*; Eng and Puar, *Left of Queer*.

2 Nelson, *The Argonauts*, 110: "How can rampant, 'deviant' sexual activity remain the marker of radicality? What sense does it make to align 'queer' with 'sexual deviance'?"

3 Halperin, *Saint Foucault*, 62.

4 Halperin, *Saint Foucault*, 64–67.

5 See Farmer, *Pathologies of Power*.

6 See, e.g., Hirsch et al., *The Secret*.

7 Buchbinder et al., "Sexual Risk, Nitrite Inhalant Use, and Lack of Circumcision Associated with HIV Seroconversion in Men Who Have Sex with Men in the United States," 83.

8 Rubin, "A Little Humility," 372–73.

9 See, in this connection, the brilliant and sensible reflections of Marjorie Levinson, "What Is a Particular?"

10 See, e.g., Halperin, *One Hundred Years of Homosexuality*; Halperin, *How to Do the History of Homosexuality*.

11 Dover, *Greek Homosexuality*.

12 Foucault, "Des caresses d'hommes considérées comme un art," reprinted in Foucault, *Dits et écrits, 1954–1988*, 4:315–16: "Bien sûr, on trouvera encore des esprits aimables pour penser qu'en somme l'homosexualité a toujours existé. . . . À de tels naïfs Dover donne une bonne leçon de nominalisme historique. Le rapport entre deux individus du même sexe est une chose. Mais aimer le même sexe que soi, prendre avec lui un plaisir, c'est autre chose, c'est toute une expérience, avec ses objets et leurs valeurs, avec la manière d'être du sujet et la conscience qu'il a de lui-même. Cette expérience est complexe, elle est diverse, elle change de formes."

13 Aristotle, *Poetics*, 9.1451b5.

14 Malcolm, *Psychoanalysis*, 127–28.

Works Cited

Buchbinder, Susan, et al. "Sexual Risk, Nitrite Inhalant Use, and Lack of Circumcision Associated with HIV Seroconversion in Men Who Have Sex with Men in the United States." *Journal of Acquired Immune Deficiency Syndromes* 39, no. 1 (May 1, 2005): 82–89.

Dover, K. J. *Greek Homosexuality*. London: Duckworth, 1978.

Eng, David L., Judith Halberstam, and José Esteban Muñoz, eds. *What's Queer about Queer Studies Now?* Special issue, *Social Text* 84–85, 23, no. 3–4 (Fall–Winter 2005).

Eng, David L., and Jasbir K. Puar. *Left of Queer*. Special issue, *Social Text* 145, 38, no. 4 (December 2020).

Farmer, Paul. *Pathologies of Power: Health, Human Rights, and the New War on the Poor*. Berkeley: University of California Press, 2003.

Foucault, Michel. "Des caresses d'hommes considérées comme un art." *Libération* 323 (June 1, 1982): 27. Reprinted in Michel Foucault, *Dits et écrits, 1954–1988*, edited by Daniel Defert and François Ewald, 4:315–17. Paris: Gallimard, 1994.

Halperin, David M. *How to Do the History of Homosexuality*. Chicago: University of Chicago Press, 2002.

———. *One Hundred Years of Homosexuality: And Other Essays on Greek Love*. New York: Routledge, 1990.

———. *Saint Foucault: Towards a Gay Hagiography*. New York: Oxford University Press, 1995.

Hirsch, Jennifer S., Holly Wardlow, Daniel Jordan Smith, Harriet M. Phinney, Shanti Parikh, and Constance A. Nathanson. *The Secret: Love, Marriage, and HIV*. Nashville, TN: Vanderbilt University Press, 2009.

Levinson, Marjorie. "What Is a Particular?" (forthcoming).

Malcolm, Janet. *Psychoanalysis: The Impossible Profession*. New York: Vintage, 1982.

Nelson, Maggie. *The Argonauts*. Minneapolis, MN: Graywolf Press, 2015.

Rubin, Gayle. "A Little Humility." In *Gay Shame*, edited by David M. Halperin and Valerie Traub, 369–73. Chicago: University of Chicago Press, 2009.

Contributors

Edwige Crucifix is an assistant professor of French and Francophone studies at Bryn Mawr College. Her research and teaching stem from an interdisciplinary interest in modes of cultural resistance, explored in previous publications dedicated to modernist aesthetics, nineteenth-century bourgeois taste, and interwar Jewish identity.

David M. Halperin is the W. H. Auden Distinguished University Professor Emeritus of the History and Theory of Sexuality, and professor emeritus of English language and literature and women's and gender studies at the University of Michigan. He is the author of several books, including *One Hundred Years of Homosexuality*, *Saint Foucault*, and *How to Be Gay*.

Elizabeth Johnstone is an independent scholar who holds an MSc in global migration from University College London and an MA in French and language and civilization from New York University. Her research explores queer Muslim community building in Europe, with a particular focus on the United Kingdom and France.

Amr Kamal is an associate professor of French and Arabic at the City College of New York and the Graduate Center, City University of New York. His research interests include nineteenth- and twentieth-century French literature, Francophone literature from the Mashreq (especially Egypt, Lebanon, and Syria), Mediterranean studies, human geography, and material culture.

Robert Phillips is chair of the Department of Anthropology and associate professor of anthropology at Ball State University. His main body of research has explored the effects of new and emerging technologies, particularly the internet, on national and religious belonging. He is the author of *Virtual Activism: Sexuality, the Internet, and a Social Movement in Singapore*.

Matthew Richardson holds a PhD in human geography and social anthropology from Newcastle University. His research explores queer Jewish self-(trans)formation in contemporary Britain with an emphasis on ritual performance. He currently works in the counseling, safeguarding, and well-being department at a college of further education in North East England.

Adi Saleem is an assistant professor of Romance languages and literatures and Judaic studies at the University of Michigan. His research focuses on the intersection of race and religion, or religion as race, particularly in relation to Jews and Muslims.

Shanon Shah is a researcher at the Information Network Focus on Religious Movements (Inform), based at the Department of Theology and Religious Studies, King's College London, and is a tutor in Islam at the University of London's divinity program. He is the author of *The Making of a Gay Muslim: Religion, Sexuality and Identity in Malaysia and Britain*.

Katrina Daly Thompson is the Evjue-Bascom Professor of the Humanities and professor of African cultural studies at the University of Wisconsin–Madison. They are the author of *Zimbabwe's Cinematic Arts: Language, Power, Identity, Popobawa: Tanzanian Talk, Global Misreadings*, and *Muslims on the Margins: Creating Queer Religious Community in North America*.

Index

Note: Page numbers appearing in *italics* refer to tables and figures.

Abby (Buttmitzvah attendee), 165–66, 169
Abdel-Jaouad, Hedi, 70n30
Abir (queer Muslim identity study participant): queerphobic violence persecution of, 187; queer-sensitive Islam interpretation of, 190–91, 193
Abraham, queer, 77–81
Abrahamic Law, in *À la recherche du temps perdu*, 79
Abu Ghraib prison, 6
academe, queer terminology in, 205, 208
"Acting Out Orientalism" (Apter), 82
Adam (queer Muslim identity study participant), 188, 193
adequation: of David, 34, 35, 39; intersubjectivity tactic, 32–35; of Keegan, 32–34, 44
Adler, Rachel, 8
African American Pentecostal church, 163
Ahmed, Leila, 12
Aldrich, Robert, 54
Alexander, Bobby, 163
Algeria, 53; *crise antijuive* in, 58; French army rape and sexual abuse in, 68n2
Alpert, Reuven, 28, 29
Altab Ali Park, 151
Anidjar, Gil, 2, 11, 28
anti-Jewish crisis (*crise antijuive*), 58
anti-Jewish league (*ligue antijuive*), 58
antisemitic violence, 127, 152, 155
antisemitism, 1; Islamophobia interrelationship with, 2–3; Jewish sexual deviance constructions as, 12–13
anti-structure: of communitas, 162; liminoid phenomena and, 162–68; social structures shaping, 165, 168
apocryphal Abrahamic scriptures, 116
Apter, Emily, 57, 82
Arab-Islamic societies, premodern, 7–8

Argonauts, The (Nelson), 205
Aristotle, 214
art: harem paintings, 99n70; Orientalist, 81–85; *À la recherche du temps perdu* referencing, 76, 78, 81
Asad, Talal, 152
Ashkenazi Jews, London East End migration of, 150
Asmara (queer Muslim identity study participant), 192, 201n15; queerness and family of, 185; on religion self-distancing, 190
Auschwitz, Jewish Muselmänner in, 2
authentication: of David, 36, 37–38; intersubjectivity tactic, 32, 36–38; of Keegan, 36–37, 38
authorization: of David, 38–40; intersubjectivity tactic, 32, 38–40

Baer, Marc David, 29
Bakalian, Anny, 161
Bangladeshi migrants, London East End community of, 150
Barthes, Roland, 86
Bat Mitzvah, Buttmitzvah play on, 154–55
Believers (*mu'minun*), 115
Belle Époque, in *À la recherche du temps perdu*, 77, 91, 94
belonging: queer Muslim citizenship regarding, 184–87; support groups regaining, 194–96
Bendahan, Blanche, 15, 71n48; *Mazaltob* by, 71n52; *Messieurs, vous êtes impuissants* by, 53, 63–68
Benhaïm, André, 99n70
berdache (boy slave), 6–7
Bethnal Green, gentrification in, 155
Bethnal Green Working Men's Club, 147. *See also* Buttmitzvah

222　Index

Bhabha, Homi, 62, 80, 197
Bible, sodomy in, 111
biblical scriptures: of Lot, 110; Qur'an
　regarding, 114, 115, 116; *À la recherche*
　du temps perdu referencing, 76, 78, 81;
　tahrif regarding, 114. *See also* scriptures,
　Abrahamic
Birth of Venus, The, 87
blood purity statutes (*limpieza de sangre*),
　1, 11
Blue (Buttmitzvah attendee), 169
Bonnett, Alastair, 31
Boone, Joseph, 68–69n6, 91–92
Botticelli, Sandro, 87
Boumendil, Rosine. *See* Rhaïs, Elissa
Boupacha, Djamila, 68n2
Bourdieu, Pierre, 88
bourgeoisie, French, 85–87, 88
boy slave (*berdache*), 6–7
Branche, Raphaëlle, 68n2
Bright, Susie, 210
Britain, 128, 151
British National Survey of Sexual Attitudes
　and Lifestyles, 180
Buchbinder, Susan, 208
Bucholtz, Mary, 31–32, 36
Bugéja, Marie, 61–62
Butler, Judith: on heteronormative subject
　formation, 80; on performativity, 79
Buttmitzvah, 17; Bat Mitzvah word play
　with, 154–55; Becky, 158; communitas
　generated by, 148, 156, 160, 168;
　domestic religion of, 159, 160; Hannah
　on, 156–57; liminality of, 149–56,
　168; liminal personae attending, 164;
　as liminoid phenomenon, 167; queer
　unwanted experience at, 165–66;
　ritual complex and, 156–61; symbols
　employed in, 160
Buttmitzvah attendees: Abby, 165–66, 169;
　Blue, 169; Hannah, 156–57; identities and
　pronouns of, 169–70; Liane, 169; O.K.,
　159, 164, 170; R., 170; T.M., 164, 170

Camus, Renaud, 3
Charlottesville, Unite the Right rally in, 3
Christian church leaders, early Islam
　reactions of, 113

Christianity, 118; Bible, 111; Islam
　distinguished from, 107; Pauline
　theology within, 112; sodomy in,
　111–12; *tahrif* regarding, 114; Tower
　Hamlets ethnoreligious demographic
　shifts of, 151. *See also* biblical scriptures;
　scriptures, Abrahamic
Cinnirella, Marco, 180–81, 199
circumcision, 87
citizenship, queer Muslim, 183; belonging
　and family regarding, 184–87; mental
　health consequences regarding, 189–90;
　queer community regarding, 187–89
Clardou, Sixfrancs (*Messieurs, vous êtes*
　impuissants character), 64–65
Clinton administration, 184
closet spectacle, in *À la recherche du temps*
　perdu, 90
Cole, Josh, 155
Collins, L., 131
collocation, corpus linguistics revealing, 130
colonial feminism, 12
colonialism: intermarriages during, 71n47;
　in Maghreb, 54, 68n3; in *Le mariage de*
　Hanifa, 62; in *À la recherche du temps*
　perdu, 92; same-sex prostitution under, 54
coloniality: of gender, 4, 5; of power, 4
coming out, 186
communitas, 153, 161; anti-structure of,
　162; Buttmitzvahs generating, 148,
　156, 160, 168; of fishing dam–building
　ritual, 162–63; institutionalization of,
　164; social structure relationship with,
　165, 166–67; staggered nature of, 166;
　subversion regarding, 163
communities, 161; corpora keyword, 134;
　Jewish, 34, 41, 113; London East End
　migrant, 149–50; Muslim, 34; queer,
　187–89
concordance: analysis, 131, 137–38; corpus
　linguistics revealing, 129
conscientização (self-conscientization), 108,
　119
corpora, 139, 140n18; Islam-related terms
　in, 133, *133*, 134, 137–38; Judaism-
　related terms in, 134, *134*, 138; keywords
　in, 132, *132*, 133, *133*, 134, *134*, 135;
　multiword keywords in, *135–36*; noun

frequencies in, *132*; political leanings of, 131; semantic mapping of, *136*, 137. See also *Guardian* corpus; *Independent* corpus; *Telegraph / Daily Mail* corpus

corpus linguistics: British media examined with, 129; keywords revealed by, 129–30

Côté de Guermantes, Le (Proust): dancer in, 83–84, 85, 96n34; Rachel in, 82–85, 96nn33–34, 97n39; theater in, 82, 96n32. See also *recherche du temps perdu, À la*

crescent symbol, Orientalist, 91, 92, 98n60

crise antijuive (anti-Jewish crisis), 58

critical discourse analysis, British media examined with, 129

cross-dressing, women, 57, 70n29

Crucifix, Edwige, 15, 216

cultural boundaries, permeability of, 27

cultural identity, 196

DADT. *See* Don't Ask, Don't Tell policy

Daily Mail corpus. See *Telegraph / Daily Mail* corpus

Daily Telegraph, 127

dancer, in *Le Côté de Guermantes*, 83–84, 85, 96n34

Daoud, Kamel, 13

David (queer-Jewish-Muslim), 26, 29, 32, 46n30; adequation of, 34, 35, 39; authentication of, 36, 37–38; authorization of, 38–40; distinction of, 42–43; on El-Tawhid Mosque, 35, 39–40, 42, 43; on Islam and Judaism, 42; Jewish and Muslim community involvement of, 34; on Jewish Sufism, 38, 39; on race, 30–31, 44; sermon of, 35, 39–40, 43

Davidman, Lynn, 161

Décret Crémieux (1870), 53, 58

DeHanas, Daniel, 149

demographics: Britain public discourse on, 151; ethnoreligious shifts in, 150–51

depression, 189

dildo, silicone, 209–10

Disraeli, Benjamin, 76

distinction: of David, 42–43; intersubjectivity tactic, 32, 40–43; of Keegan, 41–42; queer, 40–43, 44–45

Divine Interventions, 210

doctorate, 117, 118

Dolicho, Riema (*Messieurs, vous êtes impuissants* character), 64–65

Dönme, 27–28

Donner, Fred, 115

Don't Ask, Don't Tell policy (DADT), 184

double life, 190

Dover, K. J.: Foucault on, 213–14, 217n12; *Greek Homosexuality* by, 213

drag: of European women, 57; Hidayah at Pride, 197; of Scheherazade, 77, 93–94, 216

Drake, Susanna, 12–13

Dreyfus affair, Odette response to, 87–88

Driessen, Henk, 28

East End, London, 147; Buttmitzvah liminality in, 149–56, 168; ethnoreligious demographic shifts in, 150–51; immigration waves into, 149–50

Eberhardt, Isabelle, 57, 70n30

El-Rouayheb, Khaled, 8

en être, À la recherche du temps perdu usage of, 79–80, 89, 96n26, 98n53

engendering, 2–5. *See also* racing

epistemologies: alternative, 5–9; binaries of, 90; of gender and sexuality, 9

ethnicity, Tower Hamlets demographic shifts regarding, 151

Europe: history of, 1–2; Orient discursive power relations with, 76

European imperialism, over Indigenous peoples, 6–7

European masculinity, 7

Eve's Garden, 209, 210

Fakhite (*Le mariage de Hanifa* character), 60, 61, 62

family: of Asmara, 185; of Joy, 184; queer Muslim citizenship regarding, 184–87; queerness relationship with, 184–85; of Sadiya, 184–85, 186

Fanon, Frantz, 3

far-right political shifts, 199n1

fashion: of Odette, 86, 97n48; sociology and semiology of, 86

Favre, Lucienne, 54

feminism, colonial, 12

femonationalism, 12
Fille des Pachas, La (Rhaïs), 58
fishing dam–building ritual, 162–63
forums, online: queer-sensitive Islam interpretations on, 105; transgender support group, 187–88
Foucault, Michel, 213–14, 217n12
France, Tan, 134, 135
Freire, Paulo, 108
French army, rape and sexual abuse by, 68n2
French colonies, same-sex relations in, 55
French nation, in *À la recherche du temps perdu*, 75–76, 77, 90, 99n66
Frum (religious), 172n59

Garber, Marjorie, 52
gay affirmative social contexts, 180–81, 199
Gay International, Massad label of, 106
gender: in British media, 129; coloniality of, 4, 5; epistemology of, 9; in *Messieurs, vous êtes impuissants*, 66–67; performativity, 84; in *À la recherche du temps perdu*, 93; social constructionism of, 8–9; SOGI, 180, 182, *183*; transgender identity, 185, 192, 200n13
Genesis, 110
genesis amnesia, of French bourgeoisie, 88
gentrification, in Bethnal Green, 155
German, Jew, Muslim, Gay (Baer), 29
Goldberg, Harvey, 37
Good Vibrations, 209, 210
grand remplacement (great replacement theory), 3
Greece, ancient, 212–13
Greek Homosexuality (Dover), 213
Guardian corpus, 131, 139; Islam-related terms in, 133, *133*, 134, 137–38; Judaism-related terms in, 134, *134*, 138; noun frequencies in, *132*; semantic mapping of, *136*, 137. *See also* corpora; *Independent* corpus; *Telegraph / Daily Mail* corpus

hadith, 117; anti-*liwat*, 110–11; Joy interpretation of, 192–93
Hall, Kira, 31–32, 36
Hall, Stuart, 2
Halperin, David M., 9, 13–14

Hanifa (*Le mariage de Hanifa* character): Fakhite relationship with, 61, 62; hybridization of, 59–60
Hannah (Buttmitzvah attendee), 156–57
Hannan-Stavroulakis, Nikos, 28, 29
harem: paintings of, 99n70; sapphic, 55–56
hate crimes: antisemitic violence, 127, 152, 155; Islamophobic violence, 127; SOGI-based, 180. *See also* queerphobic violence
hatred, semantic mapping of, *136*
Hayes, Jarod, 80; on circumcision, 87; on queer terminology, 69n7; on Zionism discourse, 90
health insurance, 208
heteronormativity, 80, 82
Hey Alma, 155
Hidayah, 181, 194, *198*; cultural identity supported by, 196; at Pride, 182, 197, 199; Stories Events, 195
historical nominalism, 213, 214, 215
history, 1–2, 214, 215
HIV/AIDS pandemic, queer identity politics emergence from, 208–9
Holloway, Julian, 151, 160–61
Homoerotics of Orientalism, The (Boone), 91–92
homoerotic tropes, 68–69n6
homoerotic utopia, Orientalist, 56–57
homonationalism, 188–89
homophobia, 41. *See also* queerphobic violence
homosexuality: Abrahamic scriptures on, 107–9, 111; in ancient Greece, 212–13; Foucault on, 213–14, 217n12; intertextual queering of, 109–12; Islam regarding, 117; Kocher invasive examinations of, 55; narratives of, 128; in Qur'an, 109–10, 113–16; rabbinic literature interpretations against, 110; in Singaporean media, 130
Homosexuality in Islam (Kugle), 105–6, 193
hora, 171n36
Houellebecq, Michel, 92
Hughes, Aaron, 25, 27, 28
Huguenots, London East End migration of, 149
hybridization, 197; of Hanifa, 59–60; queering of, 58–63

Ibn Hazm, 110
identities, 207, 215–16; of Buttmitzvah
    attendees, 169–70; Buttmitzvah
    celebrating, 167; cultural, 196; of David,
    44; of Keegan, 31, 33, 44; Luz on, 161; of
    Maghrebi Jewish women, 52–53; queer
    identity politics, 208–9, 211; religious,
    182, *183*; transgender, 185, 192, 200n13;
    of Zara, 200n13. *See also* gender
identity conflict, 199; identity
    reconciliation, 191–93; self-distancing
    dealing with, 190–91
ideology, 215
ilm (knowledge), 120; in Islam, 107–8, 117;
    power impacting, 119
Imams: Islam queer-sensitive
    interpretations by, 193; women, 192
immigration, London East End waves of,
    149–50
incestuous feelings, in *À la recherche du
    temps perdu*, 96n19
Independent corpus, 131, 139; Islam-
    related terms in, 133, *133*, 134, 138;
    Judaism-related terms in, 134, *134*, 138;
    noun frequencies in, *132*; semantic
    mapping of, *136*, 137. *See also* corpora;
    Guardian corpus; *Telegraph / Daily
    Mail* corpus
Indigenous peoples, European imperialism
    over, 6–7
inequalities: HIV/AIDS correlation with,
    208; in knowledge claims, 108
In Search of Lost Time (Proust). See
    recherche du temps perdu, À la
intercourse, male same-sex. See *liwat*
intermarriages, during colonialism, 71n47
interstructural situation, 153
intersubjectivity tactics: adequation, 32–35;
    authentication, 32, 36–38; authorization,
    32, 38–40; Bucholtz and Hall framework
    of, 31–32, 36; distinction, 32, 40–43
intertextuality: Abrahamic scriptures read
    with, 113–16, 120; homosexuality
    queered with, 109–12
Invention of Women, The (Oyěwùmí), 5
Iraq: Keegan upbringing in, 41–42; US
    invading, 6
Iraqi Jewish community, 41

Irish migrants, London East End
    community of, 149–50
ISIL. *See* Islamic State of Iraq and the Levant
Islam, 8–9; corpora terms related to,
    133, *133*, 134, 137–38; David on,
    42; early, 113; everyday religion of,
    109; homosexuality regarding, 117;
    ilm in, 107–8, 117; queer-sensitive
    interpretations of, 105, 190–91, 192–
    93; *tahrif* in, 114; Tower Hamlets
    ethnoreligious demographic shifts of,
    150–51. *See also* Qur'an
Islamic law, illicit sexual activity hierarchy
    of, 111
Islamic State of Iraq and the Levant (ISIL), 133
Islamic Studies, 117
Islamophobia, 1, 2–3, 6, 10, 14
Islamophobic violence, 127
Israeli-Palestine conflict, Keegan on, 36–37
Isra'iliyyat (Qur'anic commentary genre), 114

Jaspal, Rusi, 180–81, 199
Jewish Chronicle, 127
Jewish communities, 34; early Islam
    reactions of, 113; Iraqi, 41
Jewish Muselmänner, in Auschwitz, 2
Jewish-Muslim relations, 3–4, 10–14, 17–18
Jewish Muslims: Dönme, 27–28; Marcus,
    29. *See also* queer-Jewish-Muslims
Jewish scriptures: Qur'an regarding, 114,
    115–16; *tahrif* regarding, 114
Jewish Sufism, David on, 38, 39
Jews. *See specific topics*
Johnson, Boris, 127
Johnstone, Elizabeth, 17, 216
Jones, L., 131
Joy (queer Muslim identity study
    participant): hadith interpretation of,
    192–93; queerness and family of, 184; on
    support groups, 194
Judaism, 8–9; corpora terms related
    to, 134, *134*, 138; David on, 42;
    rabbinic literature anti-homosexual
    interpretations in, 110; *tahrif* regarding,
    114; Tower Hamlets ethnoreligious
    demographic shifts of, 151. *See also*
    scriptures, Abrahamic
Juifs, Les (Rhaïs), 58–59

226   Index

Kamal, Amr, 15–16, 216
Kapferer, Bruce, 162
Keegan (queer-Muslim-Jewish), 26, 29; adequation of, 32–34, 44; authentication of, 36–37, 38; distinction of, 41–42; identity of, 31, 33, 44; religious practices of, 33–34
Khaled (queer Muslim identity study participant), 191
khatib (sermon giver), 35
Kik support group, 196
Klug, Brian, 25
knowledge, 107; situated, 211; validation process of, 108, 119. See also *ilm*
Kocher, Adolphe, 55, 56, 63
Kugle, Scott Siraj al-Haqq, 8; criticisms of, 106–7, 119; everyday religion focus of, 109; *Homosexuality in Islam*, 105–6, 193; *Living Out Islam* by, 106; on *liwat*, 110–11; *Progressive Muslims* by, 105

Laplanche, Jean, 78, 95n15
Lee, Daniel, 68n4
legal victories, 200n5
Levy, André, 28–29
Liane (Buttmitzvah attendee), 169
Libération, 213
ligue antijuive (anti-Jewish league), 58
liminality, 149–56, 162, 168
liminal personae, 152; Buttmitzvah attended by, 164; within interstructural spaces, 153
liminoid phenomena, 154; anti-structure and, 162–68; Buttmitzvah as, 167
limpieza de sangre (blood purity statutes), 1, 11
Living Out Islam (Kugle), 106
liwat (male same-sex intercourse), 110–11, 214
London: Tower Hamlets, 150–51. See also East End, London
Lot, in Abrahamic scriptures, 110
Lugones, María, 4
Lut, Qur'an story of, 110
Luz, Nimrod, 161

Mack, Mehammed, 12
Maghreb, 51; colonialism in, 54, 68n3; Orientalist homoerotic utopia of, 56–57;

queer, 54–58; same-sex desire in, 52, 55–58
Maghrebi Jewish women, identities of, 52–53
Maghrebi women writers, 52, 53, 61–62. *See also* Rhaïs, Elissa
Maimonedes, 39
Malaysia, 117
male gaze, in Rhaïs novels, 59–60
Marcus, Hugo, 29
mariage de Hanifa, Le (Rhaïs), 53, 63; colonial relations in, 62; Fakhite in, 60, 61, 62; Hanifa in, 59–60, 61, 62; *Messieurs, vous êtes impuissants* compared to, 67–68; race in, 61
marriage: colonialism intermarriages, 71n47; of Khaled, 191; semantic mapping of, 136
marriages of convenience (MOCs), 191
Massad, Joseph, 92, 106
Mazaltob (Bendahan), 71n52
Mazower, Mark, 27
McFarland, K. T., 11
media: on monkeypox epidemic, 206; Singaporean, 130
media, British, 16; critical discourse analysis and corpus linguistics examination method for, 129; double minorities representation in, 127–28; othering in, 139; research questions on, 130–31. See also *Guardian* corpus; *Independent* corpus; *Telegraph / Daily Mail* corpus
Memmi, Albert, 87
mental health consequences, regarding queer Muslim citizenship, 189–90
Messieurs, vous êtes impuissants (Bendahan), 53; gender in, 66–67; *Le mariage de Hanifa* compared to, 67–68; queer disguises in, 63–67; race in, 66–67; racism in, 64; sexual desire in, 65–66
Mimouna holiday, 37
"Mimuna and the Minority Status of Moroccan Jews, The" (Goldberg), 37
minorities, 160–61
minorities, double: British media representation of, 127–28; problematic binaries impacting, 152
MOCs. *See* marriages of convenience

monkeypox epidemic, 206
Moses, wife of, 87
MPV. *See* Muslims for Progressive Values
Muhammad (Prophet), 192–93
mu'minun (Believers), 115
Muslims: ban, 179; communities, 34; nonconformist, 29–30. *See also specific topics*
Muslims for Progressive Values (MPV), 30, 41
Myerhoff, Barbara G.: on communitas, 163, 165; on domestic religion, 159; on symbol complex, 158
mythmaking, in ritual complex, 158

Nahum-Claudel, Chloe, 162–63
names, 46n28, 66, 201n21
Napier, Charles, 11–12
narrative ethnography, 148–49
Nelson, Maggie, 205
Nos soeurs musulmanes (Bugéja), 62
noun frequencies, in corpora, *132*
Nycravatt, Bainur (*Messieurs, vous êtes impuissants* character), 65–66
Nycravatt, Nicole (*Messieurs, vous êtes impuissants* character), 63
Nycravatt, Soifranc (*Messieurs, vous êtes impuissants* character), 65–66
Nye, Malory, 161

Odette (*À la recherche du temps perdu* character): Dreyfus affair response of, 87–88; fashion of, 86, 97n48; Orientalist decoration of, 85–86, 97n42
O.K. (Buttmitzvah attendee), 159, 164, 170
O'Neill, Kevin, 159
online support groups, 187–88, 195–96
Orient: crescent symbol of, 91, 92, 98n60; Europe discursive power relations with, 76; in *À la recherche du temps perdu*, 75–76, 91, 92, 98n60
Orientalism, 6; in *À la recherche du temps perdu*, 76, 77, 82, 91, 95n8, 216; Said on, 2, 16, 51, 55, 76, 91; sapphic harem of, 55–56; sexualization of, 51–52, 55–57
Orientalism (Said), 2, 94

Orientalist art, everyday imitating, 81–85
Orientalist decoration, of Odette, 85–86, 97n42
Orientalist stereotypes, 82
othering, 179; in British media, 139; within gay affirmative social contexts, 181; within queer community, 187
Ottoman eunuch, 70n22
Owens, Craig, 79
Oyěwùmí, Oyèrónkẹ́, 5

paraplegic, straight African American male, 210, 211
Paris-Sodom-Istanbul, 75
Participant #3, 188, 190, 191, 201n14
Pauline theology, within Christianity, 112
Peace Iftar, 34
Peace Seders, 34
pederast, 52, 55, 69n18, 70n22
Pentecostal church, African American, 163
performativity: Butler on, 79; in *Le Côté de Guermantes*, 83, 84; gender, 84
phallic woman, 78–79, 95n15, 95n17
Phillips, Robert, 16, 211
philosophy, 214
Pillar of Salt, The (Memmi), 87
Plato, dialogues of, 212
poetry, 214
Pontalis, J. B., 78, 95n15
postsecularism, Holloway on, 151
power: coloniality of, 4; Europe and Orient discursive relations of, 76; *ilm* impacted by, 119
prayer group (zikr), 38
pre-exposure prophylaxis (PrEP), 140n17
Pride, Hidayah marching at, 182, 197, 199
Progressive Muslims (Kugle), 105
pronouns, 46n30; of Buttmitzvah attendees, 169–70; moral panic around, 4–5; of Zara, 200n13
Proust, Marcel, 16; on everyday, 81; *Le Temps retrouvé* by, 91. See also *Côté de Guermantes, Le*; *recherche du temps perdu, À la*
Puar, Jasbir, 188

228   Index

al-qanfûd, 70n25
queer, 26, 165–66; Abraham, 77–81; disguises,
   52–53, 57, 63–67; distinctions, 40–43,
   44–45; Hayes on, 69n7; identity politics,
   208–9, 211; Maghreb, 54–58; moment, 83;
   scholarship, 211–12; terminology of, 69n7,
   205–9, 210–11; theory, 13–14, 208, 214;
   Zionism, 89–90. *See also specific topics*
queer community: othering within, 187;
   queer Muslim citizenship regarding,
   187–89; racial fetishization in, 188
queering: homosexuality intertextual, 109–
   12; of hybridization, 58–63; of Jewish-
   Muslim relations, 10–14, 17–18
queer-Jewish-Muslims, 25–26, 28, 45. *See
   also* David; Keegan
queer Jews. *See specific topics*
queer Muslims. *See specific topics*
queerness, 32, 216; denial of, 191; of Joy,
   184; of Sadiya, 184–85; self-distancing
   from, 190–91
queerphobic violence, 152, 155;
   persecution, 186–87; Sadiya fear of, 186
queer-sensitive interpretations, of Islam,
   105, 190–91, 192–93
Quijano, Aníbal, 4
Qur'an: biblical scriptures regarding, 114,
   115, 116; homosexuality in, 109–10, 113–
   16; *ilm* in, 107; *Isra'iliyyat* commentary
   genre, 114; Jewish scriptures regarding,
   114, 115–16; Kugle revisionism of, 106;
   Lut story in, 110; *mu'minun* in, 115. *See
   also* scriptures, Abrahamic

R. (Buttmitzvah attendee), 170
rabbinic literature, anti-homosexual
   interpretations in, 110
race: David on, 30–31, 44; in *Le mariage
   de Hanifa*, 61; in *Messieurs, vous êtes
   impuissants*, 66–67; Quijano on, 4
Rachel (*Le Côté de Guermantes* character),
   82–85, 96nn33–34, 97n39
racial fetishization, 188
racialization, sexuality relation to, 11–12
racing, 2–5. *See also* engendering
racism: anti-Muslim, 179; in *Messieurs, vous
   êtes impuissants*, 64; religion regarding,
   10, 11, 179

Ramadan Shoebox Appeal, Hidayah, 182
rape, by French army, 68n2
recherche du temps perdu, À la (Proust),
   16, 94n1; art referenced in, 76, 78, 81;
   biblical scriptures referenced by, 76, 78,
   81; closet spectacle in, 90; drag in, 77,
   93–94, 216; *en être* usage in, 79–80, 89,
   96n26, 98n53; French nation in, 75–76,
   77, 90, 99n66; gender in, 93; incestuous
   feelings in, 96n19; Orientalism in, 76, 77,
   82, 91, 95n8, 216; Orientalist crescent
   symbol in, 91, 92, 98n60; Orient in,
   75–76, 91, 92, 98n60; phallic woman in,
   78–79; queer Abraham in, 77–81; queer
   Zionism in, 89–90; Sodom depicted
   in, 89, 91, 92, 98n52; Sodomites in, 89,
   98n52; Swann in, 85, 87, 88, 98n51; *Le
   Temps retrouvé* volume of, 91. See also
   Côté de Guermantes, Le; Odette
relative frequency (RF), 132
religion: Britain public discourse on, 151;
   domestic, 159, 160; everyday, 109, 119;
   racism regarding, 10, 11, 179; self-
   distancing from, 190–91; transgender
   support group forum stance on, 187–88
religious (*Frum*), 172n59
religious boundaries, permeability of, 27–
   29, 44
religious identities, 182, *183*
religious practices, of Keegan, 33–34
representations, 15; British media double
   minorities, 127–28; support group self,
   196–98, *198*, 199
research questions, on British media,
   130–31
RF. *See* relative frequency
Rhaïs, Elissa, 15, 71n33; *La Fille des Pachas*
   by, 58; *Les Juifs* by, 58–59; male gaze
   writing of, 59–60; *La Riffaine* by, 60. See
   also *mariage de Hanifa, Le*
Richardson, Diane, 183
Richardson, Matthew, 17, 207
Riffaine, La (Rhaïs), 60
ritual: fishing dam–building, 162–63; van
   Gennep on, 152–53
ritual complex: Buttmitzvah and, 156–61;
   symbols within, 157–58
Riviere, Joan, 84

Rose (queer Muslim identity study participant), 185–86, 195–96
Rubenstein, Jeffrey, 167
Rubin, Gayle, 209–10

Sadiya (queer Muslim identity study participant), 194; family of, 184–85, 186; on Hidayah aim, 195; queerness of, 184–85; queerphobic violence fear of, 186
Said, Edward: on Orientalism, 2, 16, 51, 55, 76, 91; *Orientalism* by, 2, 94
Saint Mary's Park, renaming of, 151
Salaam, 34
Salafism, 192
Sallé, Vincent, 95n2
same-sex desire: in Maghreb, 52, 55–58; among women, 55–58
same-sex prostitution, 54, 68n4
same-sex relations: Foucault on, 213–14, 217n12; in French colonies, 55; between women, 56
same-sex relationships, 180
sapphic harem, 55–56
Sappho, 212
Schachter-Shalomi, Zalman, 39
Scheherazade (*The Thousand and One Nights* character and *À la recherche du temps perdu* narrator), 77, 93–94, 216
scholarship, queer, 211–12
scriptures, Abrahamic, 16; apocryphal, 116; Bible, 111; on homosexuality, 107–9, 111; intertextual reading of, 113–16, 120; Sodom in, 110. *See also* biblical scriptures; Jewish scriptures; Qur'an
secularization paradigms, 152
self-conscientization (*conscientização*), 108, 119
self-distancing, identity conflict handled through, 190–91
self-representation, support group, 196–98, *198*, 199
semantic mapping: of corpora, *136*, 137; multiword keywords and, 135, *135–36*
semantic preferences, corpus linguistics revealing, 130
semiology, of fashion, 86
Semitic traits, of Swann, 88, 98n51
sermon, of David, 35, 39–40, 43

sermon giver (*khatib*), 35
Sexagon (Mack), 12
sex shops, 209
Sextius, Arène, 56
sexual abuse, by French army, 68n2
sexual colonization, 5–8
sexual desire, in *Messieurs, vous êtes impuissants*, 65–66
sexual deviance construction, Jewish, 12–13
sexual immorality, Christian conceptions of, 112
sexuality, 69n16; in ancient Greece, 212–13; in British media, 129; epistemology of, 9; Islamic law illicit, 111; in *Messieurs, vous êtes impuissants*, 66, 67; in premodern Arab-Islamic societies, 7–8; racialization relation to, 11–12. *See also* homosexuality
sexualization, of Orientalism, 51–52, 55–57
sexual orientation and gender identity (SOGI), 180, 182, *183*
Shah, Shanon, 16, 214; on problematic double minority binaries, 152; on situated knowledges, 211
Shammas, Anton, 98n60
Shared Identities (Hughes), 27, 28
Shatz, Adam, 13
Shepard, Todd, 69n16
shirk (worshiping anything other than God), 43
Shohat, Ella, 27
situated knowledges, 211
Sketch Engine, 129, 130, 131, 135
Slabodsky, Santiago, 2
Slandering the Jew (Drake), 12–13
social constructionism, of gender, 8–9
social structures, 153; anti-structure shaped by, 165, 168; communitas relationship with, 165, 166–67
Social Text, 205, 207
sociology: of fashion, 86; of religion, 117, 118
Socrates, 212
Sodom: in Abrahamic scriptures, 110; Paris-Sodom-Istanbul, 75; *À la recherche du temps perdu* depicting, 89, 91, 92, 98n52
Sodomites, in *À la recherche du temps perdu*, 89, 98n52

230 Index

sodomy, in Christianity, 111–12
SOGI. *See* sexual orientation and gender identity
solidarity, 15, 17
Southwest Asia and North Africa (SWANA), 7
spiritual traditions, 118
Spivak, Gayathri, 12
stereotypes: Arab pederast, 52, 55; of Maghrebi peoples, 52; Orientalist, 82
Stories Events, Hidayah, 195
"Straight Mind, The" (Wittig), 95n17
Strassfeld, Max, 9
Sufism, 38
suicidal thoughts, 196
support groups, 179; belonging regained through, 194–96; online, 187–88, 195–96; self-representation through, 196–98, *198*, 199; transgender, 187–88. *See also* Hidayah
SWANA. *See* Southwest Asia and North Africa
Swann (*À la recherche du temps perdu* character), 85; Odette viewed by, 87; Semitic traits of, 88, 98n51
symbols: Buttmitzvah employing, 160; complex, 158; concrete and ideological, 157–58

tahrif (distortion), 114
Talmor, Gregorio (*Messieurs, vous êtes impuissants* character), 63
Talpurs, Napier on, 11–12
Tancred (Disraeli), 76
Tardieu, Ambroise, 55
El-Tawhid Mosque, 30, 38; David on, 35, 39–40, 42, 43; sermon at, 35, 39–40, 43
Telegraph / Daily Mail corpus, 131, 139; Islam-related terms in, 133, *133*, 134, 138; Judaism-related terms in, 134, *134*, 138; noun frequencies in, *132*; semantic mapping of, *136*, 137. *See also* corpora; *Guardian* corpus; *Independent* corpus
Tell MAMA, 127
Temps retrouvé, Le (Proust), 91. See also *recherche du temps perdu, À la*
Terrorist Assemblages (Puar), 188
theater, in *Le Côté de Guermantes*, 82, 96n32

Thompson, Katrina Daly, 15, 216
Thousand and One Nights, The, 92, 93, 94, 216
T.M. (Buttmitzvah attendee), 164, 170
torture, in Abu Ghraib prison, 6
Tower Hamlets, 150–51. *See also* London
transgender identity, 185, 192, 200n13
transgender support group forum, 187–88
Trans Talmud (Strassfeld), 9
Trials of Moses, The, 87
Trump, Donald, 134, 179, 199n1
Turner, Victor, 152, 163; on interstructural situation, 153; on symbols, 157
Turnerian anthropology, of experience, 148, 168, 169

United States (US), 6
Unite the Right rally, in Charlottesville, 3

Vadakkiniyil, Dinesan, 165
van Gennep, Arnold, 152–53

Wallach, Yair, 27
Weiss, Margot, 26
Western Wall, of Jerusalem, 95n2
WhatsApp group, support groups, 195–96
Wilson, Ara, 26
Wittig, Monique, 95n17
womanhood, 95n17
women: cross-dressing, 57, 70n29; drag of, 57; Imams, 192; Maghrebi Jewish, 52–53; Maghrebi writers, 52, 53, 61–62; same-sex desire among, 55–58; same-sex relations between, 56
Woodstock generation, 165
worshiping anything other than God (*shirk*), 43
Wrocław/Breslau, anti-Muslim rally in, 3

Zahed, Ludovic-Mohamed, 8
Zara (queer Muslim identity study participant), 187–88, 192; identity and pronouns of, 200n13; Kik support group created by, 196
Zevi, Sabbatai/Shabbetai, 27–28, 29
zikr (prayer group), 38
Zionism, queer, 89–90
Zipporah (wife, of Moses), 87